Alaska's Charter Schools

Freedom and Accountability

Gordon E. Castanza, Ed. D.

PO Box 221974 Anchorage, Alaska 99522-1974

ISBN 1-888125-57-8

Library of Congress Catalog Card Number: 99-067480

Copyright 1999 by Gordon E. Castanza
—First Edition—

Cover design and all photography ©1999 Sidney H. Rittenberg

All rights reserved, including the right of reproduction in any form, or by any mechanical or electronic means including photocopying or recording, or by any information storage or retrieval system, in whole or in part in any form, and in any case not without the written permission of the author and publisher.

Manufactured in the United States of America.

Acknowledgments

In writing this book, I have been fortunate to have Dr. Carolyn Chapman, Associate Professor in the Department of Educational Leadership at the University of Nevada, Reno, as my mentor. Her experience and wisdom provided focus and support. It was a rare privilege to work closely with her. Appreciation is also extended to Dr. David Noonan, Dr. Gary Peltier, Dr. Frank Meyers, and Dr. Gus Hill, for their constructive comments and willingness to support this study.

I am also grateful to Dr. John Anttonen, Director of the School of Education, University of Alaska, Fairbanks. Dr. Anttonen made available the services of a research assistant, Mr. Li Lian Jia, and the resources of the School of Education to the study. Mr. Li assisted in the dissemination of the on-site questionnaire and he conducted several in-person interviews with the principal or lead teacher of the charter schools. Dr. Anttonen and Mr. Li have helped to strengthen and criticize drafts of this project.

I wish to acknowledge the contributions made by Dr. Karen Farley-Halverson, Principal Gustavus School, Gustavus, Alaska, and Dr. Earl Francq for their assistance and contributions of advice and of documentation of school accountability systems in Texas and Kansas.

Finally, my gratitude and love is extended to my wife, Jenny, and daughter, Chergai, for their emotional support. Without their willingness to assist in mailings of over 250 surveys, this project would have taken considerably longer. I give thanks to Jan D. Castanza, and Mr. and Mrs. John Castanza for sending me newspaper clippings and legislative transcripts of the development of charter school legislation in the states of Ohio and Washington. Their support has been a great source of motivation throughout the entire project.

Table of Contents

Acknowledgments 3
Preface 7
Chapter One—Introduction 9
    Statement of the Problem 17
    Purpose of the Study 17
    Theoretical basis of the Study 17
    Significance of the Study 17
    Limitations of the Study 18
    Delimitations of the Study 20
    Itemized checklist, Alaska Charter School Application 21
    Basic Assumptions of the Study 22
    Definition of Terms 23
    Organization of the Study 32
    Summary 33
Chapter Two—Review of the Literature 34
    Introduction 34
    Historical Perspectives 34
    Literature on the concept of freedom in education 57
    Literature on the concept of accountability in education 76
    Literature on relationship between freedom and accountability in education 109
    Summary of the review 119
Chapter Three—The Design and Methodology of the Study 120
    Introduction 120
    General Questions 120

Research Methodology 120
　　Research Procedures 121
　　Instrumentation 126
　　Selection of Participating Schools 126
　　Differential Selection of Subjects 126
　　Issues of Generalizability 126
　　Data Sources and Evidence 127
　　Data Analysis 127
　　Sample size/selection. 128
　　Subjects 128
　　Instrumentation 128
　　Procedures 128
　　Research Questions 128
　　Data Analysis 129
　　Summary 129
Chapter Four—Presentation and Analysis of Data 130
　　Introduction 130
　　Response to Data Collection Strategies 130
　　Contextual Findings 132
　　Funding to Alaska's Charter Schools 134
　　Perceived Areas of Freedom 134
　　Summary 161
Chapter Five—Summary, Conclusions and Recommendations 162
　　Summary 162
　　Research Questions 164
　　Conclusions 166
　　Recommendations 168
　　Summary 170
Appendix A—Alaska's Charter School Law 172
Appendix B—4 AAC 05.080 School Curriculum And Personnel 176
Appendix C—4 AAC 06.075 High School Graduation Requirements 177
Appendix D—Sec. 14.14.130 Chief School Administrator 178
Appendix E—4 AAC 33.110: Alaska's Charter School Regulations 179
Appendix F—Senate Bill 182 181
Appendix G—Sec. 14.30.010 When Attendance Compulsory 185

Appendix H—Standards for Evaluating State Assessment Systems 187
Appendix I—Alaska Charter Schools' Principals/Lead Teachers' Questionnaire 189
Appendix J—Alaska Charter Schools Administrator's Survey 206
Appendix K—Alaska Charter School Grantees 212
Appendix L—Chaos Theory and the Charter School 213
References 215
Endnotes 227

List of Tables

Table 1 21
Table 2 75
Table 3 79
Table 4 81
Table 5 81
Table 6 127
Table 7 131
Table 8 132
Table 9 133
Table 10 133
Table 11 135
Table 12 137
Table 13 139
Table 14 141
Table 15 143
Table 16 144
Table 17 146
Table 18 146
Table 19 147
Table 20 150
Table 21 156
Table 22 157
Table 23 158

List of Figures

Figure 1. Competing Values and School Ideals 58
Figure 2. Types of Accountability Systems 91
Figure 3. An accountability network conceptualization 94

Preface

The purpose of this study was to investigate the relationship between freedom from constraints and the amount of accountability for charter schools in Alaska. Survey responses were collected from superintendents, principals, community members, and principals/lead teachers of charter schools with respect to variables freedom and accountability.

Review of the literature focused on philosophical foundations of charter schools, Alaska legislative history, and journal articles dealing with freedom, and accountability.

Conclusions: 1. Charter schools' sponsors, and operators had little regard for accountability, and; 2. Almost 90% of the survey respondents supported some, or a lot of, freedom for charter schools. Only 4% of the respondents thought charter schools should have total freedom.

Further research on charter school innovation, and student achievement is needed. Researchers should use on-site visits, and should disaggregate the data.

Since the original draft of this project, there have been some recent developments in charter schools in Alaska. On April 14, 1998, the Nome City School District approved the application of the Anvil City Family Science Academy Charter School. The Alaska Department of Education (AK-DOE) technical review committee ruled that the application met all the requirements for approval and forwarded their recommendation to the Alaska State Board of Education (SBOE). Two months later, at its June 9, 1998 meeting in the 4th Avenue Theater in Anchorage, the SBOE approved the Anvil City Family Science Academy Charter School. At its meetings on June 3, 4, and 5, 1999 in Fairbanks, the SBOE approved the applications of the Ayaprun Elitnaurvik Yup'ik Immersion charter school in the Lower Kuskokwim School District and the Wiseman Community Charter School in the Yukon-Koyukuk School District (State Board June Meeting Actions, 1999). At the same meeting, the SBOE turned down the Craig City School District's application for a charter school. In taking this action, the SBOE was less than elastic. After July1, 1997, the Alaska Charter School regulations authorized the SBOE to approve more than seven charter schools in the geographic regions (4 AAC 33.111 (e) (i)). Even though the Ketchikan Gateway Borough School District had a charter school in the region that included Craig, the SBOE could have allowed for another charter school in this region.

Manno, Finn, Bierlein, and Vanourek (1997) forecast that as states discovered the shortcomings in their charter school laws they would tighten regulations. The AK-DOE has fulfilled this portent. In other action at its June, 1999 meeting, the SBOE opened public discussion on proposed regulation 4 AAC 33.410-490, Statewide Correspondence Study Program: "This poposal [made] several clarifications to a regulation addressing statewide correspondence study programs [including that] charter schools that offer statewide programs must comply with these regulations" (State Board June Meeting Actions, 1999). In the first test of 4 AAC 33.410-490, at a special meeting of the SBOE on July 26, 1999, it affirmed Commissioner Rick Cross' decision to accept Douglas Kemp Mertz' opinion that Eddy Jeans', AK-DOE's School Finance Manager's, notification to the Delta Cyber School of its 80% funding under AS 14.17.430 was correct. After Karen Rehfeld, Director of Education Support Services found Mr. Jeans' calculations to be correct, former Commissioner of Education, Shirley Holloway, Ph. D., appointed Mr. Mertz as a Hearing Officer on February 23, 1999.

Chapter One
Introduction

The dawn of charter school legislation was in Minnesota in 1991. By fall of 1997, 29 states as well as the District of Columbia, the Commonwealth of Puerto Rico, and the U.S. Trust Territory of Guam had enacted charter school laws. Charter school proponents say that they founded the schools to avoid state laws and regulations that they felt were obstacles to school reform. Advocates of charter schools contended that "... their autonomy will increase opportunities for student academic success, give teachers more professional opportunities for innovation in methods and measurement of student performance, guarantee fiscal responsibility, and increase competition among schools by allowing choice in the public schools" (Pratt 1996, p. 1). Charter school opponents charged that there was not enough evidence to show that charter schools worked to justify their threat to the public schools. Open enrollment was a main feature of charter schools, thus giving purpose for school choice promoters. Charter school opponents challenged the choice idea because they saw it as a danger to the goals of equity and fellowship.

This study was the first project to examine the charter schools of Alaska. The study proposed to provide descriptive information about the number and type of charter schools that furnish instruction to students and about the perceived freedom and accountability conditions that promote or hamper the charter schools' growth and performance.

The National Commission on Excellence in Education's 1983 publication of <u>A Nation at Risk: The Imperative for Education Reform</u>, hastened the U.S. public's demand for school reform and restructuring. Prior to <u>A Nation at Risk</u>, the 1957 Soviet Union's launching of Sputnik caused pundits in the United States to question the nation's resolve regarding science and mathematics education. The reform chorus has continued unabated into the 1990s. Business leaders have charged that graduates entering the workforce lack academic and social skills. State legislators and governors have passed and signed laws calling for stronger educational accountability.

In 1989, the General Assembly of the state of North Carolina passed a performance-based accountability program. The purpose of the program was:

> ... the improvement of student performance. In addition to adopting procedures for local school system participation in the Program, the State Board of Education issues guidelines for developing school improvement plans with three-year

student performance goals and annual milestones to measure progress in meeting those goals. The Board also adopts student performance indicators for measuring and assessing student performance in the participating school systems. (North Carolina State Board of Education, 1995, p. 13)

In 1990, Wisconsin joined the growing trend for state accountability systems. By 1993, its reporting system evolved into a comprehensive look at student performance indicators and opportunity-to-learn indicators. The purpose of the accountability was "... not only to measure educational success but help define achievement and performance ..." (Wisconsin Dept. of Public Instruction, 1995, p. vii).

Student Performance Indicators give readers a look at seven different measures of student achievement:
- Third Grade Reading Test
- Eighth Grade Knowledge and Concepts Examinations
- 10th Grade Knowledge and Concepts Examinations
- Enhanced American College Test (ACT)
- Advanced Placement Test
- Graduation information
- Postgraduation Follow-up data

Opportunity-To-Learn Indicators offer insight into the classes and experiences made available to students. It is divided into profiles of districts and schools and of students. District Profile information includes:
- District Staffing Ratios
- High School Graduation Requirements
- General Fund revenues
- General Fund Expenditures (Wisconsin Dept. of Public Instruction, 1995, p. vii-viii)

The California Assessment Program (CAP) came into being in the 1980s. By 1991, California threw out the CAP and brought in the California Learning Assessment System (CLAS). In 1994, the incoming governor declined to sign the funding bill for CLAS. The legislature stepped in to require districts to submit data according to the School Accountability Report Cards (SARC).

School Accountability Report Cards (SARC) ... are updated annually to provide site-specific information to the local community. There are no sanctions attached to results contained in the SARC. Its format varies by district. The state model of SARC is not mandatory (the state department of education has no oversight authority), but at least once every 3 years local boards must compare their efforts to the contemporary version of the state model. (Texas Education Agency, 1996, p. 38)

In the spring of 1996, California began the Pupil Incentive Testing Program (PITP). Under the PITP, districts received reimbursement for using off-the-shelf testing packages for grades 2-10. In the absence of legislative direction, PITP became the default testing program. As the struggles between the governor and the legislature over statewide assessment continued:

The state has curriculum frameworks and is now developing content and performance standards .... Currently, the California statewide assessment program is limited to the Golden State Examinations (GSE) and the Career-Technical Assessment Program (C-TAP). The State plans to develop a new state assessment for grades 4, 8, and 10, using a mix of methods, to produce school-level data.

The purpose of the GSE program is for awarding honors diplomas and for improvement of curriculum and instruction. The GSEs are criterion-referenced, end-of-course exams offered on a voluntary basis to students in grades 9-12 in a variety of subjects. (Neill, 1997, p. 49)

The Nevada School Accountability Law, Nevada Revised Statute 385.347, was passed in 1993. The original intent of the law was, " ... [to] provide the legislative framework under which all school districts in Nevada inform the public about their performance overall and about the performance of individual public schools within the district" (Purvis, 1997, p. vi).

In 1995, the Nevada legislature revised NRS 385.347. Because grade-level reporting included, in many instances, age-level data, the latter requirement was eliminated. The reporting of teacher-student ratios was shortened to include grades K-6. Class size data for high school classes in English, Mathematics, Science, and Social Studies was required. The requirement to report annual graduation rates was dropped and the requirement to report overall school dropout rates was added. A report on advancement rates was dropped and a report on truancy rates was added. The legislature seemed particularly interested in dis-aggregated data about violence in the schools. Instead of a single data element, districts had to report violence according to four categories: "violence to other students, violence to school staff, possession of weapons and distribution of controlled substances" (Purvis, 1997, p. 2).

With the passage of SB 482 in the spring of 1997, the Nevada legislature amended the Nevada School Accountability Law.

> It amends our current Accountability Law by strengthening it in that schools will be designated into three categories. We have a current Accountability Law which requires schools to report publicly to parents and community on achievement and other school demographics. This new provision takes it steps further by requiring improvement through a school improvement plan, appropriations of remedial funds to help and funds for teacher training/staff development. After three years of no improvement, (designation as inadequate) a school could be assigned a new administrator. (W.F. Arensdorf, personal communication, November 5, 1997)

The press reported on the Nevada Education Reform Bill of 1997 in more dramatic terms: "... schools that don't do an adequate job of educating students could incur some strict remedial measures-including firing the principal" (Hoke, 1997, p. 9A).

The 53rd legislature of the 1993 regular session of the Washington legislature passed Engrossed Substitute House Bill 1209. The Education Reform–Improvement of Student Achievement Law became effective on July 25, 1993. Section 1 of ESHB 1209 stated that:

> The legislature finds that student achievement in Washington must be improved to keep pace with societal changes, changes in the workplace, and an increasingly competitive international economy.
>
> To increase student achievement, the legislature finds that the state of Washington needs to develop a public school system that focuses more on the educational performance of students, that includes high expectations for all students,

and that provides more flexibility for school boards and educators in how instruction is provided.

At the same time that states were adopting accountability systems, the public insisted that public schools be all things to all people. While some public schools were part of cumbersome bureaucracies, others received inadequate funding to meet the goals of states' school reform regulations. Public schools were buffeted by a multitude of advocates' agendas that found their ways into school reform legislation. Charter school legislation emerged as one school reform measure that had broad political appeal.

The debates over charter schools have been contentious. While there have been numerous reports about charter schools, still little is known about these schools of choice. Individuals, groups, teachers, parents, and private companies have formed them. Charter schools have formed multi-grade classrooms and have experimented with various innovations. State legislatures have freed them from many of the constraints that have governed public schools for decades. In exchange, charter school founders have agreed to be held accountable. Roberts (1993) reported on the link between freedom and accountability, "Once approved by the State Board, a contract will be written with the local board to delineate student achievement outcomes the [charter] school will achieve. Beyond these requirements, charter schools are free from most public schools [sic] rules and regulations" (Roberts 1993, p. 43).

All across the United States, various researchers have conducted base-line, first-year (Diamond, 1994; Bierlein, 1994b; Corwin, 1994), fourth-year (Buechler, 1996) and benchmark (Buechler, 1997) studies that have indicated diverse effects of charter schools. In September 1992, California Senate Bill 1448 was passed. California became the second state to adopt a charter school law. It became effective in January 1993. Barely four months later, researchers from the Southwest Regional Laboratory published the first discussion of California's charter schools. They stated, "The issues we discuss relate to the reasons schools seek charter status, the trade offs associated with autonomy, parental involvement in charter schools, and finally, the promise and reality of parental choice in charter schools" (Corwin, 1993, p. 3). In May 1994, Marcella R. Dianda and Ronald G. Corwin published the first report (Corwin, 1994) on California's charter schools. The report provided

> ... a general impression of California's fledgling charter-school movement and suggests patterns worth following. Some trends may come to characterize charter schools in California; others may change as additional schools are chartered; and still others may be first-year phenomena that dissipate as the state's charter-school movement evolves. (Corwin, 1994, p. 51)

One year and eight months after its charter school legislation became effective, January 1993, the first overview of California's charter schools made no mention of charter school accountability or of charter school student achievement results (Diamond, 1994, p. 41). Two years and ten months after the effective date of the California charter school law, another report (Corwin, 1995) came from the Southwest Regional Laboratory. The report concerned itself with school autonomy, teacher characteristics, innovations, parent involvement, parent contracts, and student characteristics. This report omitted any mention of charter school accountability or of charter school student achievement results. This latter report received some negative criticism:

> Yet the newer report also reaches some overzealous and possibly partisan conclusions. For example, it claims "modest support for the possibility that charter schools are underserving special education students." Later in the same report it calls these "only tendencies... [that] are not statistically significant."
>
> This assessment leads us to suspect that parts of the WestEd analysis result from an agenda driven more by ideology than by close attention to the facts. The report is a good example of how the charter school world is quickly becoming vulnerable to politicized education policy research and evaluation. More opposition is apt to occur as the number of charter schools grows and they become more threatening to education "status quo." (Finn, 1996, p. 67)

The Education Commission of the States (ECS) published several issue briefs and a couple of brief studies. An early ECS study "was designed to gather and share the best available information about [charter schools]" (Medler, 1995, p. v). This study made some tentative remarks about charter school accountability and student achievement: "Charter schools use a variety of ways to report student progress. The most common are standardized tests and student portfolios, parent surveys and student demonstrations of mastery" (Medler, 1995, p. v). In a Phi Delta Kappa Educational Foundation publication the authors asserted, "A basic tenet of the charter concept is accountability for results" (Mulholland, 1995, p. 36-37).

Sage McCotter's 1996 issue brief (McCotter, 1996) failed to mention charter school accountability and student achievement. Louann A. Bierlein (Bierlein, 1996) reported on student outcomes:

> In reference to student outcomes, current information remains limited to self-reports surfacing from various charter schools. Although generalizations cannot be drawn at this point, some charter schools appear to be reporting tangible student outcomes. Several examples include:
> - City Academy, St. Paul, Minnesota, reports that of its 42 graduates to date (all former dropouts), 100% had been accepted into postsecondary programs.
> - Horizon Instructional Systems, a charter school near Sacramento, California (which uses an individualized education plan for each student), notes that its test scores increased an average of 10% over the rest of the district.
> - Vaughn Next Century Learning Center in the heart of Los Angeles, California, (an existing public school of more than 1,200 students which converted to charter status) reports that their language arts scores improved from the 9th percentile to the 39th, while its math scores increased from the 14th percentile to the 57th.
>
> Of concern however, are reports which state that a number of charter schools have not developed rigorous performance expectations for students, nor have they specified precisely the methods by which performances are to be measure. (Bierlein, 1996, p. 5)

Deborah Perkins-Gough (1997) redacted the results of the May 1997 National Study of Charter Schools first-year study and the Vanourek, Manno, Finn, and Bierlein (1997) work.

The findings from these two major national studies confirm that charter schools have taken hold as a vigorous reform effort. Charter schools are growing in number; they are serving a diverse population of students, and they are satisfying many expressed needs of their students, parents, and teachers.

Future research will be needed to indicate whether charter schools will also produce the desired benefits in terms of student achievement and academic excellence. (Perkins-Gough, 1997, p. 9)

In March 1997, the Clayton Foundation published an evaluation of Colorado's charter schools (Clayton Foundation, 1997). It contained data on the number of waivers from statutes (freedom) and on student achievement measures and data (accountability).

In June of 1997, Massachusetts reported the student achievement data for its charter schools, and Robert V. Antonucci, Commissioner of Education, made the following prefatory remarks:

This report cannot offer a definitive statement on the academic progress of students in charter schools. These early results are more suggestive than authoritative, and more data will come over the months and years ahead. Yet, there are now sufficient data to suggest answers to questions about the academic performance level of students entering charter schools, and at least preliminary data about the academic gains those students have made. (Antonucci, 1997, n.p.)

In the fall of 1997, Michigan reported its statewide test scores for charter schools: "As a group, Michigan's charter schools scored far lower than the state's schools as a whole in the percentages of students who reached the 'proficient' level on the state tests" (Schnaiberg, 1997a, p. 5).

Charter schools were a diverse lot, thus prompting Luanne A. Bierlein to warn: "... charter laws should not be lumped into a single category; all charter schools are not created equal" (Bierlein, 1995/1996, p. 90). The national charter school study confirmed this finding as one of the most troublesome problems confronting charter school researchers. There was no level playing field:

Charter schools are extremely diverse because of state and local factors. Their approaches to education often vary dramatically from one another. States play a primary role in defining the possibilities of charter schools, and states vary greatly in their approaches. (U.S. Department of Education, 1997)

Television newsmagazine reports provided coverage of successes and failures of charter schools. On September 6, 1997, John Merrow, executive producer of "The Merrow Report," produced a program on charter schools. He reported:

[Le Soeur], Minnesota's New Country School ... is free to teach any way it chooses, but it is freedom with accountability. Students have to take the state's standardized tests and meet all state graduation requirements. Students do not seem to mind that accountability accompanies freedom. ... Minnesota's charter school law attempts to balance freedom and accountability[1].... Not every state is as careful. Arizona's approach to charter schools emphasizes freedom, but pays scant attention to accountability .... It's a freewheeling, experimental atmosphere that State superintendent, Lisa Graham Keegan, embraces.[2] (Merrow, 1997)

In order to avoid the charge of synecdoche, many of California's charter schools indicated that they had petitioned for a charter to free themselves from rules and regulations (28 schools) and to gain control over decisions related to curriculum and instruction (26 schools). In sharp contrast, only one-third wanted to become legally autonomous. (Dianda, 1994, p. 42)

During an Internet on-line forum conducted in December 1996, the following exchange took place:

Pam Riley. The ASCD charter position statement indicates that charter schools have had only marginal success. That is not the experience in California or Minnesota. Would you comment on some "successes."

Molnar. Charter school successes are, at this point, largely based on anecdotal reports. Evidence from individual schools does not make a case for the reform any more than the successes of individual public schools make the case for the status quo.

Nathan. Any research is limited, as the oldest charter schools are in their 4th year, and hundreds are only in their 2nd or 3rd year. However, seven schools in California, Colorado, and Minnesota have had their charters renewed because they had a positive impact on their students. (Pool, 1996, p. 4)

Like Arizona, Alaska's charter school law was practically silent on the accountability issue, a keystone of charter school proponents' arguments. It made only two oblique mentions of accountability.

AS 14.03.255 "(c) A charter school shall operate under a contract between the charter school and the local school board. A contract must contain the following provisions ... (2) specific levels of achievement for the educational program; ... (12) a termination clause providing that the contract may be terminated by the local school board for the failure of the charter school to meet educational achievement goals or fiscal management standards, or for good cause."

The National Study of Charter Schools (1997) found that students with disabilities were generally under-represented in charter schools nationally. Minnesota and Wisconsin were exceptions. No statistics existed on this population in Alaska's charter schools.

Joe Nathan has maintained that charter schools, "... must declare what they will do for students and theoretically at least, must provide solid evidence—to families and to taxpayers—that they are doing what they promised"(Brandt, 1996, p. 5). Eighty-five percent of the State of Alaska's revenues came from oil severance taxes. These taxes largely relieved the ratepayers of Alaska from the foundation-funding burden to finance public schools in the state. Furthermore, Alaska was one of four states that were allowed to pass-through Federal Impact Aid Payments In Lieu of Taxes (PILT). In order to meet the federal disparity test, Alaska ratepayer contributions to public school financing in the organized political subdivisions in Alaska were capped at 20%. Residents of the Rural Education Attendance Areas with charter schools have contributed little or nothing to educational funding. Ratepayers' contributions were limited in Alaska's organized municipal and borough school districts. Consequently, there was a dis-connection between taxpayer financing and an expectation for accountability.

In 1997, many states revisited their charter school legislation. Recent legislative action in Colorado, S. B. 18, aimed to eliminate the powers of the local school board regarding charter school renewals. By the end of January 1997, Arizona's legislature had no less than 10 bills introduced relating to charter schools. New York, on the other hand, had no charter school law. However, Governor George Pataki introduced a charter school law that was drawing fire from local school boards and the teachers' unions. A 16 organization alliance, the Family Coalition, in Kansas, promised to advance charter school legislation.

Dianda & Corwin (1994) stressed the innovative nature of California's charter schools:

> Because they are freed from most of the rules and regulations that have presumably prevented public schools from innovating .... Within broad parameters established by charter-school laws, each school's charter spells out the outcomes against which the school is held accountable and how those outcomes will be measured .... Ideally, charter schools also enjoy operational independence from their sponsoring agencies so they can make the curricular, managerial, and fiscal decisions needed to meet the terms of their charters. (Dianda, 1994)

As legislatures gave charter schools more freedom, they believed that their operators would rise to the professional expectation that they would be more accountable. Hill, Bonan & Warner (1992) asserted that staff members would "... assume an obligation to take the initiative in assessing the needs of their students, devising appropriate services and constructing realistic expectations for success" (Hill, Bonan, & Warner, 1992, p. 24). The Education Commission of the States and the Center for School Change (1995) outlined the freedom and accountability connection in charter school contracts:

> These schools operate independently of local school districts and are designed to exist outside of most rules and regulations .... As long as the school meets the terms of its charter, it is free from much of the rules and regulations under which other public schools must operate. And unlike other schools, if a charter school fails to meet these conditions, its charter can be revoked. (Education Commission of the States & the Center for School Change, 1995, p. 3)

Pratt (1996) found that, "Proponents of school choice value freedom as the highest regarded value in the venue of public education ... [and] ... Charter schools consistently utilized student standardized testing as a means of accountability and authentic assessments, for purposes of evaluation" (Pratt, 1996, p. 183-184).

Wohlstetter and Griffin (1997) continued the emphasis on freedom and accountability of charter schools. They stated, "One of the basic premises of charter schools is that they should be allowed greater autonomy in exchange for greater accountability for results" (Wohlstetter, 1997).

Nathan (1996) outlined freedom and accountability as one of several key elements of his model charter school. Nathan stated:

In return for accountability for specific results, the state grants an up-front waiver of virtually all rules and regulations governing public schools. Aside from the basic regulations mentioned in the first item of this list [They must be nonsectarian. They cannot charge tuition. They cannot employ admissions tests, and they must be open to all kinds of students. They cannot discriminate against students on the basis of race, religion, or gender. They must use buildings that meet health, accessibility, and safety regulations.], charter schools should be exempt from state regulations about how schools operate. (Nathan, 1996, p. 3)

Statement of the Problem

Since charter school proponents assert that they desire to be held accountable in exchange for freedom (Bierlein, 1994a, p. 1-2), it is timely to investigate these issues as they emerge because this quid pro quo has yet to be demonstrated.

Purpose of the Study

The purpose of this survey study was to investigate the relationship between freedom from constraints and the amount of accountability for charter schools in Alaska.

Theoretical basis of the Study

This theory implied (Effect of a public school choice program, 1997) that charter schools led to an improvement of public school education by compelling schools and school districts to raise the quality of their educational practices. The researcher defined "freedom from constraints" generally in terms of such indicators of freedom as waivers from curriculum, teaching style, textbooks, teaching methods, district policies, collective bargaining agreements, Department of Education regulations, and state laws. The researcher defined "accountability" generally in terms of such indicators of accountability as standardized test scores, direct writing assessment scores, National Assessment of Educational Progress scores, Brigance skill inventories, student performance portfolios, drop-out reduction, graduates that go on to college, and teacher value added assessment. These terms informed the research questions that the researcher developed and used to guide this project.

The following research questions guided the study:
1. How are Alaska's charter schools held accountable and how does that accountability compare with public school accountability in general in the state?
2. What do the founders/operators of Alaska's charter schools perceive to be the importance of freedom and accountability in the implementation of their plans?
3. How do urban and rural charter schools compare in the area of perceived importance of freedom and accountability?

In the course of seeking answers to these questions, the research took turns down the various by-paths of governance, personnel, student admission, types of assessment and accountability, school and class size, philosophy and mission statements, and curriculum.

Significance of the Study

This study presented information that was collected from all of Alaska's charter schools in existence since 1996.

Evolution of Alaska's charter school law. Alaska's charter school legislation, AS 14.03.250, was passed in July 1995. The first three charter schools were approved in 1996. In the spring of 1997, 12 more charter school applications were approved.

Before the law was two years old, Senator Ward introduced Senate Bill 182. It proposed to repeal AS 14.03.250 and to create three separate charter school-approving agencies. Two of the agencies paralleled existing agencies. The bill also prohibited the charter-granting agency to require the principal to hold an Alaska administrator's certification. It also extended the sunset of the original law from 2005 to the year 2015.

Local education agency application of Alaska's charter school law. There are 53 school districts in the state of Alaska, nine of which have charter schools.[3] Each district promulgated its own charter school policies and application procedures, and defined the conditions under which they would approve a charter school application. Furthermore, each of the charter schools had extremely different instructional and curricular approaches that presented the researcher with the same confounding conditions as were found nationally.

Many times the public had access to popular reports that did not meet the peer-reviewed journals' criterion. These amounted to charter school promotional materials. They contained some references to "research" endorsements, testimonials, and anecdotal recommendations. One is prompted to ask why these evidence-free assertions were not submitted for peer review.

Numbers of approved charter schools. In spite of the pressures to change AS 14.03.250, a high demand for charter schools in Alaska has not materialized. The charter school law was passed in July 1995, but districts and the Alaska Board of Education have approved only 17 out of the 30 authorized. Given Alaska's cap of 30 was not overly generous by national standards, and the conditions of its charter school law were fairly restrictive, these schools have captivated some education reformers and charter-school advocates. However, few educational researchers have noticed them. Charter school advocates have said that charter schools hold the promise for true educational reform. Before the existing law is repealed, researchers need to explain the conditions of access to a charter school education to policy makers and the public.

Benefits of the study. Investigators need to follow the emergence of the state's charter schools; to record their evolution and the innovations they devised; and, to document their effect on public education and on student achievement. The first step in improving the adoption of an innovation is to measure its implementation with a reliable assessment procedure. The benefit is associated with the restructuring of public schools. A literature search revealed little or no significant information about the nature of charter schools. Their condition needs to be determined in order to detect their effect on the education of students. The intent of this research was to describe the character of charter schools in Alaska in terms of freedom and accountability. The results will benefit policy makers, educators, parents, community members, and students in their efforts to improve education and to amplify student achievement. It is essential, then, that some attempt is made to understand and to explore the boundaries of our own knowledge about the relationship between freedom and accountability in Alaska's charter schools.

Limitations of the Study

1. Although legislation authorized the creation of 30 charter schools, and the Alaska Board of Education had approved 17, only 15 were in existence as of May 19,

1999. At its February 17, 1998 meeting, the Alaska Board of Education ap proved the charter school applications of the Sports Program for Youth Devel opment Education and Recreation (S.P.Y.D.E.R.) Charter School and the Vil lage Charter School. Both schools were located in Anchorage. On June 22, 1998, the Anchorage School District Board of Education approved the SPYDER Charter School's request for an extension of its projected opening date for one year. Thus, the SPYDER Charter School was permitted to retain the $142,000 federal grant money it was awarded. Consequently, the population size was too small to lend itself to inferential statistical analysis.
2. The surveys were administered over a 90-day period.
3. The superintendents', community members', and principals' surveys were self-completion.
4. The charter schools' principals'/lead teachers' survey was conducted both by self-completion, telephone interview, and face-to-face interview.
5. The instruments incorporated the essential elements of extra-Alaska surveys with elements that reflected Alaskan charter school characteristics.
6. Two of the survey instruments were administered to a vertical cross-section of school districts from superintendents to building administrators.
7. One of the instruments was given to the administrators of the charter schools.
8. One of the instruments was administered to a horizontal section of the general population living in school districts with charter schools.
9. Internal validity concerns

   a. History

Senate Bill 182 was introduced near the end of the 1997 legislative session. Senator Ward, the sponsor of the bill, re-introduce the bill at the beginning of the legislative session in January 1998. In addition, Rep. Fred Dyson introduced another charter school bill, HB 441. The intent of the bill was to review:
- funding equity for charter school students;
- charter school use of existing public school facilities;
- alteration of the limit on the number of charter schools;
- extending the length of the allowable contract limits between

a charter school and a school district; and
- extending the charter school statutory sunset date.

During a lull in the legislative debate, the study was conducted in
January and February 1998. This timing precluded new legislation affecting the study.

A part of the 1994 "Improving America's Schools Act" contained the "Public Charter Schools Program." This program received $51 million in Fiscal Year 1997. In August 1996, Commissioner of Education, Dr. Shirley Holloway, applied for federal charter school grant funding. In October 1996, the Alaska Department of Education (AK-DOE) received $2.3 million in federal charter school grant funds (Appendix K). The AK-DOE planned to disburse the funds over a three-year period. Receipt of these funds provoked 12 more charter school organizers to submit their applications for approval. After approval, the total number of charter schools in Alaska was

15. Six charter schools shared the first-year allocation of $647,290. The second year allocation (FY98) was $775,450. The third year allocation (FY99) was $887,279.

President Clinton proposed "to double [the grant funds] in size in FY 1998 as part of his quest for 3,000 charter schools by the year 2000" (Finn, 1997, p. 10). However, "[u]sing the state's first independent school as a backdrop, President Clinton pledged $40 million...to establish similar charter schools nationwide, with $3.4 million going to California" (Guthrie, 1997, p. A-12). On November 7, 1997, "[t]he House passed the Charter Schools Amendments Act of 1997 (H.R. 2616)" (Charter schools, 1997). On the same date, the Senate version of the bill (S.1380) was winding its way through the Senate Labor and Human Relations Committee. Finally, during the week of November 12, 1997, President Clinton signed a spending bill that set an $80 million appropriation for charter schools: "The allotment represents an increase over the $51 million spent for fiscal 1997, but also fell short of Mr. Clinton's request of $100 million. In 1996, federal funding for charters was only $18 million" (Sack, 1997, p. 16). Some of those funds have been earmarked for Alaska (Appendix K). The study was conducted in January and February 1998, thus precluding the effect of additional funding for planning, design, and start-up expenses for charter schools.

A third external validity concern was that of the expiration of the geographical distribution clause of AS 14.03.250-275.

b. Maturation

The study was conducted over a two month period. Thus the effects of changes on the information base of the respondents were limited.

Delimitations of the Study

This study was conducted in all 53 school districts in the state of Alaska. The first phase of the research entailed a gathering of all the approved (at both the local and State Board of Education levels) and disapproved (at the local school district level) charter school applications. The researcher contacted the Alaska Department of Education's Charter School Liaison to obtain copies of the charter school applications. Mr. Harry Gamble performed these duties from the summer of 1995 to the winter of 1995-1996. In the winter of 1996, Ms. Darby Anderson, Superintendent of the Alyeska Centralized Correspondence School, performed this role. Upon Ms. Anderson's retirement in June 1996, these duties were transferred to Ms. Marjorie Menzie. Gathering the original applications was free of the inherent limitations of surveys and questionnaires. However, this method was not without its own limitations. Other than the expectations of the "Itemized Checklist" (Table 1) that the State Board of Education directed the Department of Education technical review panel to use, the charter school applications did not have to conform to any model or cover predetermined concepts. On the other hand, when viewed along side the survey results, these original source documents provided an element of stability.

The second phase entailed three separate survey instruments. Current principals or lead teachers of each charter school completed a questionnaire. Since the author was

Table 1
Itemized checklist, Alaska Charter School Application

Item	Yes	No	Criteria
1			The application contains procedures for designation of an academic policy committee including parents, teachers, and school employees.
2			Provisions of the law which describe the responsibilities of the academic policy committee are acknowledged.
2a			• Authority to select a principal
2b			• Selects, appoints or otherwise supervises employees
3			The relationship of the charter school to the rest of the district is articulated.
4			The educational program is described.
5			Provisions are made for specific levels of achievement for the educational program.
6			Admissions procedures are provided for
6a			• Admission for all eligible students (eligible student defined)
6b			• Provisions for accommodating additional students if necessary
6c			• Provisions for random drawing for enrollment when applicants exceed capacity.
7			If the charter school is the only school in the location, provisions for students who do not wish to attend the school.
8			Administrative policies are provided for which are in keeping with the law.
9			The funding allocation from the local school board and costs assignable to the charter school program budget are designated.
10			Methods by which expenditures and receipts will be accounted for are articulated.
11			The location and description of the facility are included.
12			The teacher to student ratio is articulated.
13			The number of students to be served is articulated.
14			The age group or grade level, or definition of students who will benefit from a particular teaching method or curriculum is identified.
15			Collective bargaining contract exemptions agreed to by the school district and bargaining unit are articulated. If no exemptions are agreed to, the employees of the charter school are subject to all provisions of the collective bargaining agreements in force in the school district.
16			A charter school contract termination clause is provided for.

Revised April 24, 1996

a superintendent in one of the school districts, he recused himself from the study. Therefore, 51 of the 52 superintendents of school districts in Alaska completed the questionnaire. Alaska public school principals completed the survey instrument. Community members in school districts that sponsored charter schools completed the questionnaire. An informal review of the instruments was conducted with 10 volunteers to test readability and look of the survey instruments. The charter school principal/lead teacher survey was given to the 15 charter school administrators.

Prior to administering this survey, each principal/lead teacher was contacted by a research assistant from the University of Alaska, Fairbanks. The research assistant asked if the administrator preferred a face-to-face interview, a telephone interview, or a self-completion. The researcher mailed the survey administered to the superintendents, to the principals, and to the community members. A cover letter accompanied all surveys introducing the researcher and the purpose of the survey. The letter also invited respondents to receive a copy of the abstract of the study. All surveys were accompanied with a consent form informing respondents of the purpose of the study and assuring them of the confidentiality of their responses. Questionnaires were designed and the raw data tabulated using the interview mode of the SNAP(tm) questionnaire design software.

The researcher did not know if the variables measured were normally distributed in the populations, or if the data represented an interval. The researcher also selected some subjects (principals/lead teachers of charter schools, superintendents, and public school principals) because of their membership in a group. The only subjects the researcher independently selected were the community members residing in postal zip code areas in which charter schools were located. Therefore, responses were analyzed using a non-parametric test of significance.

Delimitations included:
1. Except for the principals/lead teachers of the charter schools, all other respondents completed the survey separately.
2. The charter school principal/teacher rate of return would be greater than or equal to 70%.
3. Except for the researcher, who was a superintendent, the entire population of superintendents was contacted. It should be noted that there was one superintendent, Stephen Cathers, who shared a contract with two school districts, Unalaska City School District and Aleutian Islands Borough School District.
4. The superintendent rate of return would be greater than or equal to 70%.
5. A sample of 135 Alaska public school principals was contacted.
6. The public school principal rate of return would be greater than or equal to 70%.

Basic Assumptions of the Study

The state of Alaska has over 490 public schools and charter school legislation was passed in July 1995. With the creation of administrative regulations, the State Board of Education was ready to receive charter school applications from as many as 30 charter school founding groups. At least one group of charter school advocates, Alaskans for Educational Choice, along with the Anchorage School District, and the Alaska Department of Education, conducted informational workshops and shopping mall charter school bazaars.

Charter school organizers could choose whatever teaching style, student learning style, curricula, texts, and facilities they wanted. The enabling legislation included a concession to the National Education Association-Alaska (NEA-AK). NEA-AK had insisted that the charter school teachers would have to be covered by the sponsoring district's collective bargaining agreement. Local charter school accountability requirements were left up to the discretion of the sponsoring school board. Financial and budgetary concerns were to be addressed in the charter school contract.

Charter school laws in Arizona, Massachusetts, Michigan, and Minnesota allowed legal autonomy for their charter schools. As in Colorado, Georgia, Kansas, New Mexico, Wisconsin, and Wyoming, Alaska's charter schools were public schools within their sponsoring school districts. Alaska's charter schools were not permitted legal autonomy. They could not sue or be sued. They could not be signatories to contracts. The charter school would be responsible for its own staff development.

While it was assumed that each charter school would use certificated teachers, no teacher was compelled to teach in a charter school. Charter school employment was voluntary. Student attendance at a charter school was also voluntary. No one could compel parents to send their children to a charter school.

Definition of Terms

1. Accountability System—A set of commitments, policies, and practices that are designed to:
1. Heighten the probability of student exposure to good instructional practice in a supportive environment
2. Reduce the likelihood that harmful practices will be employed
3. Provide internal self-correctives in the system to identify, diagnose, and change courses of action that are harmful or ineffective (Darling-Hammond, 1991).

2. Action Research—is characterized by teachers identifying instructional problems, determining what current evidence is available about solving these problems, and proposing changes that might be more successful. They also implement changes and judge the success of their endeavors. Action research is not generalizable to other situations. It is relevant for one classroom or for one school. (Bryant-Booker, 1995, p. 10)

3. Autonomy—[T]he having or making of one's own laws, independence. 1. Of a state, institution, etc.: The right of self-government, of making its own laws and administering its own affairs. a. Liberty to follow one's will, personal freedom. (The compact edition of the Oxford English dictionary, 1971, p. 575)

The political independence of a nation; the right (and condition) of power of self-government. The negation of a state of political influence from without or from foreign powers. Green v. Obergfell, 73 App.D.C. 298, 121 F.2d 46, 57. (Nolan, 1990, p. 134)

… is the full development of the child's latent capacities for independent reflection and for judgment on issues of personal morality and social justice; it is the link between intellect and responsible action …. Autonomy will simply promote his personal and probably painful exploration of himself, the world, and his responsibility to that world .... Of course, no thoroughly independent mind exists; and no education, however effective, repeals the relative servitude of each of us to his particular genetic and external circumstances. The concept of autonomy nevertheless suggests an indispensable intellectual and ethical ideal-to achieve the highest degree of mental and moral self-determination and sensitivity which circumstance permits .... [A]utonomy does not imply a lack of assent to propositions (if that were possible); it merely denotes the manner in which propositions are held .... What is peculiar to autonomy is the willingness and capacity to seek and evaluate information relevant to those views and to revise or abandon an assent already given .... the autonomous mind automatically accord intellectual due process even to its ideological enemies .... But autonomy does not exclude concern for the capacity to enjoy, produce, or-especially-to love. Autonomy is wholly compatible with-often indispensable to- these other qualities .... [T]he second misconception about autonomy is to view it as a lonely separation of the individual from collective values, human support, and charity .... Indeed, the ability to keep intact one's early associations and experience and to integrate them into adult life seems often-though not inevitably-associated with autonomy .... A third misconception of autonomy is to perceive it as a threshold of personal power-as the capacity to get, learn, achieve, and create by the efficient use of one's brains, muscles, or money. (Coons, 1978, p. 71-74)

a. **Fiscal Autonomy**—the school receives "the full operating funds associated with its student enrollment" (Bierlein, 1994b, p. 35). "... every school has complete control over money allocated as a result of per-pupil funding" (McCotter, 1996, p. 1).

b. **Legal Autonomy**—the right to sue and be sued, to be a full party to a contract, to hire and fire staff including certificated teachers.

4. **Chaos**—... may best be understood as a dynamic view of phenomena that represents in the behavior of systems a midpoint between strict determinism and total randomness. Its primary point of application occurs when the condition of a system changes over time, although the term chaos is a bit of a misnomer. Conventional wisdom would associate the terms with complete randomness in the state of a system, without the possibility of prediction and control. Chaos science, however, is based on a more complex set of assumptions. On the one hand, the "noise" in a system (unexplained variance) can be shown to have a certain degree of predictability, particularly when the parameters of an open system are expanded. On the other hand, chaos implies that total prediction for many phenomena can never be achieved, no matter how precise are the measurement systems used (Pool, 1989). As observed by Crutchfield, Farmer, Packard, and Shaw (Crutchfield, 1986), "chaos provides a mechanism that allows for free will within a world governed by deterministic laws" (Gleick, 1987, p. 57).

The theory asserts that, although the initial relationships between two variables may appear simple and deterministic, a less visible nonlinear relationship may still exist. Outcomes that we cannot predict at all using traditional reductionist research design may result. (Ennis, 1992, p. 117)

Robert Poole, an editor at <u>Science</u>, has defined chaos as "deterministic randomness, that conveys a cause (determinism) behind irregular, unpredictable behavior (randomness)" (Chenery, 1991, p. 28).

5. Charter School—"an autonomous, results oriented, publicly funded school of choice that is designed and run by teachers or other operators under contract with a public sponsor" (Buechler, 1996 p. viii). However,

Defining what is or is not a charter school is complex. Cities such as Milwaukee, and public school districts, such as those in New York, have established charter-like schools if one judges by the freedom these schools have from regulations and the choice that students have to attend these schools .... There exists no consensus definition of 'charter schools' or 'charter school legislation.' (U.S. Department of Education, 1997)

[A charter school] is a publicly funded school without some of the restrictions of regular public schools-how free varies from state to state. In Alaska, such schools can hire their own principals, manage their budgets, set their own curriculum and choose text books, but must be approved by their local school district, hire teachers with Alaska certificates, and follow the pay and other rules of the teachers' contract with the larger school district. (Shinohara, 1995, p. B-1)

Charter schools are public, nonsectarian schools that do not have admissions tests but that operate under a written contract, or charter, from a local school board or some other organization, such as a state school board. These contracts specify how the school will be held accountable for improved student achievement, in exchange for a waiver of most rules and regulations governing how they operate. (Nathan, 1996, p. xiii-xiv)

Instead of being subject to regulatory control, each [charter] school operates under the terms of a charter or contract with a sponsoring agency (e.g. a local school board, county board of education, state board0. Within broad parameters established by charter-school laws, each school's charter spells out the outcomes against which the school is held accountable and how those outcomes will be measured, methods of school governance, and the policymaking and decisionmaking roles of parents and teachers. Ideally, charter schools also enjoy operational independence from their sponsoring agencies so they can make the curricular, managerial, and fiscal dicisions needed to meet the terms of their charters .... Charter schools are exempt from most of the state codes that apply to public schools in exchange for agreeing to be held accountable for publicly established outcomes. In this way, the schools are accountable to their clients-students, parents, and, more generally, taxpayers. Each school's charter spells out measurable student-learning outcomes and operating procedures the school will meet. Failure to do so can result in revocation of the charter. And there are still controls. In particular, charter schools must be tuition free, nonsectarian, nonselective in admissions, and nondiscriminatory. If they receive federal funds, they must meet the monitoring and reporting requirements associated with expending those funds. (Corwin, 1994, p. 1-2)

In its purest form, a charter school is an autonomous educational entity operating under a contract negotiated between the organizers who manage the school (teachers, parents, or others from the public or private sector[4]), and the sponsors who oversee the provisions of the charter (local school boards, state education boards, or some other public authority). Charter provisions address such issues as the school's instructional plan, specific educational outcomes and their measurement, and management and financial issues. A charter school may be formed from a school's existing personnel and facilities or from a portion thereof (for example, a school-within-a-school); or it may be a completely new entity with its own facilities. Once approved, a charter school is an independent legal entity with the ability to hire and fire, sue and be sued, award contracts for outside services, and control its own finances. Funding is based on student enrollment, as it would be for a school district .... 'Model' elements are as follows: 1. At least one other public authority besides the local school board is able to sponsor the school (for example, a county board, state board, or university). 2. The state allows a variety of public or private individuals/groups the opportunity to organize, seek sponsorship, and operate a charter school. 3. The charter school is a discrete legal entity. 4. The charter school, as a public entity, embraces the ideals of the common school. It is nonsectarian in programs and operations, tuition-free, nonselective [sic] in admissions, nondiscriminatory in practices, and accountable to a public body. 5. Each charter school is accountable for its performance, both to parents and to its sponsoring public authority. 6. In return for stricter accountability, states exempt charter schools from all state and local laws and regulations except those related to health, safety, and nondiscrimination practices, and those agreed to within the charter provisions. 7. A charter school is a school of choice for student, parents, and teachers; no one is forced to be there. 8. Each charter school receives the full operating funds associated with its student enrollment (that is, fiscal autonomy). 9. Within a charter school, teachers may be employees or owners and/or subcontractors. If previously employed in a district, they retain certain 'leave' protections (seniority, retirement benefits, and so on) should they choose to return within a designated time frame. (Bierlein, 1994b, p. 34-35)

Once granted approval, a charter school becomes an independent legal entity with the ability to hire and fire, sue and be sued, award contracts for outside services, and control its own finances .... With a focus on educational outcomes, charter schools are freed from many (or all) district and state regulations often perceived as inhibiting innovation (e.g. excessive teacher certification requirements, collective bargaining agreements, Carnegie Units, and other curriculum requirements) .... Charter schools [are a] trade-off between autonomy and accountability. After a charter school gains approval from a local school board or other authorized sponsor, the school is free to manage its own affairs, e.g. lease space, hire personnel, contract for services, enroll students0. Though the school is subject to the same audits and inspections imposed by school districts and the state, it is not held to all of the same rules and regulations. In exchange for this freedom, the charter school is held to strict accountability on student outcomes. The overall educational focus is on outcomes, not inputs. (Bierlein, 1994a, p. 1-2)

A charter is essentially a contract, negotiated between those people starting the school and the official body authorized to approve the charter. The charter spells out how the school will be run, what will be taught, how success will be measured and what students will achieve. As long as the school meets the terms of its charter, it is free from many of the rules and regulations that apply to other public schools. And, unlike other schools, if a charter school fails to meet these terms, the charter can be revoked and the school closed. (McCotter, 1996, p. 1)

[Charter schools] operate unfettered by most state and local district regulations governing other public schools. Instead, they are held accountable for improving student performance and achieving the goals of their charter contracts. (U.S. Department of Education, 1997)

6. Disparity Test—After the top 5% and the lowest 5% school districts are removed from the ordered list of per pupil expenditures, the federal disparity test enjoins states that capture Federal Impact Aid to ensure that the difference between the highest school district's per pupil expenditure and the lowest school district's per pupil expenditure does not exceed 20%. The federal regulations state:

Federal "Disparity Test"
Improving America's Schools Act of 1994
Title VIII-Impact Aid
Sec. 8001. PURPOSE

In order to fulfill the Federal responsibility to assist with the provision of educational services to federally connected children, because certain activities of the Federal Government place a financial burden on the local education agencies serving areas where such activities are carried out, and to help such children meet challenging State standards, it is the purpose of this title to provide financial assistance to local educational agencies that—
(1) experience a substantial and continuing financial burden due to the acquisition of real property by the United State;
(2) educate children who reside on Federal property and whose parents are employed on Federal property;
(3) educate children or parents who are in the military services and children who live in low-rent housing;
(4) educate heave concentrations of children whose parents are civilian employees of the Federal Government and do not reside on Federal property;
(5) experience sudden and substantial increases or decreases in enrollments because of military realignments;; or
(6) need special assistance with capital expenditures for construction activities because of the enrollments of substantial numbers of children who reside on Federal lands.

Sec 8009(b) State Equalization Plans
(2) COMPUTATION-

a. In general—For purposes of paragraph (1), a program of State aid equalizes expenditures among local education agencies if, in the second fiscal year preceding the fiscal year for which the determination is made, the amount of per-pupil expenditures made by, or per-pupil revenues available to, the local education agency in the State with the highest per-pupil expenditures or revenues did not exceed the amount of such per-pupil

expenditures made by, or per-pupil revenues available to, the local educational agency in the State with the lowest such expenditures or revenues by more than—
i. 25 percent for fiscal year 1995, 1996, or 1997; and
ii. 20 percent for fiscal year 1998 or 1999
b. OTHER FACTORS—In making a determination under this subsection, the Secretary shall—
i. Disregard local educational agencies with per-pupil expenditures or revenues above the 95th percentile or below the 5th percentile of such expenditures or revenue in the State; and
ii. Take into account the extent to which a program of State aid reflects the additional cost of providing free public education in particular types of local education agencies, such as those that are geographically isolated, or to particular types of students, such as children with disabilities.

7. Dissipative Structures—"… forms and processes which depend for their existence on irreversibility, in which order is generated out of what appears at the molecular level as the merest chaos" (Griffiths, 1991, p. 436).

8. English grant-maintained schools—The English Reform Act of 1988 … provided for a strengthening of the authority of the Department of Education in curriculum and a lessening of the power of the local education offices while concurrently increasing the autonomy of school and colleges for the purposes of efficiency and achievement of higher standards for student achievement …. The legislation stipulated that the control of the curriculum resided with the Secretary of State, the executive of the Department of Education and Science, while schools were responsible for taking the programs of study which emerge from national curriculum councils and turning them into syllabuses and working timetables. These grant-maintained schools are financed directly by the English Department of Education. The decision to become a grant-maintained school rests with the parents who vote for this status which eliminates control by the local school district. (Pratt, 1996, p. 31-32)

9. Fallacy of the Stolen Concept—The fallacy consists in using a higher-level concept while denying or ignoring its hierarchical roots, i.e., one or more of the earlier concepts on which it logically depends. [For example, the assertion that "Everything is subjective."]

The reason stolen concepts are so prevalent is that most people (and most philosophers) have no idea of the "roots" of a concept. In practice, they treat every concept as a primary, i.e., as a first-level abstraction; thus they tear the concept from any place in a hierarchy and thereby detach it from reality. Thereafter, its use is governed by caprice or unthinking habit, with no objective guidelines for the mind to follow. The result is confusion, contradiction, and the conversion of language into verbiage.

The antidote is the process of reduction. In regard to higher-level concepts, reduction completes the job of definition. The purpose of definition is to keep a concept connected to a specific group of concretes. The definition of a higher-level concept, however, counts on the relevant lower-level concepts, which must themselves be connected to concretes; otherwise, the definition is useless. Reduction is what takes a person from the initial definition through the definitions of the next lower level and then of the next, until he reaches the direct perception of reality. This is the only means by which the initial definition can be made fully clear.

[C]ertain concepts—actually, pseudo-concepts—cannot be reduced to observational data. This is the proof that such concepts are invalid.

"Invalid concepts," writes Miss Rand, are "words that represent attempts to integrate errors, contradictions, or false propositions, such as concepts originating in mysticism … -or words without specific definitions, without referents, which can mean anything to anyone, such as modern 'anti-concepts' [these are deliberately equivocal terms, such as "extremism," "McCarthyism," "isolationism"]." Any such term is detached from reality and "invalidates every proposition or process of thought in which it is used as a cognitive assertion" (Rand, 1990, p. 49). (Peikoff, 1991, p. 136-137)

10. Ideological Progressivism—"[T]he belief that providing teachers and students with greater autonomy and encouragement will spontaneously and inevitably lead to higher and more sophisticated levels of performance and is sufficient to significantly improve education" (Pogrow, 1997, p. 34).

11. Indicators of Accountability—The indicators of accountability used in this study were: standardized tests; Iowa Test of Basic Skills; California Test of Basic Skills; California Achievement Test; Miller's Analogies Test; Scholastic Aptitude Test version 9; California Test of Basic Skills - Español; Scholastic Achievement Battery - Español; Aprenda; La Prueba; state assessment program; performance-based tests developed locally; performance-based tests developed as part of a national or state effort; student portfolios; student's demonstration of their work; parent satisfaction surveys; behavioral indicators such as attendance, expulsion, and college-going rate, etc.; other.

12. Indicators of Freedom—The indicators of freedom used in this study were: total budget; purchase of supplies & equipment; school calendar; daily schedule; student assessment; student admissions; student discipline (e.g. suspension, expulsion, dress code); establishment of curriculum; hiring teaching staff; facility; instructional methods; goal attainment; same as public schools; management strategies; collective bargaining agreement; higher standards; decision making; district regulations; state regulations; Carnegie units.

13. Indicator Systems—"… progress reports that pull together various kinds of data from schools, school districts, or states; interpret the data in an appropriate context; and attempt to follow changes in those data over time" (Ramirez, 1992, p. 33).

14. Instructional Unit—The state of Alaska defines "instructional unit" in statute as a group of 13 secondary school students or a group of 17 elementary school students. Statute allocates $61,000 for each unit.

15. League of Professional Schools—"is a network of public schools in Georgia committed to making informed decisions about instructional improvement through shared governance and action research" (Bryant-Booker, 1995, p. 10).

16. Libertarianism—… is a philosophy of personal liberty-the liberty of each person to live according to his own choices, provided he does not attempt to coerce others and thus prevent them from living according to their choices. Libertarians hold this to be an inalienable right of man; thus libertarianism represents a total commitment to the concept of individual rights. (Hospers, 1971, p. 5)

17. Normal Curve Equivalents—"NCEs are similar to percentiles. They have a mean of 50 and a standard deviation of 21.06" (Karweit, 1993, p. 2).

18. Participative Decision Making—(PDM) is defined by Vroom and Yetton (1973) as a process of joint decision making by two or more parties. The amount of participation of any individual is related to the amount of influence he has on the decisions and plans agreed upon. (Bryant-Booker, 1995, p. 10)

19. Program for School Improvement—"(PSI) is a nonprofit operation focusing on the individual school as the center of improvement which is part of the School of Teacher Education in the College of Education at the University of Georgia" (Bryant-Booker, 1995, p. 11).

20. Rural—
 Sec. 14.43.700
 Definition
In AS 14.43.600 - 14.43.700, "rural" means a community with a population of 5,500 or less that is not connected by road or rail to Anchorage or Fairbanks or with a population of 1,500 or less that is connected by road or rail to Anchorage or Fairbanks.

21. School report card—i) School report cards are public statements of the condition of individual schools and the results of their educational programs.

 (1) Two kinds of report card dominate today. Individual report cards inform parents and the public about a single school. Compiled report cards, prepared for administrators and school boards, contain a uniform set of tables used to quickly compare statistics for a number of schools.

 (2) Our analysis of report cards produced 10 categories of often-reported information: Standardized Testing, Student Engagement, School Success, School Environment, Staffing and Characteristics of Teachers, Programmatic Offerings, School Facilities, Student Services, Background Characteristics of Students, and School Finances. (Jaeger, 1994, p. 42-43)

22. Shared Governance— is defined as a democratic decision-making process that ensures teachers an equal vote on issues related to the schoolwide instructional program.

22. "Strong" charter legislation—i) Seven criteria that define strong charter legislation: (1) The possibility of a non-local board sponsor or the option of an appeal process; (2) Permission for any individual or group to attempt to organize a charter proposal; (3) Automatic exemption from state and local regulations rather than case-by-case or individual appeals processes; (4) Fiscal autonomy-every school has complete control over money allocated as a result of per-pupil funding; (5) Complete legal autonomy or charter determination of the level of legal autonomy; (6) No (or very high) limits on the number of charter schools that can be formed; (7) The acceptance of some percentage of non-certified employees as teachers in charter schools. (McCotter, 1996, p. 1-2)

 All strong laws include the following provisions for charter schools:

(1) allow entities other than local school boards, such as county or state boards or universities, to sponsor charter schools-or else they provide a process to appeal rejections by the local board;

(2) allow any individual or group to make a charter proposal, rather than limiting that prerogative to select groups, such as certified teachers;

(3) exempt charter schools from nearly all state and local laws, rules, and policies, rather than requiring charter schools to seek waivers on a case-by-case basis;

(4) give charter schools legal autonomy, so that staff members are employees of the charter school (not the local district), with the charter board determining salary and contract provisions;

(5) allow individuals other than certified teachers to teach at charter schools; and

(6) do not limit the number of charter schools that can be formed in the state. (Willis, 1995, p. 5)

24. Symmetry—… symmetry is the preservation of the shape of an object even after we deform or rotate it. Several kinds of symmetries occur repeatedly in nature. The first is the symmetry of rotations and reflections …. Another type of symmetry is created by reshuffling a series of objects. (Kaku, 1994, p. 125)

A third type of symmetry is called "self similarity," "… self-similarity is symmetry across scale. It implies recursion, pattern inside of pattern" (Gleick, 1987, p. 103). A fourth type of symmetry is known as

… spontaneous symmetry breaking. This means that what appear to be a number of completely different particles at low energies are in fact found to be all the same type of particle, only in different states. At high energies all these particles behave similarly.

Up to 1956 it was believed that the laws of physics obeyed each of three symmetries called C, P., and T. The symmetry C means that the laws are the same for particles and antiparticles. The symmetry P means that the laws are the same for any situation and its mirror image (the mirror image of a particle spinning in a right-handed direction is one spinning in a left-handed direction). The symmetry T means that if you reverse the direction of motion of all particles and antiparticles, the system should go back to what it was at earlier times; in other words, the laws are the same in the forward and backward directions of time. (Hawking, 1988, p. 71)

25. System Indicators—a. … are nothing more than sets of statistics that reveal something about the condition of an educational system-a school, district, state, or nation. Indicators may cover a wide range of elements including revenues, qualifications of personnel, curriculum, dropout and graduation rates, and college attendance. Because inputs and process are believed to be related to outcomes, system indicators address all three components of the educational process. (Brown, 1990, p. 2)

26. Teleology—"The doctrine or study of ends or final causes, esp. as related to the evidences of design or purpose in nature." (The Compact Edition of the Oxford English Dictionary, 1971, p. 3251).

27. Tragedy of the Commons—

a. [a systems] archetype [that] identifies the causal connections between individual actions and the collective results (in a closed system). It hypothesizes that if the individual use of a common resource becomes too great for the system to support, the commons will become overloaded or depleted and everyone will experience diminishing benefits. (Archetype behavior pairs, 1994, p. 6)

b. In all these situations, the logic of local decision making leads inexorably to collective disaster. Hardin first coined the term to describe situations where two conditions are met: (1) there exists a "commons," a resource shared among a group of people, and (2) individual decision makers, free to dictate their own actions, achieve short-term gains from exploiting the resource but do not pay, and are often unaware of, the cost of that exploitation-except in the long run.

"... Tragedy of the Commons structures are most insidious when the coupling from individual action to collective consequence is weak in the short run, yet strong in the long run. Local managers see their actions as independent, they don't realize how they may be jeopardizing their and others' future. They fail to see how their individual "activity" will eventually reduce everyone's "gain per activity." (Senge, 1990, p. 295, 296)

28. Urban—An Alaska community with a population of 5,501 or more that is not connected by road or rail to Anchorage or Fairbanks or with a population of 1,501 or more that is connected by road or rail to Anchorage or Fairbanks. (See "Rural")

29. Value-added assessment—A Tennessee program that "... attempts to measure the 'value' a teacher adds to students over the period of a year, using sophisticated statistical techniques with norm referenced testing" (Hurst, 1994).

30. "Weak" charter legislation—legislation that:i) ... require[s] each exemption to be specified in the charter petition or require charter schools to seek exemptions or waivers through the same process traditional schools must follow .... States with weaker laws require the charter's level of fiscal autonomy to be specified in the charter petition or deny fiscal autonomy altogether. (Norris, 1996, p. 17)

Weak laws are found in states where there was a strong lobby by teacher unions, and in some cases school board associations, opposing strong legislation. Unions have feared that strong legislation will provide the local governing boards of charter schools the opportunity to employ instructors on annual contracts only and who further have the power to hire and fire employees at-will. These practices promise to erode the union power base .... The teacher unions are concerned that schools could abandon collective bargaining and hire non-certified teachers. Presently, these personnel issues center on teachers having property rights to instructional positions. (Pratt, 1996, p. 35-36)

Organization of the Study

After this introductory chapter, the review of the literature begins with the legislative history of the discussions leading to the passage of Alaska's charter school legislation. Significant points of the various Alaska Department of Education (AK-DOE) sponsored workshops follows the legislative history. What follows next is the review of the educational literature, those magazines and journals that have reported the progress of the development of the charter school movement. Following the educational literature is a review of those journal articles dealing with the independent variable, freedom and its correlates, choice and autonomy. After a review of literature on the independent variable, is a review of journal articles dealing with the dependent variable, accountability and its correlate, assessment. The next section will review the literature that relates freedom to accountability. At the end of the review will be a summary that will highlight the most significant themes and findings. In chapter three the researcher will provide a description of the design and methodology of the research project. The following chapter will present the results of the surveys. In the final chapter, the researcher will present several recommendations based on the results of the inquiry.

Summary

This study involved the collection of data in order to explore the relationship between freedom and accountability in charter schools and to describe the current status of charter schools in Alaska. The costs allied with charter schools, the need to identify efficiencies, and the call for charter school accountability were justifications for the study. The author designed survey instruments based on and adapted from national and other state's survey tools. Pertinent terms were elucidated. The following chapter provides a review of literature fitting to charter schools.

Chapter Two
Review of the Literature

Introduction

A search of the literature was conducted to explore not only what had been written about charter schools, but also what had been written about school accountability and about school choice and its synonyms: freedom and autonomy. "School choice" was generally understood to mean: "A number of alternative arrangements in which parents are permitted to choose which particular school their children will attend" ASCD, 1990 (as cited in Roberts, 1993, p. 8-9). The search of areas pertinent to the project included a review of published materials (books, journal articles, reports, conference proceedings, television documentaries, transcripts of television shows, court cases, legislative histories, states' charter school guides, charter schools' applications, state department of education informational publications, state-level and national-level studies, videotape presentations, audiotape presentations, newspaper articles, state legislation, state administrative regulations, and bills of the Alaska legislature) and of unpublished materials (studies, presentations, interviews with charter school advocates and objectors, masters' theses, and doctoral dissertations) and also an examination of Internet web sites, home-pages, and "listservs." The literature reviewed also included examination of charter school e-mail communications.

Historical Perspectives

Although the state Board of Education approved the first three charter schools in Alaska two and a half years ago, it is too early to evaluate how well Alaska's charter schools are doing to form anything but tentative findings about them. The 20th Alaska legislature's Republican majority's efforts to consolidate school districts, to form boroughs,[5] and to revise the charter school law[6] toward the end of the First Legislative Session of the 20th Legislative Session 1997, the issue of charter school legislation was still on the minds of some legislators. Senator Bert Sharp's SB 182 and Rep. Fred Dyson's HB 441 failed to get consideration in the respective legislative chambers. However, due to the short existence of Alaska's charter schools, almost no student achievement data were available.

Charter schools are a part of the dynamic system of public education. In education, as well as other disciplines, we fashion our knowledge from the core, but we learn at the perimeters. Like the ever widening circles on the surface of a pond, education has accumulated its understanding from the inside out. The study of charter schools, that has yet to have a central point, is an immature field with an ill-defined focus of understanding.

The freedom and accountability relationship in charter schools occurs in the context of human culture. People make decisions, have curiosity, have values, and form opinions. As a result, it is not likely that public education will see an infinite number of charter schools emerging from this exchange. Why is this? Reality is not reductionist; human institutions are not simple. They resist linear absolutes, they are non-Thoreauvian and "[s]imple shapes are inhuman. They fail to resonate with the way nature organizes itself or with the way human perception sees the world" (Gleick, 1987). Fullan (1993) put it another way: "What appears simple is not so—introducing a seemingly small change turns out to have wild consequences" (Fullan, 1993, p. viii).

These new theories, that parallel research in systems thinking and chaos theory, do more than just expand the range of tools available to education researchers. They insinuate ways for us to grapple with the complexity of educational issues and to transcend the limitations of earlier methods. Marion (1992) has said:

> Research in education and organization has traditionally been statistical rather than deterministic.... The questions asked and the data collected by determinists are similar to those asked by chaologists (who are themselves determinists). Social scientists, on the other hand, will have to revise the way they conceptualize questions and collect data in order to pursue chaotic descriptions of social phenomena.... The difficulty for education is that, unlike the fields where chaos data analysis is progressing, educators do not typically collect dynamic measures of phenomena.... In education, a common measurement is achievement test scores. This data is reasonably accurate (although some would argue the point) and copious, but it is not dynamic.... To experiment with chaos in a social environment, researchers will need to define appropriate measures and observational techniques for collecting the type of data needed.
>
> Flander's Interaction Analysis suggests itself. Flander's procedures collect data on a single unit of analysis (the classroom) over time. The technique could easily be applied to other variables, such as discipline, student attending, and level of tension in faculty meetings. (Marion, 1992, p. 171-173)

Furthermore, these new theories upset the stability of the prior models. The relationships between freedom and accountability were the focal points inherent in public schools. As dynamical systems, public schools preferred stability. The focal points balanced the process that led to deterministic projections of behavior. Freedom and accountability represented distinct states of public schools and the energy that went into them. On the other hand, when the charter school concept was introduced, the public school system became agitated. The public school system was forced to move away from stability, and it showed a broad range of responses. With regards to charter schools, it was the initial conditions of freedom that generated the unpredictability of the future. As the amount of freedom increased and dissipative structures began to have an effect, change began to enter the system. The change revealed itself in patterns of focal points.

Location, funding, and governance were themes that occurred quite often in the charter school debates and they regularly were the foci of attention of participants. Although charter school advocates discussed many other educational issues, position groups formed around non-educational issues. Who will pay for the charter school? Who will provide financial auditing services? Who will control governance? Who will hire and fire staff? Who will determine the course of study? Who will choose the location of the charter school?

The public school system has a favored state of constancy. Occurrences of balancing processes both create and constrain this condition. The key determiner of the constancy in public school systems was the legalized use of force within a given political region. Legislative fiat created public schools and compulsory attendance. Truancy laws (Appendix G) enjoined parents to send their children to school. As long as this mode of organization was left alone, it gave the appearance of being typical. Enter the legislature with its authority to redistribute the use of coercion to another public school entity, the charter school. Levy (1991) called public schools, "… quasi-monopolies in neighborhood attendance and accountability to government officials who have their own interests …" (Levy, 1991, p. 195). Kolderie (1990) insisted that charter schools removed the "exclusive franchise" (Kolderie, 1990) from public schools. In fact legislative fiat merely shifted or redistributed the locus of coercion to another entity. This redistribution was given the name of "freedom."

In the 1960s, another form of coercion was visited upon education. The teachers' unions, the National Education Association (NEA) and the American Federation of Teachers (AFT) convinced congress to codify organized labor's monopoly on bargaining. The charter school legislation in Alaska failed to remove labor's "exclusive franchise" that forced school boards to bargain with the teachers' unions.

The establishment of charter schools in Colorado presaged legal challenges. On August 24, 1994, Lorraine Villanueva and Jennie Vasco sought injunctive relief from the Pueblo, Colorado School District's decision to shut down a local elementary school to make way for a charter school. The parents of students who attended a Pueblo, Colorado neighborhood school that was slated to be closed in favor of a charter school challenged Colorado's charter schools act as unconstitutional and the closure decision as violative of their children's equal protection rights. The U.S. District Court rejected both challenges, but lectured the district on how it should have implemented its school closure decision to better address the concerns of students and parents. The court found:

1. closure of schools did not violate equal protection clause or in any way discriminate against Hispanic students;
2. Colorado Charter Schools Act was not unconstitutional; and
3. there was no private cause of action under Elementary and Secondary School Improvement Act Amendments. Motion for permanent injunction denied; complaint dismissed (Villaneuva v. Carere, 1994).

The portion of the decision that had the most relevance for Alaska school districts was the section commenting on the potentially discriminatory or exclusionary impact of some of the admissions procedures that the school used. These procedures included permitting parents of applicants to camp out in line to enroll their children, asking parents to disclose their place of employment, and requiring pre-acceptance interviews with parents. Those sections of the opinion dealing with school closure issues had little relevance for most Alaska districts because, outside Alaska's major metropolitan areas, closure of one district school in favor of a charter school would leave a local community with no other option for their children's attendance. Legal opinion clarified this issue:

> At the other end of the spectrum, [Alaska] school districts have an obligation to provide an alternative to a charter school's program for their students. AS 14.03.265(b) states: "A school board may not require a student to attend a charter school." This means that districts may not permit the conversion of the only school in an attendance area to a charter school without providing student access to the district's regular educational program. If that access can be provided only by requiring students to travel a significant distance from their homes, the conversion to a charter school probably imposes an unreasonable burden on those district students who do not wish to attend the school, and therefore would probably require denial of the charter school's application. The same would likely be true of a proposal to convert an existing school into a charter school, if the net result were a significant increase in the pupil/teacher ratio or in crowding of other district schools. (A. Gifford, personal communication, March 28, 1996)

Educational value systems were another determinant of the interaction between freedom and accountability in charter schools. Normative educational value orientations appeared stable because of the amount of effort that people devoted to the formative philosophical disciplines from which they emerged and the difficulty to mount the energy needed to perturb them. The desire to establish a beachhead for their individual or group value orientations, be they governance-based or ideological-based, often motivated charter school founders. These value orientations determined the decisions that charter school founders made about curriculum, instruction, and assessment. Indeed, "Teachers' own value attractors may be the most influential factors in curricular decision making .... [T]eachers' value orientations often dominate the curriculum selection process" (Ennis, 1992, p. 21). Ennis (1992) declared:

> Educational values serve as a deep attractor basin for [charter schools], effectively encouraging a stable, limited set of participant behaviors. Alternative modes of operation ... or new organizational formats, [governance], are encouraged so long as they are consistent with the set of approved policies. There is room for difference, but only within the steep walls of the deep attractor basin [the public school system]. (Ennis, 1992, p. 121)

The steep walls were the constraints or dissipative factors affecting the freedom of the charter school. Ennis (1992) has identified

> [t]hree major constraints ... the learner, the instruction, and the context.
>
> *Learner constraints* ... represent learners' unique characteristics ... individual differences associated with culture, ethnicity, gender, socioeconomic class, language, handicapping condition, and intellectual and physical ability ... that modify the learning process .... [P]erceptual differences also influence how well students understand information and find meaning.

Other hidden constraints—learner expectation, self-concept, and locus of control—diminish opportunities for students to pursue their interests

Instructional constraints ... consist of the school-and teacher-designated content, methods, and materials selected specifically for their perceived effect on student learning.

Contextual constraints ... include social, economic, and political conditions that control or facilitate opportunities for learning. (Ennis, 1992, p. 122-124)

According to Giroux, contextual constraints, such as accountability, often lead to oppression, inequality, and silencing in school and social systems" (Giroux, 1986). An example of silencing came from the Chinook Charter School in Fairbanks, Alaska:

Of the schools' 56 families, only 11 responded to an anonymous *News-Miner* survey that included questions about ethnicity, income and educational background—for fear, some parents said, of harming Chinook during its fledgling year. The teachers have coached parents, through conversation and typed memos, to keep problems within the school family. (Hower, 1997, p. A-6)

It took an enormous amount of energy, though, to disturb the constancy of the public school system. Two institutions fused to create this energy. Legislatures granted "freedom," and they disbursed funds from the public treasury. In 1996, Congress approved Pres. Clinton's request for $50 million dollars in the Improving America's Schools Act for charter school grants. Furthermore, Ennis suggested, "When two or more attractors [freedom and accountability] blend to form a unique perspective ... [that] may result in a major change or bifurcation that leads to reorganization within the system" (Ennis, 1992, p. 125).

When this "coupling" took place, there was often spillover from one focal point to another as the change appeared. This spillover was called "cascading" and it "refers to the multi-tiered influence of strange attractors [focal points] as they affect a succession of decisions ..." (Ennis, 1992, p. 126). For example, "The observable complexity in the operational curriculum results from the cascading and coupling ...within the attractors and constraints in the educational ecosystem" (Ennis, 1986, p. 38).

Legislative value systems were yet another determinant of the interaction between freedom and accountability. Political value orientations were subject to the steady state of the pendulum. Without the periodic revisiting of the "will of the people" through the ballot box, the political value orientation would appear stable and settle to a point. Absent the ballot box, legislatures will struggle to institutionalize their respective party dominants to minimize the broad swings of political positions between the far left and the far right. Political value orientations appear resolute because of the monolithic effort people have devoted to the synthesis of metaphysics, epistemology, and ethics that shows itself as a political system. Political campaigns and their corollary, political campaign contributions, represent the amount of energy people put into maintaining the political party, that is the status quo political value orientation.

One demonstration of this institutionalization is collective bargaining. Collective bargaining laws have the fundamental effect of shifting the locus of labor control from management to the individual teacher surrogate, the teachers' bargaining unit and its sponsor, the major teachers' unions. With regard to the political support for charter school legislation in Alaska, the bill's sponsors courted the support of the state's largest teachers' union, the National Education Association-Alaska (NEA-AK). The desire to maintain the labor organization's salient value orientations motivated NEA-AK. During the legislative debate on CSSB 88, Claudia Douglas, President of NEA-AK, insisted that charter schools meet certain conditions relative to the union's control of labor in the charter schools. She stated that the legislation must provide for:

> ... voluntary staff and student assignment to charter schools; direct involvement of all effected school employees in the charter schools design, implementation and government; adequate defense in regards to contract and employment provisions for all employees; and, licensed professional staff (Senate HESS, 1995, p. 1).

These value orientations determined the decisions that the teacher charter school founders and staff made about their support for labor's involvement in the governance and the pedagogical environment of the school.

The political value orientation often produced the exact opposite of what was intended. Demitchell (1997) said,

> Although the law has been the vehicle for launching school reform efforts, little attention has been paid to the way legal mechanisms enable and constrain effective school reform. For example, several state legislatures have attempted to empower teachers and create collegial school environments by passing laws that require school districts to implement site-based management. However, other laws—specifically state collective bargaining statutes—virtually mandate that teachers and school districts relate to one another as adversaries.
>
> To date, no state legislature has come to terms with this incongruity. Thus, in state after state, laws that mandate a collegial and cooperative work environment exist side by side with labor laws that make this worthy reform goal difficult to attain. (Demitchell, 1997, p. 28)

In terms of dynamic systems, the creation of charter schools came about because of the dynamics of the public school system. The "equilibrium in the system is lost when an attractor [freedom] and its concomitant constraints [accountability] are no longer adequate to maintain the status quo" (Sawada, 1985, p. 16).

During the 1960s and 1970s, Ron Edmonds and Walter Brookover led educational research into an era of rapid growth that allowed others to investigate correlational factors in education in some detail. When taken in the context of the decades of educational questioning, it is interesting that now, in the late 1990s, educators still do not have a firm grasp on education. For charter schools, the center, the correlates of effective schools, is an immense body of knowledge.

However, once education gets away from the correlates—out at the periphery—then it becomes a different story. With regards to charter schools, Alex Molnar has said, "The reality is that without an enormous increase in funding, charter schools will at best be reform at the margins" (Pool, 1996, n.p.). By 1996, charter schools saw the beginnings of massive federal support in the form of Title X, Part C of the Elementary and Secondary Education Act. Appendix L lists the amounts that Alaska's charter schools received. The Matanuska-Sustina Borough School District provided a minimum of $250,000 in lease-holder improvements to the Midnight Sun Charter School in Wasilla.

There is a cliché that people should never see how laws or sausages are made. Unfortunately, this caveat applies to Alaska's charter schools. Responding to a request from Fairbanks, Sen. Bert Sharp, R-Fairbanks, introduced the charter school bill in the Senate. "Fairbanks North Star Borough School Superintendent Rick Cross and the Fairbanks school board last fall asked Interior legislators to revive the idea of charter schools,[7] and let the issue stand on its own" (Shinohara, 1995, p. B-2). Consequently, the legislature gathered to watch Senators and Representatives in their respective chambers debate the frontiers of education. They joined to hammer out a political picture of the least known of educational phenomenon: the Alaska charter school.

Before the Alaska legislature entered the charter school arena, Alaska educators did not have a consistent and clear picture of charter schools. All they knew were the superlative assertions that pundits wrote about them. Charter schools pushed educators' understanding of schooling to its limits. Sometimes charter schools were freewheeling and sublime, other times they were erupting into lawsuits, spewing charges of financial mismanagement (Merrow, 1997).

With their exceptional features and variability, charter schools were the most fascinating schools in education. They were also enigmas. Educators understood little about charter schools and did not even know what kind of schools they arise from or develop into. Part of the problem was that charter schools were new and rare. In 1991, Minnesota became the first state to bestow charters. Milo Cutter and Terry Kraabel founded the first charter school, City Academy, in St. Paul, Minnesota in 1992.[8] This meant that the "charter school phenomena"—the extreme hyperbole, variation, and assertions—occurred during a very short time in the life of charter school legislation. However, did all schools become charter schools or just a select few? What kind of schools would charter schools become? In short, what were these new schools?

When the Alaska legislature passed CSSB 88 (FIN), not only did it provide for the creation of charter schools but it also reduced the autonomy it had granted to school boards. First, it annulled some of the powers it granted to local school districts in 4AAC[9] 05.080—School Curriculum And Personnel (Appendix B), 4AAC 06.075—High School Graduation Requirements (Appendix C), and AS[10] 14.14.130—Chief School Administrator (Appendix D), and gave them to the founders of the charter school. Second, it dictated that the local school boards accept much of the language and 14 of the terms of the contract between it and the charter school. Third, the legislature assigned responsibility for charter school accountability to the local school board. The legislature compelled school boards to accept the only term of the contract referring to the minimum requirements for charter school accountability: AS 14.03.255 (c)(2) "specific levels of achievement for the educational program" and (12) a termination clause. Fourth, the legislature enhanced the rights of the teachers' union and reduced management rights by eliminating the superintendent from the administration of one of the district's public schools. The local school district's collective bargaining agreement with the teachers' union would apply to teachers in the charter school. The Academic Policy Committee would deal directly with the school board, thus bypassing the chief school administrator of the school district. Fifth, the legislature set up the dialectic of freedom and accountability in Alaska's charter schools. Accountability was one of the most often touted ideal characteristics of charter schools.

In return for assuming accountability for student performance, charter schools are exempted from collective bargaining agreements, district policies, and most or all state education laws and regulation. They are free to manage their own budgets, hire and fire staff, set salary levels, and so forth. (Buechler, 1996, p. vii)

Joe Nathan, director of the Center for School Change at the Hubert H. Humphrey Institute of Public Affairs, University of Minnesota, stated that:

... charter schools are an especially good option because they promise two-way accountability. They must declare what they will do for students and theoretically at least, must provide solid evidence—to families and to taxpayers—that they are doing what they promised. (Brandt, 1996, p. 5)

John Merrow reported on this highly touted feature. In Minnesota, charter schools, "[are] free to teach any way [they] choose, but it is freedom with accountability" (Merrow, 1997). Louann A. Bierlein and Lori A. Mulholland specified that, "With a focus on educational outcomes, charter schools are freed from many (or all) district and state regulations often perceived as inhibiting innovation—for example, excessive teacher certification requirements, collective bargaining agreements, Carnegie units, and other curriculum requirements" (Bierlein, 1994b, p. 35).

The legislative process was completed. What remained was the drafting of the implementation regulations. Following the law's passage, the Alaska Board of Education opened a period of public comment on proposed regulations to implement the charter school act. The public had until December 4, 1995 to express an opinion.

In the meantime, the Department of Education conducted several informational workshops around the state. On Tuesday, June 6, 1995, Alaska Commissioner of Education, Dr. Shirley Holloway held the first meeting, by teleconference, in the Commissioner's conference room in Juneau, Alaska, on the drafting of Alaska's charter school regulations. Norm Palenske, then superintendent of the Matanuska-Susitna Borough School District, sent a memorandum to all superintendents that summarized the meeting. There were eight questions that were addressed.

- Who actually employs charter school teachers? Are they eligible for state teacher retirement plans? Do state collective bargaining laws cover them? If still a public school employee, could a new teacher work at a charter school for several years and suddenly be tenured without ever being evaluated by a district administrator? Who makes decisions regarding hiring and firing?
- Has the question of liability been resolved? Can the local school board be sued for the actions of charter school personnel? Are charter school teachers protected from personal liability? Who is responsible for insurance needs?
- How much authority does the school board have over charter schools? Can the board veto decisions by charter school personnel? Can the Board enforce its regulations and mandates?
- How much access will the school board have over charter school records? Can district personnel audit financial records? Will student personnel records be open to district administrators?

- Who is responsible for the fiscal integrity of the charter school? Will the charter school be incorporated to limit liability? Will the school board ultimately be responsible for unpaid debts or fiscal mismanagement?
- Who will guarantee that state and federal mandates are followed? Although most charter school laws allow waivers to many regulations, charter schools are not exempt from federal laws regarding special education and limited English proficiency students.
- How will questions of enrollment be decided? Will minorities receive equal access? If the charter school serves particular youths—gifted, special education, or at-risk, for example—how will questions of equal access be resolved?
- Does the school board retain final authority over discipline? What are the legal implications of allowing charter school administrators to handle this issue? And if a child is expelled from the charter school, can he or she transfer to the public schools? (Palenske, 1995, p. 1-2)

On June 12, 1995, Commissioner Holloway sent a letter to the June 6 teleconference participants. She stated:

The consensus of the group was that each LEA needs to develop its own policies and guidelines for charter schools, while the State will propose only the regulations that are needed to give districts some guidance .... As a result of this meeting,
- Sheila Peterson will send to all school district superintendents information that the department has received on charter schools nationwide.
- Nancy Buell will continue to work on a federal grant request proposal that will provide federal dollars to support the charter school effort.
- Harry Gamble will assemble a small working committee to begin writing draft regulations to implement SB 88.
- The committee will include Norm Palenske [superintendent of the Matanuska-Susitna Borough School District], Carol Comeau [Assistant Superintendent of the Anchorage School District], Rick Cross [Superintendent of the Fairbanks-North Star Borough School District], Bart Mwarey [Principal of Takotna School], and Sheila Peterson [Special Assistant to the Commissioner]. (Holloway, 1995, p. 1)

On September 26, 1995 the second charter school workshop, "Alaska's New Charter School Law: 'From Passage to Implementation,'" was held in the Bristol Bay Ballroom of the Anchorage Hilton Hotel. Dr. Holloway moderated a panel. William Randall, Colorado Commissioner of Education, Senator Bert Sharp, Craig Black, Assistant Attorney General, Kimberly Homme, Special Assistant to the Commissioner of Education, William Windler, Senior Consultant to the Colorado Department of Education, Duane Guiley, Director of School Finance, and Harry Gamble, Education Administrator in the Alaska Department of Education were members of the panel. The workshop covered charter school guidelines, proposals, model charters, and contracts from Colorado's charter schools.

At its meetings in Dillingham, Alaska from October 23 to 25, the Alaska Board of Education opened a period of public comment on charter schools regulations. At its December 7 and 8, 1995 meeting, the Alaska Board of Education adopted regulations, 4 AAC 33.110 (Appendix E), that required districts to establish charter school application procedures before July 1, 1996.

Thirty charter schools were allocated both to achieve geographical balance and to provide opportunities for major urban centers to operate multiple charter schools. Anchorage was allocated 10 charter schools; five in Fairbanks; three in the Kenai Peninsula Borough; three in the Matanuska-Susitna Borough; and two in Juneau. In order to achieve geographical balance for the remaining seven charter schools, the regulations organized the remaining 49 school districts into seven regions (Appendix E). The school boards in those regions were given until June 30, 1997 to propose charter schools. After July 1, 1997, the regions expired and the Alaska Board of Education used its discretion in achieving a geographical balance of approved charter schools.

Although the Alaska Board of Education was poised to approve two charter school applications at its February 20 and 22, 1996 meeting, it postponed action on the applications of the Takotna Training Center from the Iditarod Area School District and the Project Education Charter School from the Galena City School District. The postponement was predicated on the Alaska Board of Education directing the Department of Education to develop a compliance checklist (Table 1) to assure that applications met the requirements of the charter school law. Since the local school boards were the first-line authority to approve or deny a charter school application, the checklist amounted to a de facto proscription on the authority of the local board. The compliance checklist enumerated those freedom factors and accountability factors that the local school board must guarantee were contained in the charter school's application. Items 2, 2a, 2b, and 15 were those items that prescribe the freedoms of the charter school. Items 4, 5, 10, and 12 prescribed the elements of accountability that the charter school's application must contain.

By April 12, 1996, the Alaska Board of Education adopted the charter school regulations. Lieutenant Governor Fran Ulmer signed and filed them and they took effect on April 27, 1996. Local school boards were given until June 30, 1996 to develop charter school application procedures and to make them available to the public.

From the fall of 1995 to the spring of 1997, there were three charter schools approved in Alaska. At its April 16-17, 1996 meeting in Anchorage, the Alaska Board of Education approved the Chinook Charter School in Fairbanks. Although approved, the start up of the Project Education Charter School in Galena, Alaska was stalled over lease negotiations with the U.S. Air Force for the use of its decommissioned facilities in Galena, Alaska. The Takotna Training Center, a charter school located in the Iditarod Area School District, was also approved at the April 16-17, 1996 Alaska Board of Education meeting.

When the Alaska Department of Education announced the availability of federal charter school grants in the spring of 1997, 11 more charter schools received Local Education Agency and Alaska Board of Education approval in Alaska. In spite of this flurry of approvals, the Anchorage School District Board of Education disapproved the charter school application for "The Village Charter School." The North Slope Borough School District also disapproved the application of a charter school (L. Dishman, personal communication, August 1997).

On November 10, 1997, however, the Anchorage School Board finally approved the Village Charter School and the Sports Program for Youth Development Education and Recreation (SPYDER) Charter School application. At its February 17, 1998 meeting, the Alaska Board of Education approved the two charter applications, thus bringing to 17 the number of charter schools approved in the state of Alaska. The Anchorage School District Board of Education granted the SPYDER Charter School waiver of its opening for one year.

Shortly after opening in September 1998, Linda Sharp, the main organizer of the Village Charter School announced that she would close the school. In a letter that Linda Sharp, Carrie Merrill, a teacher at the Village Charter School, and Susan Anderson, President of the Academic Policy Committee, sent to the Anchorage School Board, they said, "... they decided it was better to shut down early in the school year so students could get set up in new schools" (Shinohara, 1998, p. A-1). Upon hearing of the school's closure, "Several Village Charter parents and students asked the School Board on Monday to give the school $40,000 to allow it to pay up-front costs and secure a long-term lease at another facility" (Shinohara, 1998, p. A-8).

Shortly after its opening, the Project Education Charter School posed problems for the state. Promising unfettered access to parent-selected course materials and the offer of the use of a school supplied micro-computer, the Project Education Charter School was slated to open with only 30 students. However, the popularity of its free Internet access soon inspired the school's principal, Steve Musser, to accept more students. When the numbers reached over 1,000 new students from all over the state of Alaska, the administration stopped accepting applications. Previously, these students were not state of Alaska public school attendees and, therefore, not accounted for in the school foundation funding scheme. When the Alaska Department of Education (AK-DOE) realized that it would have to request a supplemental request of approximately $11 million, it was faced with a dilemma. In its haste to present a positive acceptance of charter schools would it have to reign one in and risk the disapproval of both charter school advocates and the legislature? Or, would it jeopardize its education funding request to the governor's budget? The department responded in its capacity as a regulatory agency. However, by taking this action, the DOE asserted itself to be another body that would circumscribe the limited autonomy of charter schools.

The AK-DOE sent a team to Galena to investigate the verity of Superintendent Carl Knudsen's claims. The AK-DOE urged Superintendent Knudsen to explain the evolution of his cyber school project at the annual Alaska Association of School Administrators' conference at the Lake Lucille Best Western Inn in Wasilla, Alaska on October 10, 1997. In order to thwart Superintendent Knudsen's counting of the over 1,000 new extra-territorial students using the area cost differential of 1.32 for the Galena City Schools, Commissioner Holloway issued "Numbered Memorandum 97-12." The memorandum had the force of regulation until the Alaska Board of Education could approve the Commissioner's action. It said:

> The number of school districts offering correspondence programs to students, both within and outside of district boundaries has increased. These programs are providing a wide range of options to students and parents for receiving educational services. Current laws and regulations are not adequate to address this expanding educational alternative and several questions have been raised as a result.

The purpose of this memorandum is to inform all school districts of the Department of Education's policy regarding district-operated correspondence programs. This policy applies to all correspondence students whether they reside within or outside of the school district boundaries. Effective immediately:
1. The Department of Education will not pay the school district's area cost differential for correspondence students residing outside of the district; the area cost differential for out of district correspondence students will be 1.00;
2. The Department of Education will convene a working group to establish standards for correspondence school programs, and
3. The department of Education will prepare revisions to the Governor's Foundation Formula legislation, for introduction during the 1998 session, to determine a rate of reimbursement that will level the playing field for all correspondence programs [including the Alyeska Central Correspondence School]. (Holloway, 1997a)

In October 1997, Commissioner Holloway convened the Correspondence Schools Standards Task Force (CSSTF).[11] The purpose of the task force was to establish standards for correspondence programs and to develop a process for gaining correspondence school operation approval from the AK-DOE. The CSSTF met for the first time on November 11, 1997. The task force proposed the criteria correspondence schools would have to meet before the AK-DOE would grant approval. Both the standards and the process would eventually emerge as regulation.

At its November 11, 1997 meeting in Anchorage, the CSSTF, with the help of Harry Rogers, superintendent of the Valdez City School District, organized itself. The CSSTF held its second meeting on December 12 and 13, 1997. The committee came to consensus about the criteria correspondence programs would have to meet in order to gain approval from the AK-DOE. The criteria included:
- Standards for the correspondence program must be the same as for other district curricula.
- Local school boards must approve curricula for correspondence programs.
- A student assessment plan must be in place for the correspondence program.
- Correspondence programs must meet the same accreditation standards as other school district programs.
- Districts must document parental involvement in the planning, development, evaluation, and curricula of the correspondence program.

At the December 12-13 meeting, the CSSTF developed a timeline for obtaining AK-DOE approval. Dr. Virgie Fryrear, superintendent of the Alyeska Central School, and Tom Dahl, Assistant Attorney General, drafted a proposed regulation based on the work of the task force.

Prior to the existence of the Project Education central correspondence program, school districts were free to form their own correspondence programs without AK-DOE approval. It was clear that the thrust of this regulatory change was aimed directly at charter schools that operated correspondence study programs. As such it placed the AK-DOE as a de jure approval body for such entities. The proposed regulations would virtually guarantee the AK-DOE's hegemony over centralized correspondence programs. Dr. Fryrear and Mr. Dahl briefed the Alaska Board of Education on the proposed regulations on March 28, 1998.

While the Commissioner was going through the process to put her Numbered Memorandum 97-12 into regulation, Dr. Patrick Doyle and the Copper River School District (CRSD) protested. The Commissioner's Numbered Memorandum 97-12 limited districts operating correspondence study programs to an area cost differential of 1.0 for out-of-district students. CRSD alleged that the Commissioner had no legal authority to pay other than the district's statutory area cost differential (ACD), 1.14. As a result of the Commissioner's memorandum, the CRSD lost $99,000 in correspondence foundation funding. The AK-DOE argued that the foundation formula only permitted the ACD factor for students who resided in the district. The dispute went to an administrative hearing.

The Project Education charter school's curriculum posed another problem. Again the AK-DOE used its regulatory authority to abrogate some of the freedom, especially in education programs, the legislature gave to charter schools. Project Education offered parents the option to select from a broad range of correspondence study programs, including some from sectarian institutions. Commissioner Holloway responded with Numbered Memorandum 97-13:

> Some school districts are apparently providing correspondence curricula that has been purchased or made available from sectarian sources. Article VII, Section 1, of the Alaska State Constitution provides:
>
>> **Public Education**. The legislature shall by general law establish and maintain a system of public schools open to all children of the State, and may provide for other educational institutions. *Schools and institutions so established shall be free from sectarian control. No money shall be paid from public funds for the direct benefit of any religious or other private educational institution.* (Emphasis added in original).
>
> In consultation with the Attorney General, the Department of Education has determined that including a religious curriculum among the curricula offered by a district to correspondence students violates this constitutional provision. School Districts are instructed not to purchase sectarian curricula in accordance with AS 14.03.090, which states:
>
>> **Partisan, sectarian, or denominational doctrines prohibited**. Partisan, sectarian, or denominational doctrines may not be advocated in a public school during the hours the school is in session. A teacher or school board violating this section may not receive public money.
>
> This provision applies to any part of a curriculum produced as part of a religious curriculum, such as a math course, even though that particular part of the curriculum may not appear to have religious content. (Holloway, 1997b)

The AK-DOE has recommended changes to the correspondence study regulations to the Alaska Board of Education that bring all correspondence study programs in line with the .65 of an instructional unit funding for the Alyeska Centralized Study correspondence program. In a July 1, 1998 memorandum, Commissioner Holloway

> ... explained new Department of Education procedures for enrolling students from outside a school district's boundary .... The procedure affects programs

that enroll students from out-of-district, including correspondence study programs operated by school districts, Alyeska Central School, charter schools and school districts enrolling part-time students.

The procedures, prompted by passage of Senate Bill 36 and House Bill 367, require Department of Education approval for all correspondence study programs that enroll out-of-district students. The department will consider approving only such programs that operated during the 1997-1998 school year.

The memorandum also spells out procedures for school districts that enroll out-of-district students to enter into a cooperative arrangement with a student's home school district. The memorandum requires a district that enrolls out-of-district special education students to enroll each special education students through an individualized cooperation agreement with the student's home school district.

The memorandum also requires school districts to report to the Department of Education certain information about part-time students to assure that no student is counted more than one full student for state funding purposes. (Department of Education sets new policy for out-of-district enrollment, 1998)

In the winter of 1997, the Alaska Board of Education anticipated the provisions of Senator Sharp's SB 182 and Rep. Dyson's HB 441. It convened a Charter School Subcommittee to consider charter school issues such as funding, teacher evaluation, and facilities. Two members, Robert Gottstein, Stowell Johnstone, and the student representative, Skye Rubadeau, made up the subcommittee. Ms. Rubadeau, a student at the Juneau-Douglas High School, was the daughter of Mary Rubadeau, the superintendent of the Juneau School District, and Robert Rubadeau, an aide to Lt. Governor Fran Uhlmer. Responding to fiscal constraints, the Charter School Subcommittee elected to meet by audio conference. It held three such meetings: January 2, 1998, January 9, 1998, and January 30, 1998. The subcommittee submitted its recommendation on February 17, 1998 and they were presented to the public during the SBOEs March 27 worksession. The subcommittee made the following recommendations:

Establishment of Charter Schools
- **Limitation on Number of Charter Schools**. Eliminate the cap of 30 schools from the charter school law. There would be neither geographical boundaries nor apportionment of the charter schools. The subcommittee recommends limiting the number of charter schools that could be approved by the State Board to 20 a year.
- **Quality Controls**. Language should be added to the law which ensures that charter school educational programs will be based on state standards.
- **Teacher Certification**. Language ensuring that only certified teachers may teach in charter schools should be added to the law.
- **Conflict of Interest/Non-profits**. A guideline needs to be established for ensuring that charter schools, which have incorporated as non-profits, do not receive a disproportionate amount of funding from private sources, and therefore jeopardize their public status. (If enough outside money is generated from private sources to pay for teachers, it could be considered an issue.)
- **Contract Duration**. Current law states that the charter school law will be repealed July 1, 2005. This termination date should be eliminated.

- **Creation of an Alternative Approval Body.** An alternative approval process should be created at the local level for the approval of charter school applications. Organizers of a charter school could have two options for approval at the local level: the local school board or another body. The other body would be created by the local school board from list of nominations. Charter school organizers would have the option of going to the local school board or the alternative board for approval of an application. If the local school board did not approve an application, charter school organizers could then seek approval from the other local body. (Suggestions for composition and role of body are available from subcommittee members, Gottstein and Johnstone.)
- Dissent: Skye Rubadeau. Skye thinks that new schools should be created only by the local elected school board which she sees as ultimately responsible for the charter school. She believes that the local district's philosophy, educational goals, and student needs are all factors that could be considered in rejecting an application at the local level. She believes that while there may be a need for an appeal body, it may have more of a place at the state level.

Funding
- **Start-Up Funding.** The Department should request a reasonable amount of startup funding which would be available to support the establishment of a charter school. (Suggest $5,000 for initial application phase; $50,000 startup funds when the charter school has received both local and state approval.)
- **Local Revenues.** The law should be reworded to make it clear that local revenues, which support education, should be made available to charter schools along with the state foundation funding. (Currently, the handling of the local contribution is different from district to district.) (Alaska State Board of Education, 1998)

At the Alaska State Board of Education's (SBOE) March 28, 1998 meeting, it adopted the recommendations of the Charter School Subcommittee. The Association of Alaska School Boards (AASB) reported:

The State Board reversed its position on charter schools. On March 28 it adopted a position for amending the Alaska Charter School Act to include:
1. Lifting the current cap on the number of charter schools allowed,
2. Remove the sunset provision of 2005,
3. Create a body at the local community level to which applicants who are denied approval of a charter school application by a local board of education can appeal. The appeals body would consist of three people such as a rep from the local PTA, a teacher, and a member of the local borough assembly or city council,
4. Ensure educational programs are based on state standards,
5. Require teachers to be certificated,
6. Establish fund raising guidelines for charter schools that establish themselves as nonprofit institutions so as not to jeopardize their public school status. (Association of Alaska School Boards, 1998, p. 1-2)

The past educational history in Alaska failed to provide educators and policy makers with predictors for how future charter schools would come about. The past of Alaska educational history was made up of all the educational events that had occurred up to the time of the creation of charter schools in Alaska. The enabling event of charter schools was a combination of the passage of CSSB 88, Governor Tony Knowles' signing the act into law (AS 14.03.255), Lt. Governor Fran Uhlmer's approval of the administrative regulations, and the respective Local Education Agencies' School Board's approval of board policies. The future of Alaska's charter schools cannot be predicted by what happened before. This model suggested that research exploring the relationship between freedom and accountability in Alaska's charter schools must be informed by the past context of the charter school idea, must be cognizant of the dynamics of the present miasma of Alaska's charter schools, and be ever vigilant of their emerging future.

As of January 1997, 444 charter schools were operating nationwide (U.S. Department of Education, 1997). As of May 19, 1998, Alaska local education agencies and the Alaska Board of Education have approved 17 charter schools, and 15 of them were operating. Two school districts disapproved the applications of two charter school petitioners. After several months of school board parliamentary maneuvering, one charter school petitioner withdrew the petition.

The Alaska Board of Education's technical review committee (TRC) was a de facto approval body. The following was an example of the TRC's second tier approval powers. Upon approving a charter school application, a local school district's administration forwarded a charter school's application to the Alaska Board of Education. The Alaska Board of Education's TRC rejected the application and requested the charter school founders to revise the curriculum component of their application. After the founders made substantial revisions to the curriculum portion of their application, they resubmitted the application to the TRC. The TRC responded that the revised application was a substantial re-write and recommended that the founders take the application back to the local school board for approval. The local school board held three meetings during which they considered the re-written application. After a delay of nearly eight months, the founders eventually withdrew their application.

The state of Alaska was one of 28 states, as well as the District of Columbia, the Commonwealth of Puerto Rico, and the U.S. Trust Territory of Guam that have passed such legislation. These facts gave many people the grounds to declare that the appearance of charter schools constituted a movement or a trend.

Committee Substitute for Senate Bill 88 (CSSB 88) was read for the first time on February 15, 1995 and was referred to the Senate Health, Education, and Social Services (HESS) committee and then to the Senate Finance (FIN) committee. On February 22, 1995, at 9:06AM, Senate HESS Chairman, Sen. Lyda Green, introduced SB88 and opened the first hearing on the bill. Sen. Bert Sharp "pointed out that SB 88 would allow creativity with few limitations on setting up and operating charter schools" (Senate Health, 1995, p. 1). Sen. Judy Salo noted that "This legislation is based on the Wisconsin Charter School Law which uses an existing school within a district" (Senate HESS, 1995, p. 1). Sen. Loren Leman said he "disagreed with the Anchorage School District's Policy. All school programs should be available to all students even those that receive home schooling or attend private schools"

(Senate HESS, 1995, p. 1). Carl Rose, Executive Director of the Association of Alaska School Boards (AASB) said, "The rural communities do not expect charter schools to be part of their future .... The areas of Anchorage, Fairbanks, Mat-Su, Kenai, and Juneau are interested in charter schools" (Senate HESS, 1995, p. 1). Sen. Judy Salo asked Mr. Rose if SB 88 "would allow freedom from negotiated agreements which he had mentioned as an obstacle school board's face. Carl Rose directed the committee's attention to Section 5 subsection (b) which addresses that fear" (Senate HESS, 1995, p. 1).

Willie Anderson, representing the National Education Association for Alaska (NEA-AK),

> recognized some areas of concern ... [especially] funding ... [and] SB 88 merely implies that charter schools would be required to follow all applicable laws and regulations. He expressed the need to clarify this issue. Also there should be clarification as to how charter schools differ from what currently exists. (Senate HESS, 1995, p. 2)

Vivian Johnson, member of the Yukon Kuskokwim Health Corporation and a hospital administrator at the Bethel hospital said, "... that everyone learns in different ways. There are also numerous theories of practice for education. She envisioned charter schools in her future although, previous statements indicated that rural areas would not be interested in charter schools" (Senate HESS, 1995, p. 3).

On March 8, 1995, at 9:07AM, Senate HESS Chairman, Sen. Lyda Green opened the second hearing on CSSB 88. Sen. Bert Sharp "clarified that a proposal for a charter school must be approved by the local school board and the commissioner of education. The charter school would operate under the guidelines of the school districts" (Senate HESS, 1995, p. 1). There was some concern that charter schools might discriminate against students with low academic achievement. Claudia Douglas, President of NEA-AK, insisted that charter schools meet certain conditions:

1. no negative effect on the regular school program,
2. no diversion of current funds from public schools,
3. voluntary staff and student assignment to charter schools,
4. direct involvement of all effected school employees in the charter schools design, implementation and government,
5. adequate defense in regards to contract and employment provisions for all employees,
6. appropriate procedures for assessment and evaluation at predetermined periods within the term of the charter,
7. licensed professional staff,
8. health and safety standards for all students and employees,
9. non-discrimination and equal educational opportunities,
10. adequate defenses ensuring physical [sic] accountability,
11. adequate and equitable funding, including start up money,
12. equitable procedures regarding student admission and retention,
13. appropriate safeguards against racial and ethnic segregation. (Senate HESS, 1995, p. 1)

Ms. Douglas also said that "[t]here would be no problem with adding language that would include administrators [on the academic policy committee]" (Senate HESS, 1995, p. 1).

On March 30, 1995, Alaska legislative sponsors, Senators Bert Sharp, Steve Frank, Mike Miller, Robin Taylor, Steve Rieger, and Lyda Green, offered Senate Finance committee substitute for Senate Bill No. 88 for "an act establishing a pilot program for charter schools; and providing for an effective date," to the 19th legislature, first session. CSSB 88 was passed out of committee with "an accompanying fiscal note of $2.0 [$2,000.00] for the Department of Education .... Senators Fred Zharoff and Donley signed 'other recommendations'" (Senate HESS, 1995, p. 1). The bill passed the Senate on reconsideration (Y15 N5) on April 12, 1995. It was transmitted to the House on April 13, 1995.

The House read CSSB 88 for the first time on April 18, 1995 and it was referred to the House HESS committee and the House Finance committee. On May 2, 1995, at 2:04PM, Sen. Bert Sharp gave the sponsor's statement on CSSB 88 to the House HESS committee:

> This bill allows school districts, teachers and parents the space to be creative. It allows the charter schools to utilize existing school facilities, new facilities, and/ or the option of leasing adequate facilities owned by private enterprise within the community .... All charter school proposals must be submitted to the local school board for consideration. Upon their approval by the school board, they then must be forwarded to the commissioner of the AK-DOE for review and compliance to state law. All staffing of charter schools must be done on a volunteer basis .... The budget shall not be less than the amount generated by the students enrolled in the charter school less administrative costs retained by the local school district, determined by applying the indirect cost rate approved by the AK-DOE .... [T]he amount generated by students enrolled in charter schools is to be determined in the same manner as it would be for a student enrolled in any other school within the school district. (House HESS, 1995, p. 1)

House HESS committee co-chair, Rep. Cynthia Toohey voiced some concerns about charter schools

> ... she was very concerned that the schools are going down in value, teaching ability, and other aspects. She has often said that she does not want to detract from those concerns by passing legislation such as this. That is her fear. If charter schools are implemented, motivated children, parents and teachers will work together. That is fine. But she fears that such schools are going to jeopardize the attention that should be given to the students the current school system is producing. (House HESS, 1995, p. 1)

Senator Bert Sharp responded:

> Most of the interest in [my] community comes from the teachers who want to be involved in a school in which they can have more freedom, challenge the students and challenge themselves. They dislike the total regimentation that is applied school wide. The spec of the bill allows the school boards to relax some of the textbook requirements as long as state standards are met for education .... [I]f some experimentation was not done in an attempt to find out what works, the system is eventually doomed .... [T]he bill will allow those people to relax concerning the standards and regimentation of the schools. (House HESS, 1995, p. 1)

Following Senator Sharp's introduction, several members of the public testified in favor of the senate's version of the bill. Christine Casler testified that:

> SB 88 is essential for districts to implement updated teacher practices supported by educational research, and to allow parents choices when their children do not learn well in traditional settings. The bill would alleviate extensive waiting lists for alternative programs which now exist in some districts. (House HESS, 1995, p. 3)

Kathy [Pfundt] of Gustavus testified that:

> The idea of site-based management is a fairly new one, and it will involve parents and community members. When those entities are involved in the schools, changes can be made. It is important to have parents and communities involved and accountable. (House HESS, 1995, p. 3)

At this point, Co-chair Con Bunde noted that Gustavus is a small community with only one school. He asked Ms. Pfundt if this were a concern. She responded:

> Yes, and that she and other community members were wondering what would happen in the case of a small, single-site community if a charter school is started. She was concerned about people who move to the community and do not like the idea. She wondered what kind of problems might arise. (House HESS, 1995, p. 3)

Rep. Con Bunde said that Ms. Pfundt's concerns reflected one of his own: "If a charter school is begun where only one school exists, those who are not inclined to be part of the charter school do not have choices .... [T]hat is something to keep in mind" (House HESS, 1995, p. 3).

Annie Mackovjak, also of Gustavus, said that SB 88, "... would allow a school to try innovating teaching techniques, or even to apply old techniques, such as Montessori methods .... She sees charter schools as a potential problem in small areas" (House HESS, 1995, p. 3-4).

Co-chair Cynthia Toohey asked Sen. Sharp if there were to be a limit on the number of students in a charter school. Sen. Sharp replied,

> ... there was no limit on the number of students .... The situation is that the school board should make sure the economics are there so two schools could function within a small school district. If not [he] would assume that the school board would not approve of a charter school .... [He] assumed that the economics of having instructors in both schools would not allow the school board to even allow a charter school. (House HESS, 1995, p. 4)

Rep. Norman Rokeberg was concerned about the recruitment and certification of teachers. Co-chair Con Bunde replied that since the charter schools were public schools they would have to hire certified teachers. Rep. Rokeberg noted, however, that the bill provides for a waiver from this requirement. Sen. Sharp replied that a school board would have to abide the terms of the collective bargaining agreement with the teachers' union. Rep. Rokeberg said he was concerned about nepotism, "'Aunt Gertrude' having a position created for her in the school" (House HESS, 1995, p. 5). He was also concerned about the potential for having a mixed staff of teachers who were exempt and those who were not. He pressed Sen. Sharp to clarify this issue. Sen. Sharp admitted, "... there could be both exempt and non-exempt teachers if there is an agreement" (House HESS, 1995, p. 5).

Lynne Jensen of Gustavus was concerned about the right to appeal a decision that denied a charter school application. Sen. Sharp replied that the bill does not allow for an appeal of a local school board's decision. He felt this was necessary in order to avoid "fragmenting the community and the school system as such ... [and from] isolat[ing] the charter schools from responsibility" (House HESS, 1995, p. 6).

David Cornberg, testifying via teleconference from Fairbanks, identified himself as an independent education consultant involved in education reform. He presented the committee with three points:

> First, there are no hard and fast predictive models that show if a program is implemented today, school systems will be better in 2005 .... [T]he important thing about SB 88 from the standpoint of reform is that it be given a chance .... [S}econd point refers to the federal charter schools initiative. That initiative comes under the Improving America's Schools Act ... [but] ... that no school in a state that has no charter school legislation can apply .... [T]hird point regards the concerns with dividing the community ... the fact is that society is a democracy. In a city with 500 residents, there is only one mayor. People have to look at that. If a democratic constituency decided for a charter school, the people would have to live with that. Small communities are democracies and democracy applies to education also. (House HESS, 1995, p. 6)

Catherine Portlock from Anchorage said that charter schools would provide a no cost way of providing educational models for programs that improve education. She pointed out to the committee that children have many

> learning styles and educational needs. When a program is well suited for the child or allows for student differences, students attend more and learn more .... [W]hen parents are given choices for their children, they become more involved in their children's education, which leads to greater academic success and satisfaction with the system .... [T]eachers needs are not often considered but certainly charter schools can work with differences in teaching philosophies. When teachers feel they are valued and appropriately placed, they will be more effective and more committed .... Parents and teachers are demanding proof of improvement in school performance, but are resistant to change. Schools need to be provided for those changes, for parents, children and teachers to feel that the school system is there for them. (House HESS, 1995, p. 7)

Linda Sharp, testifying from Anchorage, said that Anchorage's 13 alternative schools are essentially charter schools and that they "... let parents, teachers and communities propose innovations" (House HESS, 1995, p. 7-8). She presented the committee with copies of articles from "Educational Digest." The articles "suggested that charter schools are the best solutions" (House HESS, 1995, p. 8). Ms. Sharp addressed some of the concerns of parents such as "creaming," by which the best students transfer to the alternative school or the charter school. She cited some anecdotal evidence to the contrary:

> ... caucasians [sic] are the minority in alternative schooling programs. The vast majority of children in her child's new alternative school are not white-European. These children also come from widely varying socioeconomic classes. (House HESS, 1995, p. 9)

Ms. Sharp asserted that "Charter schools are asking for the chance for partnerships.

When parents are asked to be a permanent part of the table, where curriculum and staffing issues are made, the parents are going to help solve the problems that arise" (House HESS, 1995, p. 9). Ms. Sharp gave as an example the 1995 National Teacher of the Year, Elaine Griffin,[12] who "was just honored because she formed partnerships with the community" (House HESS, 1995, p. 10). Ms. Sharp testified that "... there is essentially very little if any difference between the programs currently existing in Anchorage and charter schools" (House HESS, 1995, p. 10).

If there were 13 alternative schools in Anchorage and they were, according to Ms. Sharp, the same as charter schools, Rep. Gary Davis questioned the necessity of SB 88. Ms. Sharp responded,

> SB 88 merely gives the school boards a notice to pay attention and look through the proposals in an up-front way. Whenever there is a superintendent in Anchorage that favors partnerships and choices, a new one is selected every few years. At other times Anchorage has a superintendent and a school board that are afraid. They don't want to be perceived as spending money in this time of cutbacks .... SB 88 gives school districts permission to investigate these programs. (House HESS, 1995, p. 10)

> Sheila Peterson, Special Assistant to Commissioner of Education, Dr. Shirley Holloway, explained that the charter schools will also be more autonomous than alternative schools. A charter school will maintain its own financial operations and will have its own principal who will oversee the charter school's teachers.[13] ...When Commissioner Halloway [sic] looked at this legislation, she applied her test, "Is this good for kids?" She came up with a definite "yes." Charter schools are a good concept for children. It will encourage parents, teachers and communities to work together as an academic policy committee to form a charter school. (House HESS, 1995, p. 11)

Rep. Gary Davis seemed skeptical. He mused how a school district would count a charter school that only has four or five students. The minimum number of students that the law requires to form a funding unit, a new school, is eight. Ms. Peterson replied: "... at the minimum, it would be four times what an average child would be generating in that school"[14] (House HESS, 1995, p. 12). Ms. Peterson's response provoked Rep. Con Bunde to outline a possibility that, "... as there are schools in Alaska with four students[15] as the total population, it is possible that there would be charter schools composed of four, six, or eight students" (House HESS, 1995, p. 12). Ms. Peterson responded that that the school board could disapprove the charter school's application if that number of students was not in the best interest of the state.

Robert Gottstien, member of the Alaska Board of Education made several points in his testimony:

> ... the state is trying to do more with less .... Charter schools are a chance to do more with less .... [S]chools need to innovate, and learn how to produce better results. If the education community is denied by the legislature the opportunity to figure out how to do things better, then the legislature has a responsibility to figure out how to give children the opportunities they are not allowed to receive from the schools .... [C]harter schools help children in critical ways ... get more parental involvement in education. (House HESS, 1995, p. 12)

Mr. Gottstien made an oblique comparison between the former Soviet Union and public school education in Alaska:

> More power and authority is given to charter schools. Top-down decision making did not work in the Soviet Union, and it does not work in education .... [I]t must be recognized that the failures of the USSR are the same factors that public education is being criticized for. The USSR did not care about the individual. It was concerned about the general public. Public education is in that situation. Alternative schools are trying to get away from that, but public schools have never attempted to try and deal with the discrete problem of every child .... [T]he best way to solve the discrete problem of every child is to help bring the parent into the process and to give each teacher freedom to identify and deal with those problems .... Charter schools and education reform seek to do better and to create a better value and results. Charter schools can do those things more economically. Parents can do what they think is more important for their children. They do not have to decide on what is good for everyone, and how to solve everyone's problems .... If HESS Committee members are as conscientious as they appear to be in dealing with the fiscal gap, charter schools are right in line. (House HESS, 1995, p. 12-13)

Co-chair Con Bunde brought the public testimony period to an end and opened the floor for committee member discussion. Rep. Tom Brice had no objection to CSSB 88. Rep. Gary Davis (R-Soldatna) agreed with Mr. Gottstien's comments. Rep. Davis thought that

> alternatives need to be offered, and local school districts need flexibility so problems can be addressed in more conventional ways. Latitude needs to be offered and parents need involvement. One can walk into a classroom and see that there is a niche for some of those that do not belong and do not want to be in the organized, structured classroom .... SB 88 is imposing requirements for more parental and cohesive involvement from a community standpoint. (House HESS, 1995, p. 13)

Rep. Karen Robinson spoke in favor of SB 88 and moved to pass CSSB 88 (FIN) out of the House HESS committee.

Co-chair Cynthia Toohey expressed a fear of "creaming," a practice in which "... the best and the brightest were going to be put in charter schools .... But with any luck, the whole system will go charter schools ... " (House HESS, 1995, p. 14).

Rep. Norman Rokeberg was anxious about disabled children in the charter schools. Rep. Gary Davis answered his objection by directing his attention to a passage in SB 88 that read, "the charter school will comply with all state and federal requirements for the use of public funds ... " (House HESS, 1995, p. 14).

Co-chair Con Bunde was skeptical of the charter school idea because, he said,

> where he grew up, 50 years ago, they consolidated schools because it was too expensive to have what were, in essence, charter schools .... [I]f not in this year, then in five or ten years, what the costs of charter schools will be. (House HESS, 1995, p. 15)

Rep. Con Bunde felt that charter schools would split a community.

America is a melting pot. And there are two great facilities for encouraging a

> melting pot. One is the draft .... The draft is gone, and now the last remaining facet of the melting pot is the educational system. Charter schools is going to fractionalize that.... [A]t a time when people yell about diversity, charter schools look to taking 'all the math people and putting them over here, and all the art people over here. (House HESS, 1995, p. 15).

Rep. Con Bunde also was concerned about the continuity of a charter school due to the mobility of Alaska's population. When supporters of the charter school move, they leave the rest of the community to deal with continuing or dissolving the charter school. Rep. Con Bunde felt,

> that the biggest problem facing schools today is parental involvement. Therefore, charter schools take the most active parents, those who are most interested and most concerned, and pull them out of the public schools and put them into their own special little world. This is a wrong way to go. (House HESS, 1995, p. 15)

Rep. Con Bunde was also concerned with "creaming," "The area that cannot get the parents together to form a charter school becomes a dumping ground" (House Health, 1995, p. 16). He went on to point out why teachers would like a charter school, "Who would not want to teach highly motivated kids" (House Health, 1995, p. 16)? He also agreed that parents would like charter schools, but he wondered why parents were not "getting involved in their current school" (House Health, 1995, p. 16)? At the end of his comments, Co-chair Con Bunde called for a roll-call vote. The vote was 6Y 1N. CSSB 88(FIN) passed out of the House HESS committee and referred to the House Finance committee.

On May 5, 1995, Sen. Sharp presented SB 88 to the House Finance committee. His remarks echoed his presentation to the House HESS committee, but he added, "By challenging students to achieve at their capabilities, the charter school may lead the way to a more effective education system for the next century" (House Finance Committee, 1995, p. 4). The discussion in the House Finance committee was brief.

Co-chair Hanley asked if charter schools "would be optional for each school district" (House Finance Committee, 1995, p. 4). Sen. Sharp answered that it would be up to each school board whether to have a charter school or not.

Rep. Ben Grussendorf wondered if the local school district would be responsible for upkeep of the facility if the charter school deferred building maintenance for teachers' salaries or textbooks.

Rep. Brown asked Sen. Sharp about charter school's teacher tenure rights. Sen. Sharp replied that the school district's collective bargaining agreement with the teachers' union covered charter school teachers.

Rep. Paul Therriault moved to report CSSB88 (FIN) out of House Finance. The motion passed and the bill was transmitted to the House floor for a vote. On May 8, 1995, Committee Substitute for Senate Bill 88, sponsored by the Senate Finance committee received its third and final reading on the Alaska legislature's House floor. CSSB 88 passed the House on reconsideration (Y36 N2 E1 A1)[18] on May 9, 1995. The legislature approved a pilot charter schools program authorizing as many as 30 charter schools statewide.

At 1:41PM on May 15, 1995, CSSB 88 was transmitted to the Governor. Governor Tony Knowles approved the bill (Appendix A) on June 8, 1995. Section 10 of the bill took effect on June 9, 1995. Section 9 of the bill took effect on September 6, 1995. The remainder of the act, Alaska charter school law (AS 14.03.250-275), took effect on July 1, 1995, and Alaska joined 19 other states with such legislation.

Shortly before passage of the bill and for six months after passage of the bill, the Commissioner of Education, Dr. Shirley Holloway, convened a series of meetings and workshops designed to inform the public and school district officials of the charter school legislation. Dr. Holloway convened the first meeting on June 6, 1995. Several people attended via teleconference. On June 12, 1995, Dr. Holloway sent a recap of the meeting to the 11 participants that said:

> The consensus of the group was that each LEA needs to develop its own policies and guidelines for charter schools, while the State will propose only the regulations that are needed to give districts some guidance .... Harry Gamble will assemble a small working committee to begin writing draft regulations to implement SB 88. The committee will include Norm Palenske [Superintendent, Mat-Su School District], Carol Comeau [Assistant Superintendent, Anchorage School District], Rick Cross [Deputy Commissioner of Education], Bart Mwarey [Principal, Takotna School], and Sheila Peterson [Special Assistant to the Commissioner]. (Holloway, 1995)

On August 8, 1995, Commissioner Holloway invited educators from around the state to attend a workshop "on Tuesday, September 16, 1995, to discuss 'The Alaska Charter School Law: From Passage to Implementation,' at the Anchorage Hilton Hotel" (Holloway, 1995). In this letter, the Commissioner declared that the Alaska Board of Education:

> ... is not eager to regulate extensively in this area as it is the intent of the charter school law to allow schools to develop in new ways. The Board wants school districts and communities, acting within the scope of the law, to have wide latitude in interpreting the charter school law. (Holloway, 1995)

Following his attendance at the September 16 meeting, Mr. Thomas Milliron, a teacher at Cube Cove School in the Chatham School District, filed a report to the superintendent. In his report, Mr. Milliron made several observations:

> Charter schools are not independent entities .... The ball is in the court of the regional school boards in the sense that it is the regional boards that now must develop charter school application guidelines and approval criteria .... In my opinion, regional school boards should insist that the state school board provide some recommended structure for the charter school application process. Most regional school boards do not have the background or expertise to develop the application process .... A potential problem for small communities (and the state) is that an alternative to charter schools must be available to students who do not wish to attend a charter school. (Milliron, 1995)

Literature on the concept of freedom in education.

What was this idea of freedom? What did it mean in education? Before embarking on this discovery, it was useful to assert one of the ontological premises that was implied in the statement: "The reason for this is because human behavior is not only affected by the complexities of the relationships in which every person engages but also because of human teleology" (Cziko, 1992). The premise was that teleology was a subsidiary concept of the concept of free-will. Therefore, the following discussion assumed that as human beings we have free-will. This project assumed free-will as a self-evident primary. It was important to establish this up front for a couple of reasons. One, there were many skeptics who doubted it. Two, the concepts of freedom and choice cannot exist without it. To assert otherwise was to perform the "fallacy of the stolen concept."

Hospers (1971) provided the perspective of the practicing philosopher to the concept of freedom. He used the words "liberty" and "freedom" interchangeably. In this respect, his discussion will be of some benefit when we encounter Sergiovanni's model in Figure 1. Hospers said:

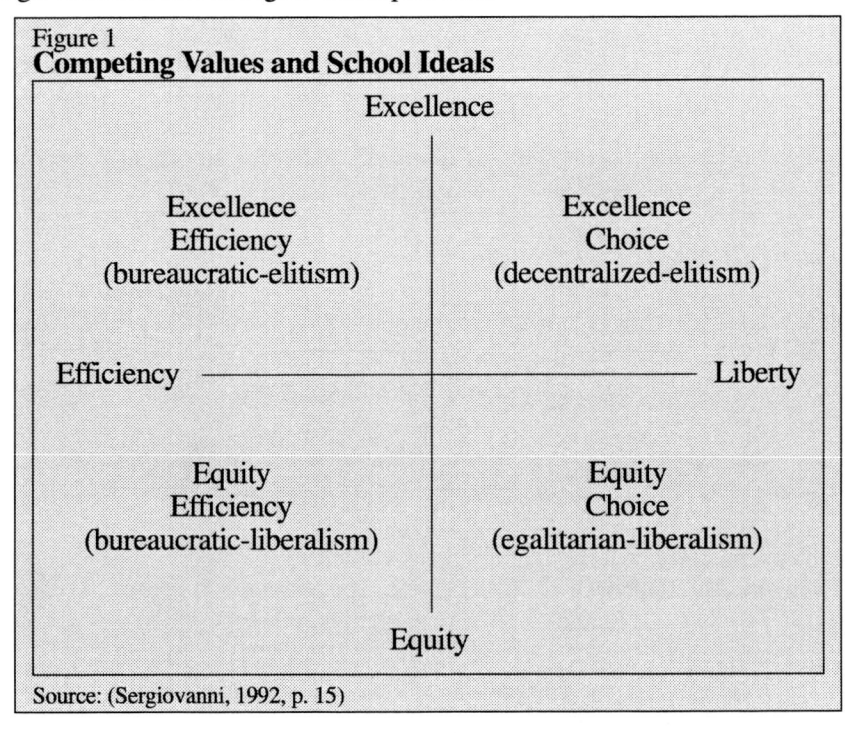

Figure 1
Competing Values and School Ideals

```
                        Excellence
                            |
        Excellence          |       Excellence
        Efficiency          |       Choice
   (bureaucratic-elitism)   |    (decentralized-elitism)
                            |
Efficiency ─────────────────┼───────────────── Liberty
                            |
         Equity             |         Equity
        Efficiency          |         Choice
  (bureaucratic-liberalism) |   (egalitarian-liberalism)
                            |
                          Equity
```

Source: (Sergiovanni, 1992, p. 15)

What, then, is liberty? In its most fundamental sense, the sense from which the other senses stem, and the sense which is also historically the earliest, liberty (or freedom) is the *absence of coercion by other human beings*. ...

This sense of liberty should be distinguished from a second one that is dependent on it. A compulsive gambler may say, in a reflective moment, "I am a slave to my desire to gamble." In one sense he is not free, because he cannot control his desires .... But the second sense is a metaphor only; the victim of powerful destructive inner drives is not a literal slave such as existed on Southern plantations before the Civil War. And it is this literal sense which concerns us in political philosophy ....

There is still a third sense of the term "liberty" which is much more easily confused with the first and original sense: liberty, or freedom, in the sense of *power* or *ability*. I am free to walk, that is, I can do so if I choose; but I am not free to fly in the air like a bird, or to make myself fifty feet tall, or to change myself into an ostrich. Doubtless the range of my choices is limited because I cannot do all these things, but I am still free in the first sense as long as no one is coercing me....I am still free in the first sense as long as I voluntarily decided to embark on the journey and no one forced me to make it. My finding myself in this position, as well as my failure to fly, is not the result of the imposition of any other human will upon mine. (Hospers, 1971, p. 10-11)

To begin the discussion of freedom in education, the researcher considered a model (Figure 1) that would help readers visualize the relationship between opposing values and mental pictures of schooling (Sergiovanni, 1992). The issue that concerned the present project was that of freedom. How did the figure help us in this regard? First, the model exhibited attributes of the symmetry of horizontal and vertical reflection, in other words, complementarity (Bronowski, 1973, p. 172). Second, it shows that the attributes were not necessarily a dialectical tension between synthesis and antithesis. Third, there was no symmetry of rotation, for example a 90^0 rotation from "efficiency" did not produce another "efficiency," but rather a phase shift to "excellence" that provided the breakdown that would eventually create chaos. Sergiovanni described the result of one such phase shift that was evident in many charter schools that those on the left support, individual management:

Excellence combined with choice describes the values of those who subscribe to elitist images but are not willing to give up control over their own destinies. What will be taught, who will be taught, and how schooling will be funded are decisions that they are unwilling to relinquish. The alternative they choose is either to leave the public schools for private schools or to convert their own public schools into the form and shape of private schools. In either case the value of equity is subordinate, for it is too threatening to the struggle for excellence. (Sergiovanni, 1992, p. 16)

Willie (1997) suggested another interpretation of the equity-excellence polarity that bore implications for charter schools. Willie speculated that the American public had focused its attention on excellence at the expense of equity, "Consequently, educational planners and policy makers have emphasized standards and qualifications, which are indicators of excellence, and ignored fairness, which is an indicator of equity" (Willie, 1997, p. 56). Pool (1996) reminded us that "Charter schools in the U.S. can never promote equity because the funding for education is perhaps the most inequitable in the developed world" (Pool, 1996, p. 4).

For the purposes of this project, the researcher was concerned with the element of liberty (freedom). Webster's defined "liberty": "freedom to choose; freedom from compulsion or constraint" (Webster's third new international dictionary of the English language unabridged, 1981, p. 779). In making this definition, Webster's gave us the conundrum of "freedom to," that is, operational freedom, and "freedom from," that is, organizational freedom. This counterpoint essentially demarcated the poles of political expression not only in general but also in the United States in particular. This philosophical definition also made "liberty" synonymous with "freedom."

A dictionary, though, did not substitute for a philosophical treatise. A short discussion of the philosophical features of these concepts provided us with what philosophy did best: gave a universal boundary for these concepts. In so doing, we discovered the roots of what at first glance looked like the intransitive system of a pendulum, that is, "It can stay in one equilibrium or the other, but not both" (Gleick, 1987, p. 169).

Upon further inspection, we came face-to-face with what Edward Lorenz called an "almost-intransitivity," that is: "An almost-intransitive system displays one sort of average behavior for a very long time, fluctuating within certain bounds. Then for no reason whatsoever, it shifts into a different sort of behavior, still fluctuating but producing another average" (Gleick, 1987, p. 170). Fullan (1993) observed that:

> Productive educational change is full of paradoxes, and components that are often not seen as going together. Caring and competence, equity and excellence, social and economic development are not mutually exclusive. On the contrary, these tensions must be reconciled into powerful new forces for growth and development. (Fullan, 1993, p. 4)

The following examination framed the discussion of the philosophical traditions of the concept of freedom. The traditions produced a tension between the Apollonian[19] view and the Dionysian[20] view. In the Apollonian tradition, the Harvard philosopher, Robert Nozik, gave a philosophical discourse equivalent to an explication of an almost-intransitive system:

> It is important and valuable that a person have a range of autonomy, a range or domain of action where he may choose as he wishes without outside forcing. Recognizing and respecting such a domain of autonomy is a response to the person as a value-seeking self .... This point does not fix the extent or content of the domain. It is important that various people recognize the same domain, though. I will not force someone about one choice but will about another, which you will not force about the other but will about the first, then although we each respect some domain or other of autonomy, there is not one domain that we both respect. So that person has no domain of autonomy within which he is free to choose without forcing or threats of force by anyone. Part of responding to another as a value-seeking self is to coordinate our specification of the respected domain with others, so that the person does have a generally recognized domain of autonomy, and also to publicly avow our respect for this domain, so that he knows he is autonomous within it and can count on that.
>
> If respecting a domain of autonomy is to be an apt response to a person as a value-seeking self, then this domain must include a range of important and significant choices (such as religious practice, place of residence, choice of mate and lifestyle, choice of occupation), as well as a vast range of trivial choices which go to make up the daily texture of our lives. The choices that are viewed as significant and central to a person's life and self-definition may vary from culture to culture—we can imagine science fiction situations where others view as trivial the choices we hold as centrally important, while viewing other choices (trivial to us) as of great significance. In that society, the domain of autonomy might appropriately be demarcated differently.
>
> There is much to be said for recognizing the widest possible domain of autonomy, limited only by the boundary of not violating the similarly specified autonomy of another. It is unclear, however, whether the recognition of the full-

est and widest possible autonomy is required by responsiveness to someone as a value-seeking self. At the least though, the limitations must be principles ones, done on the basis of general principles which, if fully followed, would not leave the domain of autonomy so shrunken as to constitute an inadequate response to a person as a value-seeking self. The range of his autonomy you respect cannot be gauged solely by the actions you do, without reference to the principles underlying your actions (and to the principles underlying those) ....

Thereby, it seems that the requirement that intrusion into autonomy be principled might establish an even wider domain of autonomy than the already wide one that needs to be recognized in order to respond to someone as a value-seeking self. This raises an interesting question about ad hoc limitations on principled reasons that purport to justify intrusions into autonomy. Suppose these reasons, if consistently and fully followed, would lead to a very extensive forcing of people's actions with a consequently greatly shrunken–too greatly, as every one would admit–domain of autonomy. Might a proponent then suggest that we not follow such reasons consistently and fully, only up to a point not beyond the point where the domain of such autonomy is shrunk to a certain specified size consonant with responding to a person as a value-seeking self? If this type of principle cannot be excluded, then (insofar as our current line of thought can say) rights need extend only so far as to constitute an adequate domain of autonomy. Even this is not a meagre (sic) result, for such a domain may be quite extensive.

The notion of respecting freedom to act within a domain of autonomy is a modern idea .... Political philosophy, as I see it, is mainly the theory of what behavior legitimately may be enforced, and of the nature of the institutional structure that stays within and support these enforceable rights. (The state usually is distinguished by political theorists as the organ of–the institutionalized monopoly over—the legitimate use of force .... The reason rights come to be so central to political philosophy, although they are not the central moral phenomena, is that the state is demarcated as the organ monopolizing the (legitimate) use of force. (Nozik, 1981, p. 501-503)

Nozik's exegesis echoed the pronouncement of one of the 20th century's state-makers. In his essay "Problems of War and Strategy," Chairman Mao Zedong bluntly pronounced, "Qiang ganzi limian chu zhengquan" (Mao, 1961, p. 224). The original Chinese literally said: "Political power comes out of guns." Chinese pundits in the United States attempted to smooth the cadence of the phrase to conform to the revolutionary patois of an Anglo audience: "Political power grows out of the barrel of a gun."

Nozik's analysis was in the political-philosophical tradition of Aristotle, John Locke, Thomas Paine, the Federalist Papers, Thomas Jefferson, John Hospers, Milton Friedman, and Ayn Rand. One of its most radical proponents, the "father of Anarcho-Capitalism," was Murray Rothbard (Rothbard, 1978). Later, Nozik went on to amplify the notions of freedom and rights in a volume that was devoted to political theory. In the beginning of this volume, Nozik made the following prefatory remark:

> The fundamental question of political philosophy, one that precedes questions about how the state should be organized, is whether there should be any state at

all. Why not have anarchy? Since anarchist theory, if tenable, undercuts the whole subject of political philosophy, it is appropriate to begin political philosophy with an examination of its major theoretical alternative. Those who consider anarchism not an unattractive doctrine will think it possible that political philosophy ends here as well. Yet, as we shall see, archists and anarchists alike, those who spring gingerly from the starting point as well as those reluctantly argued away from it, can agree that beginning the subject of political philosophy with state-of-nature theory has an explanatory purpose. (Nozik, 1974, p. 4)

While tempting, it was beyond the scope of this project to venture much farther down this road. It was sufficient to allow another theorist to provide us with glimpse of another one of the philosophical foundations for this discussion of liberty/freedom:

... the liberty human beings ought to prize and seek protection for in communities rests on a theory of negative rights. The explanation of basic rights and that of individual liberty will turn out to be mutually interdependent. For example, it is not a right to liberty in the sense of the opportunity for or power of action in general, that matters. Instead, it is the right to liberty in the sense of persons respecting each other's moral sovereignty .... That is the quintessential public good, while the opportunity for or power of action concerns a more general problem—not uniquely related to human community life-namely, human life itself. (Machan, 1989, p. xiv)

Before, leaving this phase of the discussion, Machan allowed that, "... the right to liberty... mean[s] the right to take actions that one chooses to take, not those *others* might wish and force one to take" (Machan, 1989, p. 114). Machan's viewpoint was decidedly "libertarian" and he eloquently staked out one position of those on the secular radical right.

There were two idealistic positions that were posted on the opposite end of the political spectrum. One came to us from Jean-Jacques Rousseau. Rousseau asserted the superiority of the natural over the man-made. In the Rousseauvian worldview education was to emerge from the natural dispositions of the child. In the nineteenth-century Friedrich Froebel started the Kindergarten based on the naturalistic philosophy. However, since Froebel's method did not accommodate science and mathematics, other, more structured, methods emerged, especially in Europe. In spite of the European discovery of the weaknesses of the child-centered philosophy, educators in the United States persisted and made it a new orthodoxy. In his 1996 book, The Schools We Need and Why We don't Have Them, Cromer (1998) asserted that "... the current reform movement in the United Sates is merely a continuation of failed practices that have been taught in all teachers' colleges since the 1920s" (Cromer, 1998, p. 49).

The second idealism was an expression of egalitarianism, that all children can learn at high levels of achievement. Cromer (1998) believed that if,

... you mix the idea that students don't need knowledgeable teachers, but only facilitators to help them construct their own knowledge, with the idea that all these untaught children will miraculously achieve at the highest level, then you get ... state and national standards that purport to cure our educational problems without anyone, especially the students, really trying. (Cromer, 1998, p. 50)

On the opposite side were the educational realists who believed that after the first grade what a child learns is largely non-intuitive. Without the guidance of teachers, children did not learn clairvoyantly to read, to write, and to reckon. Learners needed broad instruction and application. The idealists believed that all children needed were problem-solving skills without content. Realists, on the other hand, believed that knowledge was built on a broad foundation of facts and of specific problem-solving techniques. In other words,

> a good chess player, like a good piano player, and a good student, gets that way through countless hours of practice.
>
> The reform movement in education, which is dominated by idealists, never mentions practice. Its royal road is "inquiry."... To idealistic educators, "inquiry" is a diffuse and accommodating term that can, and does, include nonscientific methodologies. This can be seen in a unit titled "How Do Objects Fly?" given as an example of inquiry in the Massachusetts Framework. The example contains no scientific or technological inquiry at all. Students build paper airplanes, but learn nothing about air flow, pressure differences, or the Bernoulli principle. Instead, they "inquire" about the impact of air traffic on people and organisms in communities near an airport. The unit diverges away from its central question in an inherently unscientific fashion. (Cromer, 1998, p. 50-51)

In the social philosophy arena, John Rawls gave us a contemporary expression of this view. Rawls fell into the tradition of the Dionysian conviction, the political-philosophical tradition of Plato, Thomas Hobbes, Herbert Spencer, Karl Marx, Mikhail Bakunin, Pierre Joseph Proudhon, Howard Zinn, and Amitai Etzioni. One of its most radical proponents was Malcolm X. In his treatise, Rawls (1971) advanced the concept of "distributive justice":

> I shall begin by considering the role of the principles of justice. Let us assume, to fix ideas, that a society is a more or less self-sufficient association of persons who in their relations to one another recognize certain rules of conduct as binding and who for the most part act in accordance with them. Suppose further that these rules specify a system of cooperation designed to advance the good of those taking part in it. Then, although a society is a cooperative venture for mutual advantage, it is typically marked by a conflict as well as by an identity of interests. There is an identity of interests since social cooperation makes possible a better life for all than any could have if each were to live solely by his own efforts. There is a conflict of interests since persons are not indifferent as to how the greater benefits produced by their collaboration are distributed, for in order to pursue their ends they each prefer a larger to a lesser share.
>
> A set of principles is required for choosing among the various social arrangements which determine this division of advantages and for underwriting an agreement on the proper distributive shares. These principles are the principles of social justice: they provide a way of assigning rights and duties in the basic institutions of society and they define the appropriate distribution of the benefits and burdens of social cooperation (Rawls, 1971, p. 4).

While the secular radical-left position was finding its voice in the United States, it had already found expression in international circles. The rhetoric of "national liberation" in the international arena emerged as a major component of the argot of the civil rights/anti-war protest movement among the student radicals in the 1960s and 1970s. On the U.S. domestic front, the student radicals took a moral stand,

> They had been raised and schooled to believe in the promise of America, and they hated the war partly because it meant that the object of their affections, the system that rewarded their proficiency, was damaged goods. They were the inheritors of the vision of a moral America, and they did not want their moral capital squandered. (Witcover, 1998, p. 81)

The philosophical underpinnings of this point of view had long predated the protests of the 1960s and 1970s. In 1948, the United Nations adopted the "Universal Declaration of Human Rights" (UDHR). For the first time in history, the delegate nations to the United Nations systematically advanced various rights to all people of the world. During the four decades following the UDHR over 100 countries divested themselves of their colonial relationship with their host countries and gained independence. A hopeful trend ensued. Without the participation of the Western powers, the Asia-Africa Summit convened and the Non-Aligned Movement emerged. Out of these efforts, the Group of 77 was formed. The Group of 77 asserted they were their own rulers and they called for a new international political and economic order. The political appearance took the form of self-determination. The economic manifestation took the form of the right to development.

In 1960, the United Nations adopted the "Declaration on the Granting of Independence to Colonial Countries and Peoples." For the first time the United Nations affirmed the right to self-determination as a collective human right. It was a significant amplification of the traditional concept of human rights that stressed individual rights. In both the "International Covenant on Economic, Social and Cultural Rights" and the "International Covenant on Civil and Political Rights," Article 1 said, "All peoples have the rights of self-determination. By virtue of that right they freely determine their political status and freely pursue their economic, social and cultural development" (Tian, 1998, p.12).

In 1974 a special session of the UN General Assembly on Raw Materials and Development was held. The Assembly adopted the Declaration and Programme of Action on the Establishment of a New International Order. The declaration was founded on "equity, sovereignty, interdependence, common interest and cooperation among States, irrespective of their economic and social systems" (Tian, 1998, p.15).

Later in 1974, the UN adopted the Charter of Economic Right and Duties of States that lead to the UN's 1986 adoption of the "Declaration on the Right to Development." This declaration confirmed that the UN considered the right to development to be an inalienable human right. It included both the rights of nations and the individuals who made up nations. Consequently, the UN regarded the right to development to be integral to the right of self-determination. In the lexicon of the charter school advocates, the right to development was analogous to the right to form autonomous charter schools. The right of self-determination corresponded to the parents' right to educate their children. Instead of making appeals to an international assembly, charter school advocates appealed both to the electorate, through ballot initiatives, and to legislatures, through political action committees.

Pogrow (1997) described the educational manifestation of this persuasion. He called it "ideological progressivism." Pogrow asserted that when this philosophy was applied to education, the students who benefited the least were the academically disadvantaged students. He said that the reason for the movement's weakness was that:

> It provides no mechanism for increasing learning other than collaboration and democratic participation .... Ideological progressives always assert that we know 'what works' and that they are putting into place reforms to enable these things to be universally adopted .... So we end up with an amorphous and romantic reform to implement amorphous and romantic ideals. The reality is that given consistent failures of their initiatives, ideological progressives have shifted their emphasis away from student learning outcomes, which were the genesis of the progressive movement, to politically correct conceptions of how to organize schools, instruction, and teacher training. These process goals become ideological ends in and of themselves, supported by romantic visions of a new professionalism. They create a smoke screen for the movement's lack of success in enhancing learning by criticizing all the existing evaluation methods. As it becomes obvious to the profession as a whole that the techniques aren't working, pure progressives blame an absence of leadership. (Pogrow, 1997, p. 34)

Pogrow maintained that ideological progressives were stuck in a time warp of thinking that systematic curricula meant, "... the primitive, drill-based, teacher-proof curricula of the 1960s that were based on models of how rats behaved in a maze. They seem blind to the fact that the world has moved on" (Pogrow, 1997, p. 36). Pogrow continued that the ideological progressives' absolutism and distortion had a retrograde effect on education. He identified a couple of areas for special mention.

> First, these attitudes inhibit the development of new, more powerful interventions. The absence of a state-of-the-art development effort means that there is a shortage of powerful interventions schools can adopt and that large numbers of educationally disadvantaged students never get access to the types of interventions they need. The vast majority of educationally disadvantaged students have tremendous intellectual potential. Tapping that potential is not an easy process, or one that occurs from simply having good intentions or the right ideals. These are key points in the educational process where specific types of interactions need to be provided in a consistent fashion and sustained for an extended number of years for part of the school day. Some of these interactions are basic in nature, and others are more sophisticated and progressive. Systematic curricula are needed to help teachers maintain the necessary focus over time.
>
> Unfortunately, current conceptions of leadership that stress school autonomy and progressive rhetoric that makes teachers feel like second-class citizens whenever they are not creating their own interventions, make it almost impossible to implement and sustain the systematic experiences needed for a sufficient period of time. The consequences are that the ideological-progressive movement fails to enhance learning and that better interventions are not developed ....
>
> So we are left with ideological progressives talking only about professional development as an individualistic process with teachers and students spontaneously making the right decisions, which the competition, ideological conservatives, talk only about drill, vouchers, and school prayer .... As a result, education stagnates.

> Those of us who are trying to strike a balance and develop more advanced types of systems that generate progressive learning outcomes are left out in the cold. We do not meet the tests of political correctness—from either side.
>
> Progressive education has been hurt by the fact that those controlling the agenda place a premium on ideology and care more about process than outcome .... [T]he more ideologically progressive you are, the less likely it is that you will be able to produce progressive learning outcomes .... (Pogrow, 1997, p. 36)

Roberts (1993) contributed to our understanding of the "progressive movement" in general. Roberts said, "Progressives asserted that schools should seek to remediate social ills as well as servicing political, economic and cultural ends (Pulliam, 1968)" (Roberts, 1993, p. 11).

Bronowski (1973) quoted the poet William Blake:

> Knowledge is not a loose-leaf notebook of facts. Above all it is a responsibility for the integrity of what we are, primarily of what we are as ethical creatures. The personal commitment of a man to his skill, the intellectual commitment and the emotional equipment working together as one, has made the Ascent of Man. William Blake's Songs of Experience (as cited in Bronowski, 1973, p. 438)

Bronowski then eloquently warned against the dangers of turning ideology into certainty:

> There is no absolute knowledge. And those who claim it, whether they are scientists or dogmatists, open the door to tragedy. All information is imperfect. We have to treat it with humility. (Bronowski, 1973, p. 438)

Bronowski's book was turned into television's first quasi-scientific mini-series. At one point in the dramatic adaptation, Bronowski waded into a murky pond on the grounds of Poland's Auschwitz concentration camp. The crematoria were in the background. He knelt, reached into the pond and came up with a handful of jetsam:

> Into this pond were flushed the ashes of some four million people. And that was not done by gas. It was done by arrogance. It was done by dogma. It was done by ignorance. When people believe that they have absolute knowledge, with no test in reality, this is how they behave. This is what men do when they aspire to the knowledge of gods.
>
> Science is a very human form of knowledge .... Every judgment in science stands on the edge of error, and is personal. Science is a tribute to what we can know although we are fallible.
>
> I owe it as a scientist to my friend Leo Szilard, I owe it as a human being to the many members of my family who died at Auschwitz, to stand here by the pond as a survivor and a witness. We have to cure ourselves of the itch for absolute knowledge and power. (Bronowski, 1973, p. 374)

In terms of educational application, the views of the "right" and the views of the "left" delimited the discussions between the conservative (that is, those on the right) and the liberal (that is, those on the left). Spring (1997) characterized these positions as the tension between "... those who believe schooling should mold the virtuous citizen and those who believe schooling should provide the tools for the exercise of freedom" (Spring, 1997, p. 76).

Spring (1997) went on to inform us that the emergence of political parties in the

United States embraced opposing views of education as the educational theories of Horace Mann took root in the "common school" movement:

Most leaders of the common school movement were Whigs, who believed that government should intervene to maintain social order through a centrally managed school system designed to educate moral and responsible citizens. On the other hand, members of the Democratic party believed that social order would occur naturally, and therefore they believed in minimal government intervention and local control of the schools ...

Whigs were concerned with morality, duty, and the reduction of social conflict and thus wanted an educational system that would shape moral character, teach social and political duties, and reduce conflict among social classes and political groups. Whigs believed these goals could best be achieved through centralized supervision by state governments. Democrats resisted the trend toward centralization of government control and talked mainly about rights and a society of conflicting interests ...

Whigs were advocates of a positive liberalism that called for government intervention to assure the workings of a free-market economy. Therefore, Whigs believed that government should provide money for education and for internal improvements to guarantee the establishment and functioning of institutions and economic organizations essential to the development of the country ....

The Democrats represented negative liberalism and argued that government governed too much. They believed that the economy should function without any state intervention and that state monies should not be used to support a common school system ...

For Whigs, schooling was the key to an ordered society. Howe [1979] summarizes the Whigs' political campaigns as being part of "a cultural struggle to impose on the United States the standards of morality we usually term Victorian. They were standards of self-control and restraint, which dovetailed well with the economic program of the party, for they emphasized thrift, sobriety, and public responsibility" (Howe, 1979, p. 29) ....

For Whigs, true freedom occurred only when the balance of mental faculties within an individual ensured that passion did not reign over reason .... [T]he Whig position was that true freedom was possible only if individuals received a proper education and social temptations were removed....The Democrats on the other hand, believed that true freedom was possible only in a society in which there was a minimum of government interference in the social order. Democrats viewed government attempts to order society as attempts to promote and protect the special privileges of the upper class ....

According to Kaestle and Vinovskis [1980], "the Whigs argued that positive government intervention was a necessary and useful means of improving the quality of public schools throughout the commonwealth." On the other hand, Democrats felt "that any increased state interference in local educational matters created the potential, if not the reality, of a centralized state school system that would dictate how children were to be educated" (Kaestle, 1980, p. 230) ....

This debate, which has continued into the twentieth century, reflects in varying degrees the tension between those wanting popular control of the schools and little government intervention and those believing that government should work actively to ensure that the schools serve general social, political, and economic goals ....

The first major educational historian to portray the common school movement as a battle between liberals and conservatives over the extending the benefits of schooling to all people was Ellwood Cubberley in his text first published in 1919, Public Education in the United States: A Study and Interpretation of American Educational History. (Spring, 1997, p. 110-114)

Gerzon (1996) described these political struggles between the secular humanistic "left" and the fundamentalist religious "right" as manifestations of "belief systems struggling for America's soul" (Gerzon, 1996). He described the religious right as "The Religious State, Patria":

Seen through the Patrian lens, America is caught in a downward spiral of moral deterioration. Although thoughtful Patrians recognize the economic, political, and ecological factors that underlie our current predicament, they believe that the root cause of the crises in our society is the corrosive, and often explosive, moral decline. Gang murders, teen pregnancy, drug abuse, gay rights, homelessness, media violence, federal gridlock, the deficit—however far-ranging the symptoms may be, they are all part of the same disease: amorality.

The Patrian prescription for what ails America, consequently, is a return to the bedrock of moral values rooted in the Judeo-Christian tradition. Patrians believe that the United States of America is a "Christian nation." Older Patrians nostalgically recall a time when all Americans could be called together in the name of Jesus Christ, our Lord and Savior. They dream of a society in which shared moral values will once again bind together Americans—men and women, black and white, rich and poor—into one great congregation. (Gerzon, 1996, p. 11)

Gerzon described the humanistic "left" as "The Governing State, Officia":

The citizens of Officia believe in the role of government. They are committed to their conviction that the government, whatever its flaws, serves the American people. Officia is the glue that holds the Union together, the loom that weaves the diverse threads of this sprawling democracy into one fabric. The country needs the Governing State more than ever. Officials believe, because without it there would be no country ....

[T]hey resent the anti-government vigilantes for undermining the very institutions which, Officials believe, made this country great.

Officials do not consider themselves to be ideologues ... but rather "progressive pragmatists," determined to find ways of fostering social progress. Their primary faith is civic rather than religious. Although they may regard "growth" as a social goal, they ... speak of it as "growth with fairness"–a goal, they believe, which only the government can and will ensure. (Gerzon, 1996, p. 159, 160, 162)

As we have observed, there was a rich and profound theoretical context that was a prerequisite for understanding the contemporary application of liberty/freedom theory to public education in general and to charter schools in particular. Since public education in the United States was essentially a political creation, it was a coliseum for the antipodes of the political spectrum: the "Left" and the "Right."

In politics, the left espoused the ideals of personal freedoms while it demanded controls on the economic interactions of human beings. They believed that it was the individual who can manage his/her own affairs. On the other hand, the right espoused the ideas of pure economic freedoms while demanding controls on individual liberty. In educational terms, the left wanted to personalize school management, that is, for individuals to take it into their own hands. They assumed that only the individual, through his/her coterie surrogates, knew best how and what to manage in the area of educational and civil affairs. This management was done best when there was no accountability to the larger society that provided the funding for their adventure.

On the other hand, the right importuned for ideological control and restrictions, that is, governance, on personal freedoms. The right assumed that the problems of society were due to the aberrations or failures of the individual. Therefore, the right wished to have ideological control of education for the purpose of "educating the individual to conform to the needs of existing political, social, and economic organizations" (Spring, 1997, p. 106).

Echoing Spring (1997), Latham (1998) described the polarity in contemporary American education. Latham said that the forces "... rang[e] from liberal proponents of educational reform to conservative families driven by religious convictions" (Latham, 1998, p. 85). When he posited the categories of ideologues and pedagogues, Latham clarified further the conceptual front lines. On the one hand were the ideologues, who "... adhere to traditional school techniques and materials, but adapt the curriculum to their specific values and beliefs" (Latham, 1998, p. 85).

On the other hand were the pedagogues, who "... seek new ways of teaching to replace traditional instruction. Although the early growth ... was generated by reform-minded pedagogues, subsequent growth has been largely attributed to ideological parents, many of whom belong to the Christian Right" (Latham, 1998, p. 50).

Hospers (1971) contributed to our understanding of the parameters of the political "left" and the political "right."

> The ["left"], when confronted by a social problem, regularly turn toward government for a solution. Whether it is the problem of the cities, the problem of integration, the problem of poverty, the problem of housing, the problem of underdeveloped nations, and so on ad infinitum, they invoke government for solutions, at the expense of the citizenry.
>
> The ["right"] are (typically at least) not averse to using government to force their plans on others; yes, there should be censorship, they say—that is, the moral convictions of one group (the one in political power) should be forced on everyone else; yes, there should be compulsory prayers in public schools; yes, there should be foreign aid to some nations, though not as indiscriminate as the liberals would have. They would still undertake to decide these questions—such as what one shall read—not only for themselves but for others via the coercive machinery of the law. (Hospers, 1971, p. 5-6)

The above discussions of the philosophical roots of the values expressed in public education were manifest in the laws that states enacted to establish public schools in their jurisdictions. The evolution of these laws had a long history. Roberts (1993) reported:

According to Black's Law Dictionary (1990), law in the United States is determined by constitutional provisions, legislative enactments (statutes), court precedents, lawyer's opinions, and evolving customs.

Since public schools are governmental agencies, their conduct is circumscribed by precedents of law and supplemented by legal and historical traditions.

> The power of operation of the public educational system, therefore, originates with a constitutional delegation to the legislature to provide for a system of education. With legislative enactments providing the basis for public school law, it then becomes the role of the courts, through litigation, to interpret the will of the legislature. The combination of constitutions, statutes, and court or case law forms the primary legal foundation on which the public schools are based. (Alexander, 1991, p. 1)

In view of the fact that public education is an entity of state law, state statutes are a significant source of law for educators. "They are often more explicit than state constitutional provisions, and their purpose is to bring a more specific outline to broad constitutional directives or to codify case law" (LaMorte, 1990, p. 13). (Roberts, 1993, p. 29)

The discussion to this point has shown that freedom, both in general and in its particular expression with regards to charter schools, was not a political absolute, but a derivative concept. Therefore, as the political expression of freedom became more removed from the concrete muzzle of a gun, the far more "friendly" abstract arena of legal practice and jurisprudence supplanted physical coercion. The rule of law became a transformational human activity.

In the May 1994 Southwest Regional Laboratory (SWRL) report, the authors noted, "Freedom from state codes and regulations was beneficial, but district regulations and union contracts (negotiable elements under the law) were still obstacles" (Mulholland, 1996, p. 3).

In January 1995, the U.S. General Accounting Office (GAO) issued a report in response to Senator Arlen Specter's, Senator Edward M. Kennedy's, and Senator David Durenberger's request for charter school information. One part of the report focused on the issue of autonomy, which implied freedom, and found considerable variation.

> Charter schools vary considerably in their autonomy. Some operate as legally independent entities, for example, as nonprofit corporations or teacher-owned cooperative .... In contrast, some charter schools operate with no greater autonomy than many traditional public schools. Factors that influence charter schools' autonomy include their legal status and how they are approved, funded, and gain exemptions from rules. (U.S. General Accounting Office, 1995, p. 3)

Finn, Manno, Bierlein, and Vanourek (1997) put the concept of freedom in the charter school context: "... freedom means, among other things, that the charter school is not legally part of a school district (unless it wants to be), nor are its daily affairs overseen by officials other than its own" (Finn, 1997, p. 2). Waivers from rules, regulations, and policies constituted one mechanism for charter schools to assert freedom.

In Colorado, the most common requests for waivers were for:

1. Teacher evaluations: Under state code, evaluations must be conducted by a li-

censed administrator. Charter schools sought waivers from this regulation because they did not always have licensed administrators on staff. Instead, they involved parents, staff, and governing board members in the evaluation process.
2. Administrative license requirements: Waivers were sought when charter schools chose alternative management structures without a traditional principal.
3. Teacher Employment, Compensation, and Dismissal Act: When waived, charter school teachers signed annual contracts, in which salary and benefit packages were negotiated with the charter school's governing board.
4. Teacher license requirements: Waivers were sought to allow charter schools to hire teachers with other types of work experience. (Mulholland, 1996, p. 4-5)

In May 1997, Research, Policy, and Practice (RPP) International published its first-year nation-wide report on charter schools. The report found that autonomy was the major reason pre-existing public schools converted to charter school status, "Four out of five charter schools that sought autonomy from districts, state regulations or collective bargaining agreements were public school conversions" (U.S. Department of Education, 1997).

Norris' (1996) unpublished dissertation extended the work of McCune's (1994) dissertation. At the time of McCune's work there were only 31 charter schools in California. His project studied California charter schools in existence as of September 10, 1993. McCune looked at how charter school founders sought relief from "… constraints relating to credentialing requirements, labor contracts, district administrative procedures, and state code provisions" (McCune, 1994). Norris replicated McCune's project and studied the 51 additional California charter schools in existence between September 10, 1993 and September 10, 1995. Norris "study would indicate whether California's newer charter schools were taking advantage of the opportunities made available by the charter school legislation" (Norris, 1996).

California's charter school law permitted founders freedom from the requirements of much of the State of California Education Code and the regulations regarding collective bargaining. It further freed charter school founders from the constraints of: "… credentialing requirements, state education code provisions, district labor contracts, and district administrative procedures" (Norris, 1996, p. 24).

One of the first things Norris found had to do with the perceived effect of freedom for charter schools:

> In general, charter schools with high levels of autonomy were significantly more likely than low-autonomy charter schools to say they have more freedom, have district cooperation in hiring, and use parent contracts. They were also three times more likely to have an adversarial relationship with the teachers union and twice as likely to have and adversarial relationship with their school district. (Norris, 1996, p. 22)

In Corwin's (1995) study, California charter schools identified freedom as having control over:

> … instructional approaches; course offerings; selecting staff, teachers, and the principal; student discipline; use of noncertified staff; the budget; course content; student admissions; rules governing suspending and expelling students; setting

enrollment caps; reassigning and transferring teachers; expenditure of categorical funds; and custodial/maintenance services. (Corwin, 1995, p. 19-20)

Pratt (1996) paraphrased Glazer (1993), who found a few freedom options that he considered to be elements of choice: "... parents choosing among schools in large districts, schools in other districts, schools with limits to protect racial and ethnic diversity, schools with transportation or without, private schools, religious or not .... He contended that teachers would gain new freedoms as would parents" (Pratt, 1996, p. 19-20).

Pratt (1996) concluded that:

> school choice proponents endorsed the value of freedom resulting in concerns of equity and community .... Charter schools could become elitist .... Reform issues consistently evident in charter schools included on-site governance, school autonomy in personnel issues, authentic assessment for evaluation of student performance standards, and standardized testing as a benchmark for accountability" (Pratt, 1996, p. iii-iv)

Pratt also asserted that:

> The charter school movement in the United States is sustained by those committed to the value of freedom and choice .... [T]he impetus for charter schools was ignited by a variety of considerations connected to freedom. They include the concepts of free-market schools, school choice, and educational restructuring and reform to increase student achievement. "The gift of Charter Schools is the gift of freedom" (Sautter, 1993, p. 4). As suggested by Swanson and King (1991), "Freedom is the right to act in a manner of one's own choosing, not subject to undue restriction or control" (Swanson, 1991, p. 23).
>
> The freedom to create their own model of quality education has led parents, or teachers in partnership with parents, to create charter schools. They have been drawn to the freedom of the managerial design of charter schools which allocates to teachers and parents the power to make school decisions that impact the outcomes of their children's schooling. This empowerment has had great appeal to parents and teachers who believe they can influence the degree of educational excellence available to students if their educational systems are free of the constraints associated with bureaucracy in public education.
>
> Houston (1993) offered another perspective. He found a perspective of choice in the term "mystique." He contended that the American dream of choice is equated with the value of freedom, and it is this mystique that draws the proponents of choice regardless of the circumstances. (Pratt, 1996, p. 16-17)

Kolderie (1990) contended that choice by itself would not be enough. It would have to be accompanied by choices:

> *In order to create new public schools, and ultimately a new system of public education, the states would simply withdraw the local districts' exclusive franchise to own and operate public schools* (Italics in original). For choice to work—to help the student and to stimulate the district to change—the state will have to provide both choice and **choices**: allowing families to choose the schools their children attend and allowing someone other than the local district to provide schools under contract to a public agency. (Kolderie, 1990, p. 1)

Kolderie's sentiments provide a focal point for the discussion of school choice that has a complex history. One expression of the choice movement arose from business leaders who became involved in education. Their proposals took on the metaphorical patina of economics. They believed that the forces of the marketplace that created the most vigorous economy in the world would "... also generate 'excellent' schools with high scoring students" (Wells, 1993, p. 29).

In their 1990 study, Chubb and Moe concluded that the most effective school was the most autonomous. They also claimed that there was a link between parental choice and involvement and student achievement (Chubb, 1990). Tovey (1995) differed with Chubb and Moe (1990) and maintained that autonomy in Southern schools led to segregation in the 1960s. This phenomenon, called "white flight," took place as desegregation efforts were forced on schools in the South. Caucasian parents withdrew their children from their neighborhood schools and moved to the suburbs to assure that their children would attend schools with a predominant Caucasian student population. Southern parents also enrolled their children in private schools. In many urban centers of the United States today this practice still was in vogue, although the justification was somewhat different. The North Carolina charter school legislation contained a provision for racial balance: "... North Carolina law says that within a year after a charter opens, its enrollment 'shall reasonably reflect' the racial and ethnic composition of the general population within the county-wide district boundaries or the district's racial and ethnic composition" (Schnaiberg, 1998b, p. 22). Instead of "white flight," 12 of the 33 charter schools operating in North Carolina were "... more than 85 percent black" (Schnaiberg, 1998b, p. 22).

In reaction to this phenomenon,
> In July, the state school board voted to allow a statewide charter school advisory committee to determine on a school-by-school basis whether a charter school's racial imbalance is justified and what action, if any, the state should take.
>
> The Raleigh-based North Carolina Foundation for Individual Rights, a conservative nonprofit legal group, plans to file a lawsuit to block the state from enforcing the law's racial-balance provision. Additionally, a bill is moving through the legislature that would soften the provision to require only that schools make a "good faith effort" toward achieving diversity. But both critics and supporters of the proposed change say it is unlikely to survive the legislative process.
>
> While the state wrestles with the issue, charter schools are not sure what, if any, steps to take as the next school year approaches, said Jack Daly, the executive director of the legal group challenging the state law. (Schnaiberg, 1998b, p. 22)

In early 1998, the North Carolina Charter School Advisory Committee (NCCSAC) looked carefully at closing down the School in the Community charter school in Chapel Hill. The NCCSAC considered reports of problems with the charter school's attendance rules, student records, curriculum and discipline policies, and operations. Mike Fedewa, the chairman of the Charter School Advisory Committee and school superintendent for the Catholic Diocese of Raleigh, reported that the Committee had a "... pretty frank discussion ... We still have concerns about them, but it was encouraging. They aren't in denial about the issues they need to address (School in community gets reprieve, 1998, p. A-1)." The NCCSAC also considered "... whether to revoke the charter of Bonner Academy in Raleigh. State officials are investigating whether Linda Bonner, the school's founder, falsified a student's record (School in community gets reprieve, 1998, p. A-10)."

Tovey (1995) warned that: "The new choice programs of the 1990s, if not carefully monitored, could further that same goal [of white flight]" (Tovey, 1995, p. 1). In at least one urban school system, Tovey's caution was borne out. In the third year of his superintendency, Seattle schools' superintendent, John Stanford, a retired Brigadier General of the U.S. Army and a non-educator "... has taken measures to make schools safer, boost academic achievement, and give parents more control over curriculum" (Teichroeb, 1997, p. A-1).

In spite of these efforts, Mr. Stanford discovered, "Private school enrollment is climbing in Seattle despite an effort to make the city's public schools safer, more challenging and more attractive" (Teichroeb, 1997, p. A-1). Seattle School Board president, Linda Harris reacted with, "If people don't get what they want, they flee to the private schools" (Teichroeb, 1997, p. A-1). The comparative demographics were interesting: "While most private schools are predominantly white, 59 percent of Seattle's public school students are non-white" (Teichroeb, 1997, p. A-1).

In a background paper aimed at school choice advocates, the Heritage Foundation pointed out some of the downsides of public school choice. The Heritage Foundation (1991) explored three areas of concern: "(1) discrimination, (2) desegregation, and (3) the religious conundrum" (Education choice: A background paper, 1991, p. 13). Elmore (1990) said that school choice promoted social stratification along the lines of race, social group, and ethnicity.

Another researcher, Paul (Hill, 1994) pointed out other reasons why the issue of school choice became a topic of discussion. Pratt (1996) paraphrased Hill's findings: "... schools do not presently exist by design but rather as a result of layers of rules, state regulations, federal and state court orders, teacher collective bargaining contracts, and other constraints that delimit efficiency and productivity" (Pratt, 1996, p. 26). Consequently, school teachers and administrators were more concerned with complying with the prescriptions rather than with student achievement. After all, their jobs depended on their ability to show that they went along with the rules. Perhaps most confounding of school choice was Pratt's (1996) finding that "... documentation of the success of school choice is obviously absent in the research literature" (Pratt, 1996, p. 29).

Pratt (1996) also found that there was considerably more literature on school autonomy than on accountability. The predominant feature of autonomy that received most of the attention was that of school governance, specifically in the form of site-based management (SBM). The main problem with using SBM as a governance principle was that it was a floating abstraction, that is, there were no specific perceptual concretes that lent them to objective understanding. In other words, "Site-based management defies specific definition because of the lack of agreement on 'what it is, how to do it, or even why to do it' (David, 1995, p. 4)" (Pratt, 1996, p. 48). Pratt helped us to understand that the purpose of such governance reforms was the improvement of student achievement.

Pratt (1996) stated that school choice was subsumed under the pillar of freedom in the argument of charter school promoters.

The issue of school choice as a philosophy reviewed in the literature indicated its strong influence as a philosophy tied to charter schools. Proponents of school choice value the freedom it provides to parents and students. Parents feel not only empowered by the freedom to choose but also righteous in the consistency of freedom of choice and democracy. Parents who feel that their locally assigned school does not meet their educational focus resent the lack of freedom to choose a school in the best interests of their children. (Pratt, 1996, p. 166-167)

However, the charter school ideal encompassed more than just school choice. It included decentralized governance in some form of site-based management. It assumed that parents would have a high amount of participation in the operations of the school. Finally, charter school operators would agree to a high amount of scrutiny in terms of student achievement and accountability.

Because of their support for equity in education, the skeptics of the charter school idea raised a cautionary voice. They were chary of elitism. They were concerned about the exacerbating effects on those students who were from the low socio-economic stratum of the community. They felt that the charter school concept destroyed a sense of community cohesion. Lastly, they were circumspect of charter school patrons stealthily using them as a ruse to intensify segregation.

In her analysis of the six states with "strong" charter school legislation, Pratt (1996) found four common themes. Roberts (1993) found similar themes in legislation concerned with public school reform (Table 2).

Table 2.
Common themes occurring in charter schools and charter school legislation

Pratt	Rogers
Governance of Charter Schools, including the degree of parental involvement	School-based management, parental involvement, parental choice
Degree of control that the school's governing body had over personnel and other issues	Curriculum, personnel roles, teacher certification, restructuring
The methods of student assessment	
The consistency of requiring accountability for student achievement	Accountability

Source: (Pratt, 1996, p. 170)

While charter school proponents were ostensibly touting the virtues of parental choice and teacher academic freedom, Pratt (1996) found some teacher working conditions and professional anomalies.

Several charters presented unusual conditions expected of employees. One school's charter designated that there was a nine-year implied teacher commitment to the school. Another school's charter stated that instructors may not have another job without the written consent of the Board. Another stated that the principal and teachers were expected to be on campus from 8 a.m. to 5 p.m. minimally. The principal and teachers at this school were paid cash bonuses for outstanding student achievement. Another school paid bonuses for improvements to the curriculum. Still another paid cash bonuses to teachers and the principal for an outstanding year-end portfolio. (Pratt, 1996, p. 173)

Literature on the concept of accountability in education.

Roberts (1993) defined "accountability" as: "An organizing principle which involves standards setting and performance reporting. It is often connected to school sites being given increased responsibility (Herrington, 1992; Rothman, 1993)" (Roberts, 1993, p. 6). Rothman (1995) defined "accountability" as: "... the process by which school districts and states [or other constituents such as parents] attempt to ensure that schools and school systems meet their goals" (Rothman, 1995, p. 189).

The accountability movement came into prominence in the 1970s. It was then that states started to exert more control over the schools. Roberts (1993) reported:

Between 1969 and 1976, over 4,000 articles and books were written on the application of accountability to education. With its mandates for planning, assessment, programmed-based budgeting, and public reporting, accountability provided a way for states to establish a well-defined role, concentrate on standards setting and performance reporting, and leverage influence without violating local control (Herrington, 1992). (Roberts, 1993, p. 14)

The following critique reviewed the broad history of the importance, nationally and in Alaska, shown for school- and district-level accountability that led to this project's emphasis on accountability of the fifteen charter schools in Alaska. It presented research on the use of school- and district-level accountability systems to develop a consistent accountability mechanism to better evaluate how Alaska's charter schools adhered to their promise to improve student achievement and to use their financial resources.

The aim of this analysis was to uncover the elements of this accountability mechanism compared to those that existed in other states, and compared to the criteria for effectiveness drawn from research and other literature. First, the examination provided the context for a future project to analyze student and charter school performance through an overview of the development of educational performance indicators[21] and indicator systems[22] nationally and in Alaska. Second, this explication documented the evolution of the Alaska "school report card" system, critiqued its current status, and explored its adequacy to provide the public and educational policy-makers with accountability information upon which they determined the effectiveness of charter schools in Alaska.

The limited autonomy[23] the legislature gave to charter schools created challenges for holding them accountable for student achievement. Linda G. Morra, Director of the federal Health, Education, and Human Services Division, testified before the Subcommittee on Labor, Health and Human Services, Education, and Related Agencies about some of those challenges:

The extent to which charter schools can be held accountable depends on how the schools assess student performance and report results. Charter schools vary in how specifically they state student performance objectives and assessment methods. Also, some charter schools have their assessment systems in place and have begun collecting data; others ... including some schools already open ... are still developing their assessment systems. Because charter schools' efforts to assess and report student performance are fairly recent, it is too early to tell if the schools will meet their student performance objectives.

In addition, several important questions about charter schools' accountability systems remain. First, are charter schools collecting adequate baseline data to determine changes in student performance? ... Second, will charter schools report data by race, gender, or socioeconomic status so that the performance of specific student groups may be assessed? No state laws require charter schools to do so; some have no reporting requirements; and most leave the nature of reporting to local discretion. Third, what are the implications of requiring charter schools to meet state performance standards and to use standardized, norm-referenced tests? (Morra, 1995, p. 4)

The first historical accounts of accountability appeared in the works of Sun Tzu ("The Art of War") and Attila the Hun. The Gilead guards used accountability when they encountered deserters from the tribe of Ephraim as they crossed the Jordan River:

Are you a member of the tribe of Ephraim? They asked. If the man replied that he was not, then they demanded, "Say Shibboleth." But if he could not pronounce the "sh" and said Sibboleth instead of Shibboleth he was dragged away and killed.

As a result 42,000 people of Ephraim died there at that time. (Judges 12:5-6)

These chronicles had a unique military flavor and application. They were the beginnings of the discussion of accountability as a tool of administration to report the status of their efforts to improve the performance of their charges to their patrons. The inchoate contemporary discussion of accountability may be traced to the launch of Sputnik in 1959. This benchmark event provoked Americans to become uncomfortable with the quasi-education system not only in the United States as a whole but also in the individual states in particular.

No less a person than Bill Walsh, former head coach of the San Francisco 49ers National Football League team, has shared his thoughts on accountability. While waxing about the philosophy of being a head coach, Mr. Walsh counseled:

Be accountable. You must accept responsibility for those matters over which you are in charge. Deflecting blame, even if you are not responsible for a particular occurrence, is often viewed as a sign of weakness by both your staff and your players.

Whatever the situation, offering apparently well-reasoned excuses and plausible alibis to explain your failings is simply irresponsible. "Passing the buck" when times get tough will not enhance the level of respect you engender from others. If you expect loyalty from your staff and your players, you must show it to them first by being accountable for your own actions.

The factor that is most often at the heart of accountability issues is the team's win-loss record. However unfair it may seem that you are held responsible for something that is not totally within your control, the responsibility comes with the position. If the team wins, you get much of the credit; if it loses, you get most of the criticism.

You should remember that ultimately, you are responsible for the performance of your players. As such, fair or not, it is logical that you would be held accountable for whether their performances led to the requisite number of victories. (Walsh, 1998, p. 17)

In 1966, J.S. Coleman, under the auspices of the National Center for Educational Statistics (NCES), issued his Equality of Educational Opportunity (Coleman, 1966). Coleman suggested that it was the "nurture" factor of family socio-economic status that held the most influence over student achievement. Because of the "nature" factor, the schools were off the hook because they had no control over the students' family backgrounds. Coleman's work, however, inspired educational researchers, notably Ron Edmonds (Edmonds, 1979), and Brookover and Lezotte (Brookover, 1979) in the 1970s to look at features of schools that may also contribute to student performance. This subsequent research challenged the Coleman work on the premise that there were things within the control of the schools that could be done to improve student achievement.

For the decade of the 1970s, national education watchers used the results of the National Assessment of Educational Progress (NAEP) to measure student achievement. The NAEP gave an annual summary of student achievement in four subject areas. Throughout the 1970s, the NAEP reported declines in American students' test scores in science and mathematics. These results alarmed many Americans particularly as they compared those test scores with those of students of other developed nations in the world.

In 1981, Secretary of Education, Terrell H. Bell, impaneled the National Commission on Excellence in Education (NCEE). The NCEE focused on educational quality in the schools of the United States and started the first phase of national attention on education. On April 26, 1983, the NCEE published A Nation at Risk: The Imperative for Education Reform. The report listed some suggestions for lifting the declining student scores in the schools of the United States. A Nation at Risk heightened the public's concern that foreign countries were surpassing the perceived hegemony the United States enjoyed in trade, business, science, and technology. Some of the report's recommendations were to:

> (a) require high school students to take four years of English, three years of math, three years of science, three years of social studies, and one-half of a year of computer science; (b) adopt hard and measurable standards; (c) lengthen the school day and school year; (d) improve teacher training; and (e) require educator and legislator responsibility for leadership and financial aid. (National Commission on Excellence in Education, 1983)

Several other reports were published between 1986 and 1992. The Carnegie Forum on Education and the Economy's Task Force on Teaching as a Profession unveiled *A Nation Prepared: Teachers for the 21st Century*. Thus began the second phase of national attention on education. The authors of the report were concerned about the quality of teachers and the institutions preparing teacher hopefuls for the teaching profession. *A Nation Prepared* also gave a framework for school districts to encourage the professionalization of teaching that included salary enhancements, freedom, and chances for career advancement (Carnegie Forum on Education and the Economy, 1986).

In October 1989, President Bush and the governors of the states met at the National Governors summit at the University of Virginia in Charlottesville, Virginia.

The summit provided the foundation for the first national education goals (Table 3). It also provided the impetus for a national accountability system.

Table 3
The National Education Goals

1. All children in America will start school ready to learn.
2. The high school graduation rate will increase to at least 90 percent.
3. American students will leave grades 4, 8, and 12 having demonstrated competency in challenging subject matter, including English, mathematics, science, history, and geography; and every school in America will ensure that all students learn to use their minds well, so they may be prepared for responsible citizenship, further learning, and productive employment in our modern economy.
4. U.S. students will be first in the world in mathematics and science achievement.
5. Every adult American will be literate and will possess the knowledge and skills necessary to compete in a global economy and exercise the rights and responsibilities of citizenship.
6. Every school in America will be free of drugs and violence and will offer a disciplined environment conductive to learning.

TWO GOALS ADDED LATER
By the year 2000:

7. The nation's teaching force will have access to programs for the continued improvement of their professional skills and the opportunity to acquire the knowledge and skills needed to instruct and prepare all American students for the next century.
8. Every school will promote partnerships that will increase parental involvement and participation in promoting the social, emotional, and academic growth of children.

The National Center for Education Statistics (NCES) in the U.S. Department of Education was then asked to meet this fresh demand for more descriptive, more detailed, more accurate, and more quickly produced empirical data. The NCES identified:

[I]ndicators as statistics that have been adjudged as important in that they inform on the health and quality of education and they monitor important developments in education. They include some basis for comparison, for a relationship is built in-frequently against a standard or in terms of time; but at least as importantly, across subpopulations, across states, or across countries. Indicators feed into our understanding of how we are performing not only overall in education, but also how we are reaching all the different children in our diverse society. (Griffith, 1990, p. 4)

In retrospect, it can be seen that these indicators were for summative and system-based evaluation rather than for formative evaluation in classrooms and in schools. They could monitor without necessarily generating improvement. Their development was given high priority at the NCES through three projects: indicators publications, an expert indicators panel, and international indicators. (Macpherson, 1996, p. 84)

Macpherson went on to say that the result of this effort was the creation of a disjointed policy. He gave three reasons:

> Performance data provides evidence of (a) the values preferred by those with the power to define them as policy and the structures to operationalize them, (b) the values actually being served, (c) the gap between them, and (d) what needs to be attended to close the gap ....
>
> Second, state political and educational leaders were antagonized when they were not involved centrally in deciding what data categories were to be used ....
>
> Third, the output measures used, such as drop-out rates and average Scholastic Aptitude test scores, were shown to be technically inadequate. They did not measure performances and services in a full and trustworthy manner. On the other hand, all stakeholders had reasons to fear the use of alternative, arbitrary, and feral processes or criteria.
>
> Overall, these three reasons gave the impression that people held systems theories of accountability that gave high priority to threshold criteria and processes that traversed political, professional, and technical dimensions. (Macpherson, 1996, p. 84-85)

Why? As Cibulka (1991) noted, it was:

> [T]o reconcile the conflicting purposes to which accountability reporting can be put, and ... arduous is the task of aligning the purpose with larger policy design and successful policy settlement .... Embedded in the controversy is the deeper, often unstated issue, of whether educators, elected officials, or individual parents should have primary power over access to and uses of performance information. This is a political problem at the heart of democratic theory .... One thing seems certain, performance information is reshaping the character of educational politics. (Cibulka, 1991, p. 198-199)

In 1991, President Bush unveiled a long-term approach that stressed:

1. using 15 world-class accountability standards (Table 4) to measure and compare results, and to make changes where necessary;
2. creating new schools along the lines of Washington State's "Schools for the 21st Century," Theodore Sizer's "Coalition of Essential Schools," Henry Levin's "Accelerated Schools," and others;
3. encouraging adults who have not completed school to do so, encouraging people to acquire parenting skills, to be better neighbors, and to practice citizenship and friendship; and,
4. creating communities friendly to learning.

After President Bush's Charlottesville summit, the formulation of the national education goals, and the unveiling of America 2000, the Secretary of Education presented the first of two Commission on Achieving Necessary Skills (SCANS) reports: *What Work Requires of Schools*. The first SCANS report (Table 5) emphasized that education needed to change according to the needs of employers. Students would need to learn successful job performance skills so they could compete in the world job market (U.S. Department of Labor, 1991).

Table 4
America 2000 15-Point Accountability Plan

- World class standards
- American achievement tests
- Encourage test use by colleges, universities, and employers
- Presidential citations for educational excellence
- Presidential achievement scholarships
- Report cards
- Changes in the National Assessment of Educational Progress
- New choice incentives and choice applied to Chapter I
- Educational flexibility legislation to support the school as site of reform
- Merit Schools Program to reward school that move toward the goals
- Governors' academies for school leaders
- Governors' academies for teachers
- Differential pay for teachers
- Alternative certification for teachers and principals
- Honor outstanding teachers in the five core course areas

Table 5.
SCANS Workplace Know-How

The SCANS suggested that job performance depended on an employee having certain foundations and competencies.

Foundation	
Basic Skills	reading, writing, mathematics, speaking, and listening
Thinking Skills	thinking creatively, making decisions, solving problems, seeing things in the mind's eye, knowing how to learn, and reasoning
Personal Qualities	individual responsibility, self-esteem, sociability, self-management, and integrity
Competencies	
Resources	allocating time, money, materials, space, and staff
Interpersonal Skills	working on teams, teaching others, serving customers, leading, negotiating, and working well with people from culturally diverse backgrounds
Information	acquiring and evaluating data, organizing and maintaining files, interpreting and communicating, and using computers to process information
Systems	understand social, organizational, and technological systems, monitoring and correcting performance, and designing or improving systems
Technology	selecting equipment and tools, applying technology to specific tasks, and maintaining and troubleshooting technologies

In 1992, the second SCANS report was published. It defined the abilities, outlooks and understanding need for workplace success. It also weighed the estimate of students' practical knowledge to be successful (U.S. Department of Labor, 1992).

A common theme of all the reports was that of accountability and the indicators to recognize it. Coincident to the first SCANS report, the first discussion of accountability indicators took place. The National Center for Education Statistics' (NCES) *Education Counts: an Indicator System to Monitor the Nation's Educational Health*, reported that indicator systems of accountability should be built on how students acquired knowledge, skills, and character and became ready for school. The report also called for teacher preparation institutions to improve, for communities to support learning, and for education and the economy to become more productive (National Center for Education Statistics, 1991). The agenda the NCES established was based on two assumptions: "… a comprehensive causal story of educational systems was available [and] the specifications of a remedial accountability subsystem" (Macpherson, 1996, p. 86).

As if the use of accountability data were not enough for domestic comparison, the Organization for Economic Cooperation and Development (OECD) expanded the development of education indicators for comparisons between developed countries. The OECD influenced thought on accountability systems based on "the need for both external coherence and the internal use of students' interests to justify policy …."

By the time of the OECD contribution, it was becoming clear that a permissible theory of accountability "… had to accommodate economic, political, educational, national, regional, and personal dimensions… [that] placed more emphasis on curriculum content, learning exposure time, higher-order thinking skills, decision making at the school site, and the role of teachers" (Macpherson, 1996, p. 86).

In 1988, California voters approved Proposition 98 that required accountability reports to assess 13 performance domains. The California accountability system became the classic example of an accountability system. It relied on four elements:

Quality Indicator Reports provided the percentages of students enrolled in academic courses, meeting graduation requirements and enrolled in pre-university courses; standardized test scores in reading and math; Scholastic Aptitude Test scores; achievement test scores; advanced-placement test scores; and drop-out and attendance rates.

Californian Assessment Program (CAP). The criterion-referenced test tested samples of children in grades 3, 6, 8, and 12 to identify changes to student learning in math, language, history/social studies, and science.

School Accountability Report Cards. Schools assess and report publicly on four input factors: (expenditure and services, development of staff and curriculum, availability of substitute teachers, and availability of qualified support staff), six process factors (facilities, discipline, and climate; class sizes and teaching loads; teaching materials; assigning teachers outside areas of competence; evaluation and development of teachers; and quality of teaching and leadership), and two outcome factors (student achievement in basic skills and academic subjects and drop-out rates) ….

An annual research report on the Conditions of Education in California by the

Policy Analysis for Californian Education center (PACE). It adds trend data to detailed discussions of inputs, processes and outputs, and analyses of major state initiatives. (Macpherson, 1996, p. 87)

In January 1992, the National Council on Education Standards and Testing (NCEST) released *Raising Standards for American Education.* NCEST filled out the work of the 1989 Charlottesville education summit. NCEST assisted the National Education Goals Panel (NEGP) that reached the conclusion that in order to measure headway on national goals three and four (Table 3) nation-wide standards needed to be defined for student achievement in English, mathematics, science, history, and geography.

This tableau of national committee projects provided the context for the growing intensity of research and development on the accountability elements measuring educational quality and school effectiveness. In the 1980s, the public demonstrated its desire for school accountability. As a result of such labors, some cardinal components emerged in the corpus of information about indicator systems and how professionals used them. The underlying premise of accountability in public education was that efficiency would result if one ignored the conundrum of oversight bodies compelling schools to operate in the miasma of the quasi-free market. In other words, information about school performance motivated parents and educators to focus resources on those schools most in need of improvement.

When taken together, the work of several authors and agencies (Oakes, 1986; David, 1988; SREB, 1992; Texas Education Agency, 1994; and Massell, 1994), identified several features of educational performance indicators and the accountability instruments that used them:

Articulation of system purposes .... [O]ne should expect to see all purposes or intended uses of the system clearly and formally spelled out, particularly for those whose performance is being gauged. Simultaneously, there should be sensitivity to unintended effects of system implementation, such as unnecessary narrowing of the curriculum or excessive testing.

System feasibility. Many discrete criteria are encompassed by system feasibility. Among them are the following: the "buy in' or consensus that exists to support the indicator system's continued existence; the economics of the system, including

(a) the use of simplistic, readily quantifiable indicators that measure enduring features of schooling,
(b) the use of standardized definitions and data collection procedures,
(c) the resources needed to operate the system, particularly collecting and maintaining large volumes of data over time,
(d) timelines of data collection and reporting,
(e) the overall unity or integration of the system to prevent losses associated with poor coordination or poor planning (e.g. avoiding excessive student testing with lost instructional time; the legality of the system (whether it is in compliance with current law).

Validity. In this context the term "validity" refers to the overall soundness of the system. Specific criteria within this area of concern the following: face validity and fairness in comparisons, including acknowledgment and (where possible) accommodation of diversity within the system; validity in measurement-particularly measurement of student learning-including reliability and system stability; appropriate use of the data and/or valid application of the findings, such that data interpretation (including the application of standards to data) leads to reasonable conclusions and reasonable courses of action.

Articulation of responsibilities ... includes clear identification in policy of local-, as well as of state-level, responsibilities. For example, increased accountability of schools for results may or may not be accompanied in policy with increased local flexibility to design programs that are responsive to student needs. Whether or not development and use of locally appropriate accountability systems is encouraged should be clearly stated as well.

Utility ... incorporates a wide range of specific criteria, including each of the following: the establishment of built-in points of reference for interpreting results on the indicators; generation of reports that are understandable or "customer friendly"; creating conditions that facilitate indicators' use in planning and decision making so that the data have a direct, rather than indirect, influence on policy (this is linked to the issue of timeliness of data collection and reporting); provision for locally-specific information as well as for information that is common across units, whether those units are schools, districts, or some other level of the system; establishment a priori of the ways that those at the local level should use or respond to the information, i.e. will local schools have to disseminate the information to parents? Do campus improvement plans have to address results on the indicators? Should schools or districts increase their program evaluation efforts to better understand what programs and/or processes contribute to their results on the indicators?; the establishment a priori of what formal consequences, if any are to be applied to the results on the indicators, such as how accreditation status and campus ratings are determined from the data; acknowledgment of informal consequences of having received the information and the opportunities for change that arise from having received certain ratings; capacity for responsiveness on the part of the indicator system itself, i.e. not only tolerance for change but allowance for regular change and refinement based on the data as well as a longer-term perspective on systemic improvement.

Attending to as many of these criteria as possible up front, in the development of an indicator system that is to be used for performance monitoring, may well be associated with not only the quality but also the longevity of the system. (Texas Education Agency, 1996, p. 8-9)

Historically, the theory of accountability assumed a relationship between the dispenser of something of value and a sponsor who had the option to compensate, discipline, or remove the provider. Other writers have asserted that a school accountability system ought to include four features:

1. Information about the organization's performance (e.g., test scores).
2. Standards for judging the quality or degree of success of organizational performance (e.g., a mean achievement score higher than other schools with comparable demographic characteristics).
3. Significant consequences to the organization (i.e. rewards and sanctions such

as bonuses to teachers in the school) for its success or failure in meeting specified standards.
4. An agent or constituency that receives information on organizational performance, judges the extent to which standards have been met, and distributes rewards and sanctions (e.g., the state department of instruction). (Newmann, 1997, p. 43)

Baratz-Snowden (1990) added what became known as the "five 'apple' criteria" (Mehrens, 1992, p. 6): "Any assessment to be used for accountability purposes has to be administratively feasible, professionally credible, publicly acceptable, legally defensible, and economically affordable" (Baratz-Snowden, 1990) quoted in (Mehrens, 1992, p. 3).

With regards to the "legally defensible" criteria, Mehrens provided an interesting caveat:

'Legally, performance assessment is considered a test' (Nathan, 1986, p. 1). Whether this is how all courts would decide the issue, prudent individuals developing performance assessments for high-stakes decisions would be wise to act as if this were the case.[24] Psychometric experts for plaintiffs generally attack tests based on whether or not the *Standards for Educational and Psychological Testing* (AERA, 1985) have been followed. One would expect them to do the same for performance assessments. That performance assessments will meet the various psychometric standards of reliability, validity, etc., has not been adequately demonstrated.

Other legal concerns also need to be considered. For example, if there is any disparate impact on protected groups, how might one deal with the fact that observers (graders) may be aware of the group status of the group status of the students? If there is debate about the scoring process, will there be documentation of the performance so rescoring can occur? (Mehrens, 1992, p. 6)

DeMoulin and Kendall (1993) leveled severe criticism of the accountability systems that states created:

Accountability is a concept that has been used as a finger-pointing instrument to deny responsibility for involvement and to blame others for lack of institutional advancement. It is also concerned with the product of the institutions as well as the participants within the institutions. Accountability for educational success is not limited to the education sector; all society must assume responsibility for providing an adequate environment for education. (DeMoulin, 1993, p. 697)

Newmann, King, and Rigdon (1997) provided a way of testing for accountability in a particular school, presumably even in a charter school. They recommended that:

... a complete school accountability system should include at least four parts:
1. Information about the organization's performance (e.g. test scores).
2. Standards for judging the quality or degree of success of organizational performance (e.g. mean achievement score higher than other schools with comparable demographic characteristics).
3. Significant consequences to the organization (i.e. rewards and sanctions such as bonuses to teachers in the school) for its success or failure in meeting specific standards.
4. An agent or constituency that receives information on organizational performance,

judges the extent to which standards have been met, and distributes rewards and sanctions (e.g. the state department of instruction. (Newmann, 1997, p.43)

They also suggested ways to test for these components,

... to measure the extent to which all four components of accountability are present for a school and to examine the extent to which strength of accountability is associated with a common measure of student achievement, independent or other facts that affect student achievement, in a large number of schools. (Newmann, 1997, p. 44)

They recognized that the four components would not be sufficient. They enumerated the three problem areas of implementation, organizational capacity, and internal accountability.

... controversy persists on how to implement standards and what the specific standards should be ....[The] dispute continues over whether school performance should be judged according to individual student improvement or on absolute performance standards; whether it should be judged relative to the social background of the student population.

[With regards to] organizational capacity ... [f]irst, the standards themselves must call for more ambitious, high-quality intellectual work for all students. Stricter accountability to deliver mediocre curriculum, or to expect more challenging academic work only from economically privileged students, would be no advance. Second, even if external authorities provided higher quality standards and inducements, many schools would lack the capacity to meet them. To meet higher standards, major advances will be needed in the quality of technical resources (such as curriculum and assessment materials, laboratory equipment, library and computing facilities), in professional development for staff, and in finding ways to balance strong external accountability with significant autonomy for schools to craft programs that respond to their unique social contexts ....

Proposed ingredients of organizational capacity include teachers' professional knowledge and skills, effective leadership, availability of technical and financial resources, and organizational autonomy to act according to demands of the local context .... The critical defining feature of organizational capacity is the degree to which the human, technical, and social resources of an organization are organized into an effective collective enterprise. (Newmann, 1997, p. 46-47)

The Consortium for Policy Research in Education (CPRE) (1997) studied the accountability systems of charter school sponsors in California, Massachusetts, and Minnesota. They concluded that the requirements were "... relatively weak .... [And] [s]ponsoring agencies have focused to date more on standards of fiscal management and, to a lesser degree, on general probity and scandal avoidance than on reasonable progress toward schools' meeting their own student goals" (Wohlstetter, 1997, p. 4). In the area of charter school accountability, the CPRE suggested that the accountability factors that held the most promise for supporting exemplary teaching and learning were:

clear performance standards which can be used to determine if the school is meeting its goals; assessments of student performance linked to the school's educational goals; rewards for schools and teachers based on performance; and, clear consequences for failure of school to perform. (Wohlstetter, 1997, p. 8)

When applied to charter school accountability in Alaska, educators could use the above indicators to identify strong and weak spots in each charter school. After using them, educators could use them for suggesting policy changes and for identifying areas where more information was needed.

However, they had problems as well as benefits. These consequences became more evident in light of the fact that Alaska's charter school legislation left it up to the local school boards to determine the level of accountability they expected from the charter school they sponsored. Although it has never been tested, the implication of this provision of the charter school legislation was that charter schools were practically exempt from the requirements of Alaska's school accountability law, also known as AS 14.03.120 the *School District Report Card to the Public*.

Furthermore, an examination of the provisions of the Alaska's school accountability law revealed that it was of little guidance to school boards in the formulation of their own charter school accountability system. However, Alaska was not unique in this deficiency. Manno, Finn, Bierlein, and Vanourek (1997) found: "The problem that charter schools face ... is that many states and communities have not yet installed ... essential components [of accountability]—either for their charter schools or for regular public schools" (Manno, 1997, p. 12). In New Jersey, researchers found that "... charter schools ... are not publicly accountable" (Charter schools, 1998, p. 16).

The Sixteenth Alaska Legislature formed the Joint Committee on School Performance to identify priorities for school improvement. Through a series of public hearings and discussions with various education groups, the Committee formulated recommendations that focused on the performance of students. The Sixteenth Alaska Legislature acted on the recommendations from the Joint Committee and enacted Chapter 173. The legislation amended AS 14.03 with the addition of Sec 14.03.120. During the 1992 Legislative Session, AS 14.03.120 was amended to require school districts to submit summaries and evaluations of their environmental education curriculum. In addition, the State School Board amended 4 AAC 06.160, the dropout regulation, to require school districts to include the information as part of the *School District Report Card to the Public*. School districts were required annually to:

- submit an Education Plan to the Department of Education (DOE) and make it available to the local public
- have each school conduct a public meeting at which the school's performance and the performance of the school's students are shared with the community, and forward a school-level report of performance to the district superintendent
- submit a *School District Report Card to the Public* to the DOE and make it available to the local public

The *School District Report Card to the Public* did not specify the content of the school level performance report. However, district's had discretion in determining the content of the report that statute required a district to present to its local community. The information in these reports was transmitted to the Legislature, the Governor, and made available to the public in a summary comparison report that the DOE prepared. The summary comparison report was based on the information received from the school districts' *Education Plans* and *School District Report Card to the Public*. It was distributed to the public each January.

The annual *School District Report Card to the Public* required districts to report the following information: comments on school performance; meaningful parent involvement; indicators of performance the school district selects; environmental education curriculum; change in enrollment; attendance rate; dropout rate; ninth-grade cohort graduation rate; percent of students promoted to the next grade; and, percent of district students in the top and bottom quartile of standardized national achievement examinations.

The collection and reporting of this information was an important professional responsibility. Individuals and organizations both in state and nationally used the information to judge the status of education in Alaska.

The annual *Education Plan* required districts to report information to the DOE and to make it available to the public. The data included district goals and priorities for improving education; a plan for achieving district goals and priorities; a means for measuring progress toward district goals and priorities; the relationship of district goals or priorities to state goals, found in 4 AAC 04.010, and the Governor's Quality Schools Initiative; and student, parent, and community member participation in the preparation of the report. The DOE summarized the districts' education plans in the annual publication, *Summary of Alaska's Public School Districts' Report Cards to the Public*.

Education planning that best served the schools in Alaska occurred in a variety of ways. Individual district goals varied in the length of time it took to meet the established criteria. Because a fully implemented comprehensive goal demanded resources, a district may choose to have as many or as few goals as they deemed appropriate. School districts have used a flexible format for education planning that met its specific needs.

In theory, the purposes of the Alaska's school accountability law were to:
1. encourage the school district to envision and develop local educational plans that are unique to each district's culture, geography, and climate, and that will graduate world-class students;
2. empower the public with the knowledge that the skills and subjects included in legislation are of great importance to education, in order that the public will be able to participate in local educational planning with more authority and effect; and
3. set standards against which the public, district, teachers, and students can measure the quality of education that students receive.

However, when these purposes were compared to the features of a quality accountability system, certain weakness became evident.

Technically, the Alaska school accountability system did not measure areas where theory and empirical knowledge were relatively weak or highly complex, such as the quality of teaching, the quality of the curriculum, and students' acquisition of higher-order thinking skills. Since Alaska school districts had the flexibility to use a format for education planning that met their specific needs, there was no uniform understanding of definitions, there were no goals that sufficiently echoed the goals of education, and there were no procedures that guaranteed objective comparisons of widely varying factors. Furthermore, Alaska's political and educational history seemed to require broad agreement on goals or standards for each indicator. However, this time-consuming and complicated agreement was lacking.

In another area, the Alaska school accountability system provided no connection between accountability indicators and incentives or disincentives. Sergiovanni (1992) saw this as a major component of an accountability system:

> ... a related issue is the extent to which program improvement should be rewarded in the funding system. Should there be incentives for improvement in student performance or some other factor? It is attractive to many policy makers to link increased state support for education with demonstrated increases in student performance. But attempts to implement this rationale bump into a multitude of tough measurement questions: What are the appropriate standards of performance? How do we fairly measure these standards across disparate schools with different student populations? How can discretion be given to local school authorities to meet meaningful state goals? (Sergiovanni, 1992, p. 408)

When the Alaska Department of Education (AKDOE) published the *Summary of Alaska's Public School Districts' Report Cards to the Public*, there were no internal and no external pressures for schools to improve. Whatever the indicators measured was of almost no value to educators to determine to which areas they should devote their attention. There was little danger of the accidental effect of curriculum tightening and the indicators did not influence local policy-making justifying the expenditure of resources.

Brown (1990) suggested some reasons for the weaknesses of local report card systems, such as that used in Alaska, were due to their nature as a purely political strategy. Brown said,

> However, who the intended targets are is unclear–apparently anyone who will react. So far, it seems that this strategy works best on discrete measures, such as improving attendance and dropout rates where public and professional attention is focused by publishing district or school results. Similarly, many districts and schools have focused a lot of attention on directly preparing students for standardized tests. What this strategy has not yet done is encourage many schools or districts to take a broad response to the indicators and generate an overall school improvement effort–one that re-analyses the function and design of the educational system. (Brown, 1990, p. 5)

Ramirez (1992) pointed out one of the reasons for the weakness of Alaska's school accountability system, "... to be effective, indicator systems can't be built solely around achievement test results" (Ramirez, 1992, p. 34).

However, some of the weaknesses of Alaska's accountability system were also its strengths. It avoided any questions of its validity when used for comparisons of states, districts, or schools with significantly different demographic attributes. Nevertheless, this characteristic did little to dissuade politicians from using the results for demagogic purposes.

Additionally, Alaska's school accountability system did not ease the difficulty of determining the cause of differences in outcomes. Even though it was generally recognized that "outcome indicators will, in general, not tell the extent to which the program has caused the observed outcomes" (Pollitt, 1995, p. 143), Alaska's educators and policy makers had no basis for planning what to do differently to improve results. This condition may be a deliberate attempt to avoid the friction between policy makers and school leaders. However, this situation decreased consensus building and long-term political support for the educational system. The current attitude of the majority of the members of the Alaska legislature represented the public's dissatisfaction with the school system in Alaska. The *Summary of Alaska's Public School Districts' Report Cards to the Public* provided no succor from this segment of society.

Since Alaska's school accountability system provided no guidance for the establishment of criteria for an accountability system to measure the relative merits of Alaska's charter schools, it was evident that there was a clear need to do so.

Brown (1990) shed some light on the issue of accountability system indicators or accountability measures. Brown said:

> System indicators are only one element of an accountability process. To be genuinely effective, they must take into account the essential relationships among actors in the educational arena, the nature of work in education, and the specific responsibilities of all actors. (Brown, 1990, p. 1)

Because the discussion of accountability measures that incorporate system indicators was at an abstract level, Brown concluded that the attraction for their use would have the political appeal of "policy Platonism"–"treating policy regimes as ideal types" (MacCoun, 1997, p. 48). They satisfied the public's demand for quick solutions. "The danger," Brown asserted, in virtual confirmation of chaos theory, "is that as more specific demands of accountability are placed on the schools, schools will be made even less effective by being forced to respond to conflicting or impossible demands" (Brown, 1990, p. 2).

By the time of Brown's exegesis, accountability systems had evolved from a focus on adequacy and equity, that is the input resources, to a focus on site-based management and decision-making, that is process, to a focus on ends, that is outcomes.

When Brown gave an operational overview of the nature of public education, she inadvertently contributed to the argument that education must be viewed as a dynamic system:

> Education, like other public agencies, is subject to multiple demands, multiple constituencies, and multiple control systems .... In education, the normal complexity of a public agency is compounded by the fact that we are trying to educate human beings with their different skills, interests, and resources instead of making robots or processing tax forms. (Brown, 1990, p. 2)

Consequently, Brown believed, a set of system indicators would have maximum utility only if they were closely linked to the performance of the education system:

> Indicators of system performance are those input and process variables which are believed to be related to quality education and student learning. Such variables include teacher training and experience, attendance, courses or subjects offered and taken, student background characteristics, and scores on standardized achievement tests. There are many other statistics which educa-

tional administrators must collect, such as the age and condition of facilities and detailed accounting records of revenues and expenditures, which are important for addressing other policy concerns—but these should be included as system indicators only if they are directly related to outcomes in education. (Brown, 1990, p. 2)

Brown suggested that organizational accountability must clearly state, "... who is responsible to whom for what" (Brown, 1990, p. 3), and must, at a minimum, contain the following components:

1. **Key Actors.** Who is holding whom responsible? In education, potential actors include teachers, principals, administrators, superintendents, board members, and legislators.
2. **Goals.** What is supposed to be accomplished? Goals might focus on increased graduation requirements, higher test scores, increased problem solving skills, higher attendance, etc.
3. **Resources.** Does the person or the agency have access to necessary resources and control over key components? Educators need a variety of materials, supplies, personnel and community resources, and decision making authority to be effective.
4. **Pre-determined Standards.** How will we know if the goals are met? Policymakers and educators need to specify targets or objectives for action on a short-term basis.
5. **Rewards/sanctions.** What is the controlling actor's response to success or failure? Are successes openly rewarded and failures openly sanctioned? Policy makers have a fairly broad repertoire of possible responses including promotion, salary increases, increased responsibility, loss of control, further training, reprimand, probation, or termination. (Brown, 1990, p. 3)

Romzek and Dubnick (1987), quoted in Brown (1990) developed a matrix to illustrate the bureaucratic, legal, professional, and political approaches for accomplishing public accountability (Romzek, 1987). These approaches were organized along the quadratic dimensions of locus of control and degree of control (Figure 2).

Figure 2.
Types of Accountability Systems

| | | Source of Agency Control ||
		Internal	External
Degree of Control Over Agency Actions	High	Bureaucratic	Legal
	Low	Professional	Political

Source: (Brown, 1990, p. 3)

A <u>bureaucratic</u> [an internal organizational control mechanism] strategy focuses attention on the priorities of those at the top of the bureaucratic hierarchy. It assumes an authoritative relationship between a superior and a subordinate and close supervision or a surrogate system of rules. A bureaucratic strategy is most appropriate when there is a high degree of control between the supervisor and the subordinate and the nature of the activity is fairly routinized and predictable.

A legal [an external organizational control mechanism] accountability strategy is similar to the bureaucratic model, but is based on a fundamentally different relationship between the actors. Legal accountability assumes that the controlling actor or agency is outside the agency and has the authority to impose contractual sanctions on the agency being controlled. This relationship depends on a process of rewards or punishments to induce compliance.

Professional [an internal organizational control mechanism] accountability is more appropriately used by school districts in areas which are highly technical or complex and where the subordinate is expected to use a high level of individual judgment to make complex decisions....Professional accountability mechanisms work most effectively when there are a clear set of outcomes by which employees are evaluated with periodic evaluation of progress toward these outcomes. Within most school districts there are elements of a professional accountability system for teachers and principals; however, they are usually undercut by a focus on adherence to rules rather than furtherance of the school's goals. Sanctions are unevenly applied and more often take the form of a transfer than increased training or firing.

Rewards are limited to recognition of a few very special teachers and principals each year. Complicating the use of more elaborate reward structures is the resistance of teachers to a differentiated structure of salary and responsibility.

A political strategy is an external accountability mechanism. Actors outside the agency attempt to impose control on the actions of the agency or its employees. In a political situation, the rewards and punishments are uncertain and subject to the vagaries of the political system. (Brown, 1990, p. 3-4)

Two years later, Darling-Hammond and Snyder (1992) restated the five types of accountability systems that function in education:

- **Political accountability**. Legislators and school board members, for example, must regularly stand for education.
- **Legal accountability**. Citizens can ask the courts to hear complaints about the public schools' violation of laws, say, regarding desegregation or provision of appropriate services to a handicapped student.
- **Bureaucratic accountability**. District and state education offices promulgate rules and regulations intended to ensure that school activities meet standards and follow set procedures.
- **Professional accountability**. Teachers and other school staff must acquire specialized knowledge, pass certification exams, and uphold professional standards of practice.
- **Market accountability**. Parents and students may choose the courses or schools they believe are most appropriate. They may also be involved in other more direct means of participating in school decision making. (Darling-Hammond, 1992, p. 15)

Each strategy had its focus and application. However, Brown suggested that because public education, and by implication charter schools, were elaborate organizations,

... multiple accountability strategies are needed to hold the whole system accountable. Policymakers need to think, not in terms of one accountability strategy or mechanism, but in terms of an accountability system in which several accountability strategies are used to monitor different functions and different parts of the educational process .... For a system to be held fully accountable, these mechanisms must also be integrated with each other so that all aspects of the institution are under control and operating under a consistent set of expectations .... Without this coordination, schools will be held accountable to splintered and conflicting demands. (Brown, 1990, p. 4)

After Brown discussed the available accountability strategies, she suggested the limitations of each:

Bureaucratic and legal strategies can effectively induce the desired behavior, but the emphasis on rules and regulations can inhibit the development of creative solutions. A tendency to over-specification, as rules proliferate, can also lead to inefficiency. The cost of monitoring can outweigh the benefits.

A professional or political strategy gives maximum latitude for developing creative solutions, but there is not much accounting for the way these solutions are derived .... It is difficult to impose sanctions on professional employees when there has been little supervision, no prior agreed-upon outcomes, and few examples that the goals are attainable. A political strategy avoids the danger of over-specification with the problems of uncertainty and vagueness. Expectations may be so unclear and the imposition of sanctions so unpredictable that there is little inducement for compliance. (Brown, 1990, p. 6)

Brown concluded that the choices for state and district policy makers are limited to those between the bureaucratic-legal model and the professional-political model. If the bureaucratic-legal model is adopted, then the policy makers, "... assume a direct supervisory/contractual relationship and routinized procedures governed by consistent rules and regulations" (Brown, 1990, p. 6).

The risk of this choice is that there is,

A high degree of institutionalization through rules and regulations guarantees that the resources of the system are distributed in a prescribed way and that procedural requirements associated with fairness and good instruction are followed. Yet, these very rules and regulations focus attention on intermediate goals and may encumber the creativity of educators in reaching better outcomes. (Brown, 1990, p. 6)

On the other hand, if the professional-political model is adopted, policy makers, "... assume indirect control of the day-to-day operations while maintaining control of the final outcomes of the system. Detailed rules and regulations are sacrificed to trust in the expertise of personnel and a reliance on rewards and sanctions for control" (Brown, 1990, p. 6). The risk of this choice is that,

A relaxation of the rules through reliance on professional or political models raises the specter of funds used inappropriately, discrimination, and elaborately designed but ineffective programs. Neither alternative in its extreme is acceptable. (Brown, 1990, p. 6)

Newmann, et al. (1997) suggested that researchers judge accountability of public schools, and, by composition, charter schools, with the following criteria. Did a school's accountability system have:

- Explicit standards for student performance, provisions for information on stu-

dent performance, and consequences to the school or teachers for student success or failure.
- Information, standards, and/or consequences that were required by an external agent (district and/or state) or developed by the school itself, or both.
- An external agent that required something specific beyond mandatory standardized testing as part of the school's accountability system or that required the school to develop its own accountability system. (Newmann, 1997, p. 49-50)

For the purposes of this project, the following findings of the Newmann study on accountability and organizational capacity were noted as having implications for charter school accountability:

1. Only seven of the twenty schools had strong accountability systems.
2. Schools varied considerably in the extent of organizational capacity.
3. School accountability and organizational capacity are not necessarily related.
4. Schools with strong external accountability tended to be low in organizational capacity.
5. Strong internal accountability advanced organizational capacity in schools. (Newmann, 1997, p. 50-58)

Newmann et al. also found:

> ... external accountability alone offers no assurance that a school faculty will have adequate technical knowledge and skill, sufficient authority to deploy resources wisely, or shared commitment to a clear purpose for student learning .... [S]trong external accountability is difficult to implement, and even when it is implemented, it can present serious obstacles to or undermine a school's organizational capacity. We showed that when highly specific prescriptive standards connected to high-stakes consequences are mandated by external authorities, this can deny school staff both the "ownership" or commitment and the authority it needs to work collaboratively to achieve a clear purpose for student learning. (Newmann, 1997, p. 62)

DeMoulin and Kendall (1993) added their theory of the "sociological network" to the debate. Their theory, illustrated in Figure 3, complemented Newmann's findings:

Figure 3.
An accountability network conceptualization

CONCERNED	Educational Attitude	UNCONCERNED
(high interest)	**students**	(low interest)
(student minded)	**teachers**	(self minded)
(functional)	**administrators**	(dysfunctional)
(progressive)	**preparatory programs for educators**	(traditional)
(outcome oriented)	**federal, state and/or local government**	(voter oriented)
(active)	**community**	(inactive)

Source: (DeMoulin, 1993, p. 692)

Unfortunately, one direction of that commitment (the performance level of each segment) characterizes an unconcern (apathetic) attitude toward educational success. The ideal situation therefore is for the accountability network to work collectively and not separately. Collective participation would enhance educational opportunity by instituting consistent and effective measures for obtaining student achievement.

Effectiveness, in this instance, is directed toward the outcome of mutually agreed upon long- and short-term goals (one long-term goal being the perpetuation of the network), the processes and procedures with which to achieve the goals, proper evaluation methods to analyze progress and commitment and responsiveness that accountability will take precedence. (DeMoulin, 1990, p. 693)

While President Bush's "America 2000" efforts and President Clinton's "Goals 2000" strategies persisted to carry the national and international school accountability programs forward, critical members of the educational research community continued to uncover major flaws in the assumptions of those policy initiatives with regards to school accountability. The first fault was with internal validity. Because those responsible for the administration of the tests were omitted from the discussions, they resisted or did not believe in the tests. As a result, "Some people in schools were manipulating testing procedures and misusing results" (Macpherson, 1996, p. 88).

Secondly, the issue of appropriate comparability of results arose. When students were not beginning from the same point, the question here was how could comparability advocates assure validity? The schools did not receive the same fiscal support. Programmatic emphases were different. There was no consistency between the schools' missions, purposes, and goals. Furthermore, the reliance on multiple-choice tests "... were found to be narrowing and partitioning the curriculum into unrelated fragments" (Macpherson, 1996, p. 88).

Another problem that was discovered:
> ... was that the profession was avoiding any real evaluation of its own pedagogical and leadership practices .... [A]lthough autonomy is believed to be a threshold condition of professionalism, it creates an accountability policy that is implausible in broader contexts and undercuts efforts to boost the external legitimacy of schools. (Macpherson, 1996, p. 88)

Kaagen and Coley (Kaagen, 1989) identified another problem: theoretical inconsistency. Although the school accountability measures in California, Connecticut, New York, and South Carolina were considered to be the most sophisticated, they "... were based on very different theories of how schooling worked and the unique goals and priorities of each state. Political conditions appeared to be antagonistic to the development of a nationally accepted and comprehensive systems theory of accountability" (Macpherson, 1996, p. 88). California, for example, in 1983, began its school reform efforts with the passage of SB 813, the Hughes-Hart Education Reform Act. However, it had no provisions for accountability. In other words the political milieus were so split that the internal dynamics in each state created unique features that obviated national accountability standards.

McLaughlin (1991) discussed the five emerging themes of high-stakes accountability, the first four were:

1. *It matters what you measure* ... [T]esting focuses practice and curriculum—and not always in ways that serve learners or society well. Tests have narrowed the curriculum to the specific topics that they cover, and in some cases tests have turned the minimum curriculum, as expressed by test content, into the maximum.
2. *Don't confuse standardization with standards.* Almost all test-based accountability schemes in use today employ standardized measures that ignore the complexity and individuality of classrooms and constrain teachers' effort to develop classroom activities appropriate to their students.
3. *Tests constitute a limited level for reform.* In the absence of adequate supports for [school accountability], telling teachers to try harder—to achieve "world class standards"—misperceives the problem .... [T]his approach demands accountability for outputs while ignoring society's accountability for inputs. Consequently, even the best of testing strategies can do little more than document the substantial inequalities that exist throughout the U.S. school system and assume away the fundamental needs for adequate resources to support the endeavor.
4. *Test-based accountability plans often misplace trust and protection.* ... existing high-stakes tests and test-based accountability plans work to undermine rather than to enhance the nation's education system. Ironically, accountability schemes that rely on existing technology trust the system (the rules, regulations, and standardized procedures) more than they trust teachers to make appropriate, educationally sound choices. And, ironically, they protect that system, through such policies as tightened standards for course taking and graduation, more than they protect the students served by the system. (McLaughlin, 1991, p. 248-250)

McLaughlin (1991) went on to suggest that reliance on high-stakes accountability plans produced undesirable results, such as:

- perverting incentives for teachers—encouraging them to avoid difficult students and difficult schools;
- discouraging classroom innovation, risk-taking, and invention;
- allocating "failure" disproportionately to nontraditional or at-risk students who need classroom activities constructed with an eye to their particular abilities, motivations, and interests;
- forcing out of the curriculum the very kinds of learning-higher-order thinking and problem solving-that learning theorists and others say are most important to "increased national competitiveness" and success in the world marketplace. (McLaughlin, 1991, p. 250-251)

The fifth emerging theme of high-stakes accountability was:

The process of setting standards is as important as the standards themselves. Almost four decades of experience with planned efforts to reform education have taught us that 1) teachers are not inclined to take responsibility for carrying out goals and objectives about which they have had no say and 2) teachers have important knowledge and expertise to contribute to the enterprise—knowledge about the students they serve, about the curricula they teach, about the contexts of instruction, and about meaningful forms of assessment. We have also learned that change hinges on the smallest unit: the classroom teacher. Teachers' voices and teachers' views are essential to the enterprise. (McLaughlin, 1991, p. 251)

Mehrens (1992) added a point of affirmation to McLaughlin's first emerging theme, "It matters what you measure," and called it the "Lake Wobegon Effect." The "Lake Wobegon Effect" stated that "[h]igh-stakes tests can lead to teachers teaching too closely to the test, thus raising scores without raising the inferred achievement" (Mehrens, 1992, p. 5).

Although Ramirez' (1992) advice was directed at the nation's school boards, it was equally as valid for state-level policy makers contemplating an external accountability system. Ramirez' advice held lessons for charter school accountability as well. Ramirez said that his concerns were not only the most apparent, but also the most completely relevant:

- *Data collection can be difficult and costly.* Be sure that the data you choose to collect and track are necessary, useful, and not already available in existing data bases.
- *Information gathering can intrude on instruction and learning, which constitute the school's primary purpose.* Completing report forms, administering tests, and performing other number-crunching tasks can overwhelm your staff and leave inadequate time for students.
- *Not all data are comparable.* You might not be able to compare statistics for different groups of students because sampling methods might vary or different types and percentages of students might participate.
- *Don't let your indicator system become a hostage to political pressure.* The stakes involved are high, and not everyone will be pleased with the information you might uncover. Still, you must strive to maintain the credibility and integrity of the data by not allowing political influence to distort information.
- *Set standards for the collection, treatment, and use of data.* You can avoid many of these problems by using broadly agreed-on standards. Establish these standards among data collectors and researchers to ensure effective and efficient collection and reporting of information.
- *Never let dry statistics replace good judgment and common sense.* Decisions that combine good data and sound judgment will be the most productive .... Policymakers must have solid information with which to make decisions, but they also need to consult with the professionals and clients their decisions will affect. (Ramirez, 1992, p. 35)

In 1992, Gregory Anrig, former president of the Educational Testing Service, gave a speech to the 1992 National School Boards Association national convention. In this speech, Anrig (1992) provided some warnings to those who would use tests for high-stakes decisions:

Some policymakers and business leaders still believe they can force schools to reform by imposing tests on them and by using the test results as a basis for high-stakes decisions about students, teachers, and schools. But using tests to drive education reform is reckless driving. It won't work, and it has at least two dangerous side effects: It will demoralize our best teachers, and it will distort the kind of learning the national goals call for ....

Accountability means more than testing. It means providing the public with enough information so citizens can reach a fair judgment on their own. It involves multiple indicators and multiple sources of information about the complexities of student achievement—not a single number on a test score. (Anrig, 1992, p. 35)

Karweit (1993) argued that her work in analyzing the effects of federal Chapter 1 accountability had general implications for the entire field of school accountability. Karweit suggested that current accountability systems have major weaknesses, but she suggested some areas for improvement:

- *Provide internal self-correctives in the system to identify, diagnose, and change courses of action that are harmful or ineffective.* This objective is central to any accountability system ... [and there are] three impediments: 1. Lack of timely and relevant information for self-correction .... The tests are not integrated with the instructional system in a meaningful or productive way .... [T]he performance measures used in standardized tests measure relative, not absolute performance .... At the same time, the accountability system does not routinely consider the wealth of performance data generated and maintained in the classroom. This information may be more appropriate for taking corrective action, but it is ignored in the normal course of evaluation .... [S]ome appeal process, based on the work that teachers and students carry out each day, may help reconnect the assessment system to the instructional system and thereby provide the potential for a self-corrective loop. 2. Lack of credible tests .... The tests are so discredited in many quarters that no one believes the results indicate anything about the performance within a school .... Until the tests are held to be valid for measuring attainment and judging improvement in school functioning, the tests remain as hurdles, not standards. 3. Lack of linkages among staff development, classroom practices, and assessment.

- *Reduce the likelihood that harmful practices will be employed....* . Errors in measurement, regression artifacts, size of school, and random sampling fluctuations contribute to the misidentification of schools are documented by several authors (Davis, 1991); (Heid, 1991) .... A starting point for developing such a system is the recognition that there will probably never be a perfect measure of anything as complex as student performance .... One approach would be to develop systems that would rely upon multiple measures, taken on multiple occasions, using a variety of instruments.

- *Heighten the probability of student exposure to good instructional practice in a supportive environment* .... [A]s schools attempt to change their program and focus, there is generally a settling-in year when performance data may not reflect positive results .... Such a situation can be highly demoralizing. Again, schools need to have a workable appeal process that would allow for the incorporation of other evidence of effectiveness .... The potential for appeal could therefore serve as an important motivator for use of alternative assessments. One way to increase the robustness of the system is to allow greater participation by a range of interested individuals in the generation and use of accountability data .... Because access to information is typically centrally controlled by the test and evaluation divisions in schools, there is usually a top-down strategy for access to and generation of data …. Ideally, the information flows within the accountability system would allow for greater communication among the various interest parties and more equitable generation and access to information. Information systems to allow such an exchange to take place are technically feasible, but raise numerous political and confidentiality concerns. Nonetheless, some significant change in the management and flow of information for decision making must occur if meaningful connections among staff development, assessment, and instruction are to be carried out in future accountability systems. (Karweit, 1993, p. 6-10)

Streshly and Newcomer (1994) thought that local education agencies and communities had only two tools to accomplish accountability:

1. By prescribing teaching methodology and establishing an expensive superstructure of supervision with a sufficiently narrow span of control to allow direct supervision of all personnel to see that the tasks are being carried out in the prescribed manner; or
2. By establishing desired quality standards for learning outcomes and products and requiring professional staff to develop plans for achieving the established standards, including agreement on criteria by which accountability may be determined. (Streshly, 1994, p. 67)

Henry (1996) provided another critique of accountability. He theorized that extrinsic standards, impositions, and rewards did not motivate the educational system to produce consistent results.

High-stakes accountability relies on extrinsic motivation and can devolve into instrumental rationality. Satisfying external demands can become the primary goal to be achieved either by accepting the charge for school improvement or by acting in ways that fulfill the primary goal without necessarily accepting the charge for improvement-in a word, gamesmanship. Instrumental rationality can take over when avoiding the consequences of failure to meet performance standards displaces to goal of school improvement. (Henry, 1996, p. 10)

Henry explicated that the purposes of external accountability systems were:

… to monitor the performance of schools and districts as reforms are attempted and to provide a tool for school improvement. The school improvement function is most commonly carried out by setting standards and regulations at the state level. These are the familiar high-stakes accountability systems ….

These systems use information as a trigger for increased state control of schools … use student outcomes and other systematically gathered data to make overall judgment of school or district performance; sanctions are then imposed on poor performers, with the ultimate sanction being state takeover of the district …. Top-down accountability focuses its improvement efforts on the lowest of the low-performing schools. It has no means for improving any other schools. Moreover, its negative focus and high stakes can lead to resistance to furnishing information to the public.

Top-down/bottom-up systems were created to increase local participation in the process and to avoid some of the adverse consequences of the top-down system …. [T]he authority for making judgments about adequate performance, as well as for devising and implementing improvement plans, lies with the local agencies.

High-stakes accountability systems of both kinds attempt to leverage school improvement principally by the threat of loss of funding or loss of control.

Both of these accountability systems are founded on a "closed system" approach to educational progress. Schools are extracted from the community, and information flows internally. Authoritative bodies set standards, review progress, and assess penalties. If necessary, local educators are coerced into participating. (Henry, 1996, p. 86)

Henry (1996) went on to suggest a constructive alternative, "community accountability," because it was an "open system" and it "relie[d] on the intrinsic motivation associated with the value of education" (Henry, 1996, p. 89).

It relies on an open flow of information between the public schools and the public. The data that support the information system are indicators of student performance and other variables that can aid the interpretation of performance results. This information can then be used to support enlightened action rather than expanded control. (Henry, 1996, p. 87)

Henry proposed the main constituents of community accountability:

First, indicators of the performance of schools and school systems must be derived from data on student achievement and opportunities to learn. Examples of such indicators include the percentage of students taking Advanced Placement courses, the percentage of Advanced Placement enrollees who pass the exam, and the percentage of students who are two or more years over age by the end of the third grade. In addition, test results, graduation rates, percentage of advanced or college-prep diplomas, and follow-up information on graduates could all be included as indicators ....

[**Second**], the process of developing indicators should include as many voices and as much depth as possible ... [to] foster high levels of commitment from those involved, especially of teachers who can be expected to be wary of accountability systems.

[**Third**] [i]ndicators should be easily interpretable by a variety of audiences, they should represent outcomes that are clearly in the best interests of students, and they should contain incentives to improve practices. Along with indicators of school performance, the accountability system will need indicators of community performance and other contextual indicators that relate to education. Public education takes place in the larger context of the society it serves, and results cannot be interpreted without an accounting of the community that surrounds the school and of the larger social forces that affect the schools ....

Schools are often seen as remedies for the sometimes intractable, sometimes merely political difficult, ills of society, and the consequences are occasionally ludicrous .... Society deposits drugs, violence, intolerance, and other problems at the schools' doorsteps. A community accountability system must acknowledge the influence of society on a school's ability to educate by measuring community characteristics that had intruded into the schools ....

Thus a second ingredient in community accountability must be additional indicators that demonstrate the impact on performance indicators of the difficulty of the educational task. Unless some account is taken of the differences in the educational tasks that confront educators, performance indicators can become indicators of privilege ....

A third ingredient for community accountability is widespread reporting of the performance information that can stimulate enlightened action both inside and outside the education system. (Henry, 1996, p. 87-88)

DeMoulin and Kendall (1993) echoed Henry's observation that communities must also be held accountable:

Accountability in education is a term that has usually been allocated to those individuals who are answerable for the degree of educational success. However, those individuals who have been answerable have usually been educators. Other members of society may have a somewhat recognized relationship with education, but have not or will not share the obligation. Subsequently, accountability carries an educational stigma that implies partitioning of responsibility by a populace who has stereotyped the degree of educational success to individuals affiliated with education—namely, teachers and administrators. It has been this conviction that has led to an accountability phobia which is destined to immobilize any true educational reform.

Perhaps this phobia has resulted from an ongoing sociological perspective implying that only educators should be held accountable for student achievement; perhaps it has flourished because educators have been relatively easy scapegoats. Whatever the rationality, accountability in education cannot be isolated to one particular segment of society; rather, all of society must be held accountable for the past, present and future status of education because "its obligations extend not just to a particular group of share holders or sponsors, but to the public at large" (Berkley, 1978, p. 11). (DeMoulin, 1993, p. 689)

DeMoulin and Kendall (1993) posited that the improvement of student achievement is a function of the effect of the "sociological network." The sociological network is made up of: (1) community members; (2) federal, state and local politicians; (3) university personnel; (4) administrators; (5) teachers; and (6) students (DeMoulin, 1993, p. 689-690). DeMoulin's and Kendall's model representing the scope of responsibility of an integrated sociological network is illustrated in Figure 3. The developmental implications of this model would apply to both school districts and charter schools. DeMoulin (1990) asserted that, "The success of one level is contingent upon the successful commitment of the preceding level. Hence, each segment of the network must fulfill its commitment in order for the network to operate in equilibrium" (DeMoulin, 1990).

However, in order for this success to take place, players have to change their behavior. Community and business members have to become actively involved in setting the goals, vision, and mission of the schools. Government leaders must concern themselves with the principles of instruction rather than the pragmatics of re-election. Teacher preparation institutions need to do early screening of teacher candidates. Administrators need to enhance their human, conceptual, and technical skills as well as work toward "... a disciplined, positive environment for educational opportunity" (DeMoulin, 1993, p. 694). Teachers must recapture a sense of collegiality and redesign their pedagogy to be student-centered. Finally, "... the educational environment must heighten student interest, self esteem and a general capacity for learning" (DeMoulin, 1993, p. 694).

In December 1994, the Minnesota House of Representatives' Research Department published a report that admitted:

> Accountability is not easy. While charter schools must meet student outcomes defined in their charter based on agreed-upon assessment methods, review of the contracts showed that some outcomes and assessments could be improved. Also, researchers noted that the resources needed to adequately evaluate outcomes may deter districts from sponsoring charter schools. (Mulholland, 1996, p. 3)

The 1995 (GAO) report found that there was considerable variation in the amount of accountability in charter schools:

> Charter schools also vary in how they plan to measure student performance and how specifically they state those plans. They expect to use a wide variety of assessment methods and measure a wide variety of student outcomes; many schools will include achievement on standardized tests. Some schools have their assessment systems in place; others—including some schools already open—are still developing their assessment systems. Whether charter schools will be held accountable for student performance depends on the quality of assessments and completeness of reporting and remains an issue. (U.S. General Accounting Office, 1995, p. 3)

The GAO report identified several assessment instruments that charter schools used, "portfolios, exhibitions, demonstrations of students' work, and often standardized achievement tests" (U.S. General Accounting Office, 1995, p. 15). The report also criticized charter school accountability for a lack of dis-aggregated baseline data.

Levy (1991) pointed out that, for charter schools, the [e]emphasis on the perverting impact of accountability to officials whose own self-interest logically drives them to stress noneducational factors is a centerpiece of the voguish public choice model, as elaborated by Michaelsen (Boyd, 1989), who probably treats the model too uncritically. (Levy, 1991, p. 195)

Further research suggested that Alaska's school accountability system was inadequate. The National Center for Fair & Open Testing (1997) used five standards (Appendix H) to evaluate the appropriateness of state accountability systems and their contribution to the improvement of student achievement. The evaluation found that "Alaska's assessment program needs a complete overhaul. Planned changes do not solve existing problems, particularly the reliance on an NRT–the CAT. In addition, they add a major problem–a mandated high school graduation test" (Neill, 1997, p. 42). Sandham (1998) repeated this criticism in an Education Week report that gave Alaska's school accountability a grade of "D+" (Sandham, 1998).

Finn, Bierlein, Manno, and Vanourek (1997) added an admonition that confirmed the findings of Neill (1997) with regards to charter schools:

> Only where a state has solid educational standards and good assessments in place will we ever have truly satisfactory information about the performance of charter schools vis-à-vis conventional schools. This admonition goes far beyond the charter law itself, of course, but is probably central to the long-term viability of the charter idea. (Finn, 1997, p. 3)

In order to meet the needs of this new "... horse-trade of operational freedom in return for tangible performance ... " (Manno, 1997, p. 1), Manno, Finn, Bierlein, and Vanourek (1997) discovered that among the states with strong charter school legislation, four criteria for accountability were common: "satisfactory academic progress by students, evidence of success in meeting other goals specific to the particular school's design and promises; responsible use of public funds; and compliance with laws and regulations that have not been waived" (Manno, 1997, p. 12).

To assist charter school watchers to recognize when students achieved "satisfactory academic progress," Manno, et al. recommended that this criteria include "... standards, testing, and consequences ..." (Manno, 1997, p. 12). The satisfactory academic progress included both content and performance. Content goals spelled out the skills and knowledge that teachers should expect students to attain at predetermined benchmarks along their academic careers. Performance goals, on the other hand, defined the level of proficiency each student would need to attain before they could progress to the next level. In their study, Manno, et al., were disappointed to find: "Many of the charter documents we read are filled with prose—sometimes quite elegant—that outlines a compelling educational philosophy. Far fewer of them demonstrated a clear sense of what comes next: coherent content and performance standards" (Manno, 1997, p. 13).

Regarding the "evidence of success" criterion, Manno, et al. suggested that it would provide documentation as to whether a charter school met its goals. Manno, et al. found that charter schools used both traditional and non-traditional assessment methods. The typical traditional instruments included norm-referenced and criterion-referenced tests of both basic and "higher order" thinking skills. Open-ended essay type questions were also included on some tests. The non-traditional methods included "... portfolios, performance assessments, individual evaluations, exhibitions, self reports, and teacher observations" (Manno, 1997, p. 13). Some charter schools used a combination of assessment approaches such as "... the Stanford Achievement Test, the Integrated Assessment System from Harcourt Brace, parent satisfaction surveys, and protocols and rubrics for the detailed (and well developed) standards they've created" (Manno, 1997, p. 14).

Manno, et al. pointed out, however, that the charter schools using non-traditional assessment methods ran the risk of using "... indicators whose reliability is not proven–or whose results are not comparable–[and] may cause doubts about the school's reported successes" (Manno, 1997, p. 14). The "evidence of success" often was more rhetoric than substance: "Most [charter] schools say they will combine a variety of assessment tools, with some also pledging to develop their own innovative instruments and approaches. These promises often verge on the grandiose" (Manno, 1997, p. 13).

Manno, et al. asserted that "... any serious accountability system must have real stakes and consequences for everyone involved" (Manno, 1997, p. 12). For charter schools, they found that charter school operators had little appreciation for coming up with consequences for a lack of achievement:

> Deciding how consequences will be integrated into the student accountability system is a task yet to be taken seriously by many of the charter schools .... This shortcoming

is most evident in schools that, to begin, do not have (or perhaps believe in) a rigorous set of standards with a supporting curriculum. (Manno, 1997, p. 14)

They expressed concern that in the long run this deficiency would be counter to the claims of the market-based advocates:

> Laxity is also a constant temptation for schools that are having trouble attracting and keeping enough students—and thus cannot afford to lose many. This could lead to grade inflation, lack of enforcement of discipline, cooked report cards, falsely positive teacher feedback, and a general tendency to soft-pedal individual accountability for the consequences of a student's actions, lest a family pick up its marbles and depart. Thus can the marketplace work against serious standards and consequences. (Manno, 1997, p. 14)

Manno, et al. found a connection between states with "weak" charter school laws, and thus no succor from compliance with governmental rules on everything from fire codes to waste water quality, and the number of charter schools in those states. On the other hand, even charter school operators in states with "strong" charter school laws encountered state department regulators who rendered a narrow interpretation of the regulations. "In short, rule-compliance accountability remains an enormous problem area, even in the states with 'stronger' laws. Unsolved, it portends the re-regulation of charter schools in the name of accountability" (Manno, 1997, p. 17).

Supovitz (1997) argued that the pluralistic nature of society in the United States demanded a multi-pronged approach to assessment. He said:

> Of course standardized tests are biased. But it is not just standardized tests—any single testing method is biased because it applies just one approach to getting at student knowledge and achievement. Any single testing method has its own particular set of blinders. Since the bias in testing is intrinsic in the form of assessment used, we cannot eliminate this problem simply by changing the questions asked. Rather, we must ask the questions in many different ways. (Supovitz, 1997, p. 34)

> As is widely acknowledged, testing drives instruction. Teachers change their curriculum to prepare students for state and district assessments. So the indicators of student achievement chosen by state- and district-level policy makers send signals to teachers about what they should spend class time preparing their students for. (Supovitz, 1997, p. 37)

Supovitz cautioned that the amount of bias in testing became a question because there was no way to tell for certain what a student was truly capable of doing. Therefore, Supovitz recommended that there be more research that compared various types of assessment approaches. He also counseled that alternative assessments must also pass the muster of reliability and validity. One of his final pronouncements, that would have interesting implications for charter schools that used standardized testing, was that, "In the end, the larger, more intractable sources of disparities in student performance stem from broad social and educational inequities" (Supovitz, 1997, p. 37).

Bryant-Booker (1995) studied the relationship between participative management and student achievement and came to a conclusion that had implications for charter schools as a school reform strategy:

Because the society in which we live expects that any intervention should have positive measurable outcomes, it is important to recognize that if participative management is to survive the latest wave of educational reform, student outcomes must be enhanced as a result of this intervention. Accountability is a byword of this decade. If sharing of decisions is a viable vehicle for change, the effects of this change must move the educational organization toward accomplishment of its primary goal of preparing students to lead successful, productive lives in a democratic society. Student achievement and teacher effectiveness must be enhanced by this change. Do organizational conditions which lead to greater satisfaction among teachers also contribute to the quality of education for students? (Bryant-Booker, 1995, p. 3)

Bryant-Booker raised an interesting question: "participative management has not been found to lead consistently to increased organizational effectiveness. If participation in decision making does not lead to increased effectiveness, why should an organization involve subordinates in making decisions" (Bryant-Booker, 1995, p. 27, 22)? Furthermore, "[w]hile most authors are in agreement that teachers are critical to school improvement and should be involved in decision making, the degree of involvement and the extent to which teachers should have the final authority are issues of debate" (Bryant-Booker, 1995, p. 28). Bryant-Booker suggested that there were at least eight categories educators perceived to have a relationship between teacher involvement in decision making and student achievement: "growth, instructional focus, research by teachers, students as the focus of decisions, interest and concern of teachers, sharing and collaborating, teacher empowerment, and collaboration with others" (Bryant-Booker, 1995, p. 61). She concluded, "when schools employ these practices, student outcomes may be positively impacted" (Bryant-Booker, 1995, p. 131).

Pratt (1996) referred to Newman's work on the factors affecting student achievement in schools that had undergone restructuring. Newman's research hinted, "… that group effort within the professional community that is committed to and focuses on the depth of student learning is the key element related to student achievement" (Pratt, 1996, p. 44). Pratt went on to list a number of assessment tools that the charter schools in six states with "strong" charter school laws enumerated. These assessment instruments covered a wide range from portfolios and exhibitions to student projects that members of the community reviewed. Pratt found, however, that the most common tool that charter schools used to assess student achievement were the students' scores on standardized tests. Pratt discovered that as the mission and goals of the charter school were narrowly focused on specific programmatic definitions, so too were the methods of assessment. Pratt ascertained that, "… the administration of an evaluation of standardized tests were the most consistent form of student assessment" (Pratt, 1996, p. 173-174).

Pratt (1996) determined that many charter schools were using authentic assessments. The types of authentic assessments that charter schools were using included "… portfolio assessment, exhibitions, and student projects" (Pratt, 1996, p. 174). These specialized forms of assessment occurred more often in charter schools with specialized programs of study.

In light of the residential program of the Galena, Alaska, Project Education charter school, Pratt (1996) found that, "One school with a residential program required students to self assess, write a personal mission statement, be cognizant of their own learning styles, and demonstrate fiscal responsibility" (Pratt, 1996, p. 174).

Pratt (1996) found that Massachusetts' charter school law specified "performance standards, state and district testing, and portfolio requirements ... the legislation also specified that teachers and administrators were to be held accountable for students' educational outcomes" (Pratt, 1996, p. 178). Manno, et al. (1997) announced their praise of the Massachusetts charter school accountability system:

> ... we believe that the Massachusetts model [for charter school accountability] is the best we have seen. (Its main shortcoming, due to be corrected within the next year or two, stems from the lack of any state-wide testing program to accompany the Commonwealth's mostly excellent new state-wide academic standards. (Manno, 1997, p. 17)

By February 1997, Massachusetts Department of Education Associate Commissioner, Scott Hamilton, issued a technical advisory[25] to all charter schools that outlined how the department was going to conduct charter school evaluations:

> The Board of Education is obligated by Massachusetts General Law, Chapter 71, Section 89, and attendance regulations to conduct an ongoing review of charter schools and, by the fifth year of a school's operation, decided whether its charter should be renewed.
>
> A decision of whether to renew a charter will be based on a simple and straightforward evaluation that is guided by three central questions:
> 1. **Is the academic program a success?**
>   • Has the school made reasonable progress in meeting internally established goals over its first four years of operation?
>   • Is student performance significantly improved and/or persistently strong on internal and external academic assessments?
> 2. **Is the school a viable organization?**
>   • Is the school financially solvent and stable?
>   • Is enrollment stable and near capacity?
>   • Is school governance sound and are professional staff competent and resourceful?
> 3. **Is the school faithful to the terms of its charter?**
>   • Are the school's program and operation consistent with the terms of its charter?
>   • Is the school within the bounds of essential statutory and regulatory requirements? (Hamilton, 1997a, p. 3)

Associate Commissioner Hamilton communicated the department's sensitivity to the unique nature of Massachusetts charter schools. He assured them that the department would work with each school to develop its accountability contract. He pledged that the contract would contain:

> ... clear, concrete and measurable school performance objectives ... [that] will reflect an emphasis on student achievement, but may also pertain to student attendance, parental satisfaction and participation, safety and order, mobilization

of private resources, school environment, staff development, facility improvement, or fiscal management

This accountability contract will also describe the measures the school will use to document progress toward those objectives, including credible student assessment tools for annually tracking student performance (including, but not limited to, standardized tests). Charter schools must report their objectives and progress toward them in the annual report due August 1st of each year (to be followed with a financial audit several months later). (Hamilton, 1997a, p. 2)

Only the Massachusetts charter school accountability system contained the added feature of annual site visits. A small group made up of "... one parent, teacher, school leader, business person, and [a] public official" (Hamilton, 1997a, p. 2) toured each charter school. The purpose of the team's site visit was "to augment and verify the information contained in the annual report ... help educate the general public ... and provide a charter school with critical feedback from a jury of objective peers" (Hamilton, 1997a, p. 2).

Associate Commissioner Hamilton seemed mindful of the accountability literature that stressed outputs. In a rare instance of perspicacity, he reminded and he forecast for charter school operators that:

A charter school should be judged primarily on the academic progress of its students, not by how much it pays its teachers or how well it complies with conventional educational practices and procedures ....

This freedom-for-accountability exchange has the potential to utterly transform public education. With charter schools leading the way, perhaps the day is not far off when all public schools will be given the freedom charter schools enjoy in exchange for real accountability for results. (Hamilton, 1997a, p. 2)

Hamilton's sentiments, informed by several years of educational experience, were asymptotic to the pedestrian understanding that Shaw (1997) expressed:

It may seem neat and easy to use standardized tests as THE measure of school quality—and it's done every day in arenas from parent conversations to real-estate offices to the media. But that approach is foolhardy rather than foolproof. Even the Educational Testing Service–publishers of the Graduate Record Exam (GRE), the Scholastic Assessment Test (SAT) and many other tests–recently wrote that it is a myth to think that any test is a single, unequivocal yardstick by which we can measure all comers ....

[O]ne very important point about evaluating school quality [is]: How students score depends to a large extent on their background, with the school playing a supporting, but usually not a defining role. Without being able to separate the role home plays in test performance from what the school contributes, test scores don't tell us nearly what we need to evaluate a school ....

But neither the CTBS (Comprehensive Test of Basic Skills) nor many other standardized tests can measure what many say are the most important goals of education, such as students' ability to apply what they have learned, to analyze a problem and communicate their solution.

Such standardized tests can say only whether students are getting closer to or further from performing as well as other students across the nation—and not necessarily whether they are achieving what they need for the future ....

> In general students' economic and social backgrounds still play a big role in performance ....
>
> But ... such scores can't be used in a vacuum, or as a substitute for deeper evaluations of schools and schooling. They are a tool, like a thermometer, that tell us only when we need to look closer. (Shaw, 1997, p. F-3)

Manno, Finn, Bierlein, and Vanourek (1997) found that accountability was the most problematic issue facing both charter schools and the charter school movement. They announced that the mixture of freedom and accountability was almost exclusive to the charter school movement:

> But what exactly does it mean for a school to be "held accountable for results"? At the heart of this is ... the horse-trade of operational freedom in return for tangible performance, a combination seldom seen in conventional public education where institutional freedom is rare and serious attention to results is spotty .... [I]n this combination ... lies much uncharted territory, some genuine dilemmas, and more than a little risk. (Manno, 1997, p. 1)

Milwaukee's Public Policy Forum released its study "Choice school accountability" in February 1998. The Public Policy Forum recommended that schools of choice adopt accountability guidelines that said:

- Choice schools should be required to make public information on their missions, philosophies, governing structures, curricula and teaching methods, teacher and administrator qualifications, finances, aggregate test scores, and attendance, graduation, expulsion, and suspension rates.
- A public board made up of private and public school representatives should be created to gather and make public the information about participating schools.
- Schools should be given a year to meet the reporting requirements. If they fail to comply, taxpayer money should be revoked. (Schnaiberg, 1998a)

When viewed in light of the National Association of School Boards of Education Study Group on Statewide Assessment's (NASBE-SGSA) 1998 report on state accountability systems, Alaska's student assessment was seen as falling short of the standard. By implication, Alaska's accountability for charter schools would gain some valuable suggestions from the group's recommendations. The NASBE-SGSA looked at the nationwide elements of assessment systems and concluded with some proposals for effective state assessment programs:

> The Study Group believes that in spite of the present diversity among state assessment systems, highly effective state assessment systems share several characteristics. For example, an effective state assessment system is aligned with rigorous state standards; addresses specific goals and purposes; balances validity, reliability, and efficiency; has mechanisms to encourage schools and districts to align their instruction and evaluation with the state system; and has a clear relationship with national and international measures of student performance .... Finally, the Study Group concludes that states need to devise mechanisms to conscientiously limit the use of alternative and accommodated assessments to include only those students whose knowledge and skills cannot be fairly assessed by standard means. (Statewide assessment systems study, 1998)

Literature on the relationship between freedom and accountability in education.
In 1994, Congress re-authorized the Elementary and Secondary Education Act (ESEA) as the Improving America's Schools Act (IASA). Title X of the act provided for 10% of the $5.4 million Congress allocated ($15 million was authorized) to be spent for funding the National Study of Charter Schools. The U.S. Department of Education (1997) sponsored the study. The purpose of the study was "... to collect data from all 252 charter schools in operation across the nation as of January 1, 1996" (U.S. Department of Education, 1997). Research, Policy, and Practice (RPP) International, in a joint venture with the University of Minnesota's Center for Applied Research and Educational Improvement (CAREI) and the Institute for Responsive Education (IRE), received the award to conduct a four-year study from September 1995 to September 1999. RPP published the first-year report in May 1997. It provided descriptive data about 30 charter schools. This was less than 10% of the total nationwide and did not include any charter schools in Alaska. The study proposed to include an additional 20 charter schools in the second year. This number severely restricted the generalizability of the study's results. Although the 1997 RPP International report promised to provide information on charter schools' affect on student achievement, it postponed reporting this information for a future study.

Several incidents have recently occurred that cast a shadow over the amount of freedom and the accountability in the nation's charter schools. Arizona and Washington, D.C. have some of the nation's "strongest" charter school laws. They permit almost unlimited freedom and autonomy for their charter schools. Roberts (1993) reported, "One of the most popular concepts [for charter schools] is decentralization of authority" (Roberts, 1993, p. 31). It did not take long for at least two examples to emerge that illustrated the hazards when license was confused with freedom. On Sunday, November 2, 1997, the television news magazine show "60-Minutes," ran a segment about the principal, Mary A.T. Anigbo, of the Marcus Garvey Public Charter School in Washington, D.C. Charter schools in the nation's capitol were virtually free from the district school board oversight. Ms. Anigbo and three members of the school's staff were convicted[26] of assaulting Susan Ferrechio, an education reporter for The Washington Times, and two police officers. Henry Hoberman, attorney for The Washington Times said that the assailants were, "... the principal, her staff, and a group of students punched, kicked, beat, pummeled, pulled her hair and forcibly dragged her down the hall of the school and threw her out the door" (Naphin, 1997, p. 3). In describing charter schools in Washington, D.C., Morley Safer asserted that:

> Even though they were set up with public money, charter schools are often accountable to virtually no one. That was the case with the Marcus Garvey school in Washington, established to try to shore up DC's crumbling school system. The question facing the city's board of education is: Can it allow a school to continue, no matter how effective some claim it to be, when the principal of that school has become a law unto herself? ...
>
> [T]hat lady [Anigbo] continues to run the school. And there's little anyone can do because under its charter, the Marcus Garvey principal can do just about anything she wants, and Don Reeves, president of the DC school board, can't lay a

glove on her. All he can do is close the school down. (Naphin, 1997, p. 2, 4)

When Mr. Safer asked Mr. Reeves if the school board could remove the principal, Mr. Reeves responded, "No. The-the-the charter school's board of trustees is– has exclusive a–authority over personnel issues in the school. All we can do is suggest or recommend that they do that" (Naphin, 1997, p. 4). Later, viewers learn that the likelihood of Ms. Angibo's ouster is highly unlikely because, "... it was Mary Anigbo who appointed the board. And the chairman of the board is her own brother, Richard Duckett, and he says she stays as principal" (Naphin, 1997, p. 5). Mr. Jay Silberman, a Washington, D.C. board member, and Mr. Safer amplified on the freedoms that the city's charter schools enjoyed and the restrictions on the board's authority:

> The board doesn't approve, disapprove, review staff, period, at all under this law. The teachers can be anybody they choose. The law does not require, nor does it give any qualitative standard to measure, that any applicant had a clear police record of–of felonies, misdemeanors or anything else.
>
> Which is why Anigbo was able to create her own curriculum, which emphasizes black history; have her brother as chairman of the board; her niece as a secretary; and her nephew as a maintenance man, even though he was a convicted armed robber, carjacker and was charged with drug dealing. As a charter school, that's nobody's business, even though it's funded by taxpayers. (Naphin, 1997, p. 6)

The Washington, D.C. school board had only one option available: close the Marcus Garvey Public Charter School. However, "The board voted last Thursday not to revoke the school's charter after the school's trustees agreed to put Ms. Anigbo on leave without pay for 30 days and on probation for another 60 days" (D.C. school retains charter, 1997, p. 4). In January 1998. The school's own board of trustees chose to fire Principal Mary A.T. Anigbo and three other staff members because of "... a recent internal audit that raised questions of mismanagement" (Charter school principal fired, 1998). Ultimately, during the week of May 18, 1998, "School board members in the District of Columbia... revoked the charter of an Afro-centric charter school with a troubled past" (Charter revoked in D.C., 1998).

In January 1998, the Cypress Youth Lodge Charter School in Dallas, Texas reverted its charter to the Texas Education Agency. Although approved in 1996, the school never opened its doors. In spite of numerous extensions it received from the state, the school could not find an adequate place to hold its classes. Consequently, "[t]he school's organizers are negotiating a plan with the Texas Education Agency and the state's attorney general's office to repay the $240,000 in state aid that the school has received since 1996" (Texas school loses charter, 1998).

Decentralization of authority, or site-based management, to teachers has long been a goal of teacher unions. American Federation of Teachers President Albert Shanker said:

> The only thing that's going to turn the schools around is to start turning over the decision making as to what works and what doesn't work over to the people who are actually doing the work and know what's happening in the classrooms. We ought to have the power to make decisions because we know more-more about

what distinguishes a good textbook from a poor one, more about all of the issues in education. (Roberts, 1993, p. 33)

Roberts (1993) defined "Site-based management [as] a form of decentralization in which planning, budgeting and accountability are devolved to the individual school (Lane & Walberg, 1989)" (Roberts, 1993, p. 33).

In another television news magazine, The Merrow Report, producer John Merrow noted that "Arizona's approach to charter schools emphasizes freedom, but pays scant attention to accountability .... It's a freewheeling, experimental atmosphere that State superintendent, Lisa Graham Keegan, embraces" (Merrow, 1997). Pratt (1996), however, noted at least one area in which accountability was explicit. The "Arizona charter school legislation required that each charter school provide an outline of the criteria used to measure the effectiveness of the school" (Pratt, 1996, p. 175). Pratt found that of the seven Arizona charter schools she surveyed, they stated that they used the Arizona assessment system for accountability.

In an incident involving Dr. Lawndia White Venerable, founder of Phoenix, Arizona's Citizen 2000 charter school, opened in August 1995, the citizens of Arizona discovered the "Tragedy of the Commons"[27] systems archetype. Dr. White was indicted on charges of fraud.

In addition to the broad freedoms allowed Arizona's charter schools, they were permitted to operate for profit. Dr. Venerable attempted to operate Citizen 2000 as a profit making business. Initially, the teachers were excited about the new-found freedoms in Citizen 2000. However, shortly after opening, the teachers noticed some major flaws in the assumptions of freedom. One teacher, Eric Helming, reported:

You can buy into a dream, but if it does not have an attendance policy or a discipline policy to back it up, that dream doesn't mean anything. And those concrete things were never hammered out. And that's really when things started to unravel …. It was wonderful on paper. Certainly the product that she had displayed to parents, you know, things that were written in pamphlets or in brochures or in staff handbook, that was fantastic. (Merrow, 1997)

In order to help put the dream together, Dr. Venerable received $2.4 million from the State of Arizona. Dr. Venerable's concept of how to run the school as a business included hiring her own family members, sister, mother-in-law, mother, brother-in-law, and her fiancé. Her rationale was: "When I looked at this business called school I saw it as being literally a monumental task, a task that I couldn't perform by myself. When you do hire family members, they don't ask you for overtime" (Merrow, 1997). Dr. Venerable, who paid herself $89,000, hired her sister to be the assistant principal. She paid her $79,000. These salaries surpassed those of comparable positions in the Phoenix public schools by $20,000. However, Dr. Venerable did clearly state those salaries in her application. Even though it had a chance to object to the salaries, the state of Arizona approved Citizen 2000's charter school application.

Dr. Venerable was free to spend the money that her reported 495 students generated. She spent some of that money on renovations to her mother's house. She claimed that this was a repayment of a loan that she had given to the school. Dr. Venerable made a crucial business mistake. Contrary to Arizona State law, she commingled her funds with those of the school and did not keep them separate. Mr. Merrow reported:

Superintendent [of Public Instruction] [Lisa Graham] Keegan and the State of Arizona knew what was going on at Citizen 2000, but the Arizona State Board of Education, which was legally responsible for this charter school did nothing.

Six months after the school opened, Arizona's Auditor General issued a public report declaring that Citizen 2000 was out of compliance with the law.[28] Four months later, the Auditor General asked the State Board to take action against Citizen 2000. It held meetings, but took no action. (Merrow, 1997)

In the meantime, Dr. Venerable shut down the high school and eliminated four grades. When the stripped down school opened again, Dr. Venerable reported an estimated student enrollment of 495. The State did not question her and provided her with the first installment of the funding for the school. However, in the fall of 1996, when the school opened for the second year, it only had 247 students. Teacher Erick Helming stated:

A lot of our problems came with attendance. So these students were counted. We counted them. The administration counted them. The school board counted them. So they were counted like gold and in the very end they were treated like dirt. (Merrow, 1997)

On November 19, 1996, Citizen 2000 Charter School closed its doors. Dr. Lawndia White Venerable declared bankruptcy. The State School Board was left holding the bag and the job of finding classrooms for the 220 students who needed to complete the school year.

When asked to comment on this incident, Ted Kolderie of the Center for Policy Studies said that:

We tend to blame failures on the operator. In any kind of arrangement like this you can have bad buyers. You can have dumb buyers, careless buyers. It is important to have the accountability question run also to the people who granted the approval in the first place. (Merrow, 1997)

Arizona state Senator Mary Hartley, a Democrat from Northwest Phoenix, in hindsight stated: "From the moment I read the charter I don't think they should have been allowed to have a charter" (Merrow, 1997). Senator Hartley believed that there was too much freedom and too little accountability:

Red flags were there when the legislation went into place. And I think that we will find that just as in every other area there are people that find ways to maximize opportunities that poor legislation allows. And I think this is the case. (Merrow, 1997)

Although the Arizona State Board of Education did not close the Citizen 2000 charter school, the problems with the school were not unique to it. Six other charter schools in Arizona were also in trouble, but the Sate Board of Education took no action. Without an accountability model, the Board had no basis for taking action. This situation left the charter schools in the dark about accountability.

This situation illustrated the dangers of license. As people extended the idea of freedom to positive infinity, the degree of accountability approached negative infinity. The organizational mortar of the Citizen 2000 charter school almost immediately began to crumble. In addition to the wide range of freedom that the Arizona charter school law permitted Dr. White in her charter school, the ultimate in business accountability, bankruptcy, ensued. Manno, et al., found that:

> Of those schools that do have fiscal accountability, a small number deal poorly with accountability: in three of the five schools that have been closed (Edutrain in Los Angeles, Citizen 2000 in Phoenix, and Windows in San Diego), mishandled finances was the reason. (Manno, 1997, p. 16)

The Horizon Charter School was a foil to the Citizen 2000 Charter School. Unlike Citizen 2000, Horizon was a non-profit K-12 school located in Chandler, a suburb of Phoenix, serving 408 students. It had its own school board that hired and set the salaries of the staff. The teachers were free to draft their own curriculum. John Merrow commented: "Is Horizon Charter School overly preoccupied with accountability? Probably not. It's trying to find the right balance of freedom and accountability hoping to deliver on the charter school promise" (Merrow, 1997).

Other problems beset Arizona's charter schools. The Window Rock Unified School District discovered problems with charter schools situated hundreds of miles removed from the district's headquarters. In 1998, the district closed seven charter schools it had sponsored. It notified several others that the district would cancel their contracts at the end of the 1998-1999 school year. Window Rock Superintendent, Paul Hanley, said, "I'm down on absentee, long-distance fatherhood. I can't say what they're doing and how they're doing it" (Chmelynski, 1998, p. 5).

Hanley reported that he did not find out until his return from vacation in January that the Alternative Learning Charter School group had closed down the Benson charter school on the day before New Years. The director said that the, "proposed site was inadequate" (Chmelynski, 1998, p. 5). Hanley reported that the school "filed for bankruptcy [and] owes the Window Rock district about $180,000" (Chmelynski, 1998, p. 5). Arizona's charter schools are legally autonomous, and, consequently, the sponsoring districts are not responsible for their debts. However, Hanley highlighted a grave concern for his district, "the state might withhold as much as $500,000 from the Window Rock district because it overpaid the Arizona Career and Technology charter school in Mesa" (Chmelynski, 1998, p. 5).

The Arizona Career and Technology High School ceased operation in January 1998 and by May 1998 the district revoked its charter. Superintendent Paul Hanley said that the district revoked the charter because: "… the school filed inflated student-attendance figures, resulting in the 300-student school's receiving more than its fair share of state aid. In addition, district officials at the March 30 revocation hearing said the Mesa facility was unsafe" (Ariz. school loses charter, p. 4).

Citing that "… the long-distance administrative over-sight has become a problem" (Chmelynski, 1998, p. 5), the Snowflake school district superintendent, Lawrence Bassett, informed seven charter school operators that they would have to find another sponsor. Bassett said, "… we have encouraged the one farthest away from us to find a different sponsor because of the distance problem" (Chmelynski, 1998, p. 5).

Other examples of the boundaries emerging from the emphasis on charter school "freedom" have developed. Michigan Auditor General, Thomas H. McTavish, cited Central Michigan University for 19 recommendations including that it "… hired uncertified teachers and did not complete criminal-background checks on some employees" (Mich. audit finds charter school problems, 1997, p. 12). As of April

1998, the Michigan Department of Education was proceeding with its investigation of the allegations:

> ... that six of the state's charter schools have hired noncertified teachers.
>
> A preliminary investigation into 132 teachers identified in a previous complaint found that six of the teachers had been denied a teaching permit and that no records could be found for five other teachers. (Charter teachers scrutinized, p. 28)

In Massachusetts, the Boston Renaissance Charter School "... violated federal laws that protect children with disabilities from discrimination" (Schnaiberg, 1997b, p. 3; Johnson, 1997, p. 30). Charter schools' compliance with the federal Individuals with Disabilities Education Act, section 504 of the Rehabilitation Act of 1973 (Section 504), and the Americans with Disabilities Act guidelines seemed to be a problem elsewhere. McKinney (1996) reported, "... during the 1995-1996 school year, only 262 children (4 percent) of the approximately 7,000 students enrolled in Arizona charter schools were being served as special education students" (McKinney, 1996, p. 22). McKinney (1996) found,

> The marketplace concept that drives charter school legislation is stood on its head and proves to be a disincentive when it comes to serving children with disabilities.
>
> The evidence from Arizona and nationwide demonstrates that children with disabilities do not have equal access to charter schools. Charter school operators are avoiding potentially high-cost students rather than serving them, and charter school operators are unaware of and unprepared to meet their responsibilities regarding children with disabilities. (McKinney, 1996, p. 25)

Kaplan (1997) reported an incident in which an Arizona charter school operator violated the rights of students:

> By now, you may have heard the story of Marian Lamb, a charter school teacher and director from Ventana Academic School that got into trouble with the law. It is a tragedy when any individual violates the rights of another. It is particularly egregious when adults violate the rights of children. (Kaplan, 1997, p. 1)

Kaplan maintained that no amount of accountability or controls would have prevented this unfortunate incident. He noted that not even the public schools made this guarantee. Therefore, he asserted that parental support would serve as a safety check on charter schools.

Legal opinion (Childs & Reagle, 1997) specifically targeted the issue of the responsibility of charter schools to comply with civil rights laws. Charter schools were not exempt from constitutional mandates, federal laws and regulations such as the 14th Amendment equal protection clause, the Voting Rights Act of 1965, Title VI, Title IX, and other anti-discrimination legislation:

> ... the Voting Rights Act requires any jurisdiction covered under the Act (typically those states with a history of denying individuals the right to vote on the basis of race, such as most of the southeastern states) to submit any law or policy change affecting voting for pre-clearance with the U.S. Attorney General or the U.S. District Court for the District of Columbia prior to its implementation, in order to ensure that the change affecting voting will not erode minority voting power .... Consequently, legislation providing for charter school governance by a body elected by a limited constituency—such as charter school employees and

students' parents—may run afoul of the Voting Rights Act's pre-clearance requirement, as well as the constitutional principle of one person, one-vote.

Additionally, many school districts, especially those in the South and in urban areas, operate under desegregation agreements with the Department of Education's Office for Civil Rights .... Recently, the Office for Civil Rights reaffirmed its position that both charter schools and school districts must comply with desegregation agreement requirements, as well as with Title VI and Title IX. (Childs, 1997, p. 6)

In the fall of 1997, Arizona's state school board annulled the contract of a second charter school, CLIN Success School. "State officials maintain(ed) that the school ha[d] violated its charter and ha[d] not abided by federal and state special education rules" (Ariz. wants four-campus charter school closed, 1997, p. 4). The CLIN Success School served expelled students and students who were either on probation or parole.

Similarly, North Carolina found that there was a dark side to the freedoms given to charter schools:

At least five of the state's existing 34 [charter] schools are struggling, said Grova Bridgers, director of the charter school office within the state Department of Public Instruction ... at some point we need to decide whether they should be allowed to keep their charters.

In the Triangle, Bonner Academy in Wake County and School in the Community in Orange County are "in deep trouble," Bridgers told members of the Charter School Advisory Committee.

A third school outside the Triangle is running into problems serving special education students and two others are struggling to make payroll, Bridgers said ....

Bridgers said the problems at Bonner are more directly related to violations of specific operating and management rules that he declined to specify ....

Linda Bonner of Bonner Academy could not be reached for comment ....

Still, the difficulties make it clear that North Carolina needs to establish some way to monitor, help and punish schools when the need arises, said Mike Fedewa, superintendent of schools for the Catholic Diocese of Raleigh and chairman of the state Charter School Advisory Committee.

"It sounds great to say either you live up to your charter or the state can shut you down," Fedewa said. "But we need to have some kind of a process here to accomplish that. And what if we don't want to shut down a school but see a need for improvements? How do we go about that? This is new ground for everyone."

"I'm not opposed to charter schools, but I feel they should compete with public schools on a level playing field," said Wake schools Superintendent Jim Surratt. "If fewer rules and regulations make a better school, then we would like the same opportunity to run our schools that way. What is this going to do to improve public education in this country? That's the question that matters most." (Simmons, 1998).

The Los Angeles, CA school board canceled the Edutrain charter school contract when a state auditor found that it "... received money for more students that it actually had in regular attendance .... [And] the principal... leased a sports car and hired a bodyguard with school funds" (Saks, 1998, p. 14).

Other examples of the boundaries emerging from charter school "accountability" have developed. Michigan's state proficiency tests found that "Michigan's charter schools scored far lower than the state's schools as a whole on the percentages of students who reached the 'proficient' level on the state tests" (Schnaiberg, 1997c, p. 5).

Finn, Bierlein, Manno, and Vanourek (1997) warned:

> Although charter schools should have most laws and regulations waived, those regulations that remain (e.g. civil-rights laws, background checks of school personnel) must be scrupulously enforced. Honest enforcement mustn't be undermined by, say, legislated exemptions, unduly long waiting periods, or forgiveness provisions designed to allow misfunctioning charter schools to evade accountability. The charter movement is not well-served by tolerating schools that misuse public funds, discriminate on illegal grounds, or fail to ensure the well-being of their students. (Finn, 1997, p. 4)

In the spring of 1998, "Drexel University and Foundations, a Mount Laurel, N.J.,-based nonprofit organization that promotes educational innovation" (Accountability for charter schools, 1998, p. 9), held a national charter school conference in Atlantic City, N.J. The attendees heard the message that in order to assure the survival of charters schools, they must "… make sure the organizers are accountable for their schools' success" (Accountability for charter schools, 1998, p. 9). One of the conference's presenters, Bruno Manno, stated, "The accountability issue, more than any other, will make or break the charter movement" (Accountability for charter schools, 1998, p. 9). At the time of the conference, there were about 800 operating charter schools in 30 states. Manno reported that

> [a]bout 12 have been forced to close … because of either fiscal problems or the academic underachievement of their students.
>
> For charter schools … accountability is the key to fending off criticism and staying alive. Establishing goals—for students, teachers, and parents—and maintaining fiscal responsibility are among the key elements of success to charter schools. These elements…will break down resistance to charter schools from the community and those within the school system. (Accountability for charter schools, 1998, p. 9)

Features the charter school advocates often mentioned as indispensable for freedom in charter schools were those of teacher empowerment, site-based management, participative decision making, and shared decision making. Bryant-Booker (1995) encapsulated these ideas under the concept of shared governance and examined its relationship to teacher effectiveness and student achievement in the League of Professional Schools. She concluded that student achievement would be enhanced,

> as a result of shared governance …. When certain conditions are present…focus on instruction, students as the focus of the initiative, changes derived from the interest and concern of teachers, the use of data to make decisions, staff development to acquire knowledge and skills, structured decision-making groups, and collaboration and support of groups outside the school. (Bryant-Booker, 1995, p. 123-124)

One of the themes of educational reform that charter school advocates espoused was that of the virtue of the free-market. Moutray (1996) contributed an econometric analysis of the effects of quasi-market-based educational reforms. He found that:

> ... the literature lacks substantive empirical evidence on the success of educational reform in improving school outcomes. There are several reasons for this. The first is that a true "open" school choice plan, which would permit choice in both public and private schools for all students, does not exist in the United States ....
>
> Second, the first experiments in reform that do exist are recent, and therefore, there is little post-reform data.
>
> Another problem is the difficulty measuring performance. For instance, it is not obvious how best to model exogenous factors such as the role of the family. This measurement debate has been well-documented in the literature; it is perhaps best summarized in (Hanushek, 1986). In addition, the lack of data often limits the choice of possible variables; on example of this is using test scores to assess the performance of an individual school. For instance, while many researchers criticize the use of test scores as a measure of a school's performance, it is nonetheless important to know the effects of various school reforms on this type of output measure. (Moutray, 1996, p. 5-6)

Moutray explicitly followed the example of Grosskopf, Hayes, Taylor, and Weber (1995). He modelled and computed: "... the effect of changing from a centralized system (in which individual schools have virtually no control over their budgets) to a decentralized system where schools are given discretion over how their budgets are to be spent" (Moutray, 1996, p. 8).

Moutray used computational techniques called the output distance function and the indirect output distance function that were "based on Shephard distance functions" (Moutray, 1996, p. 27). The output distance function was given as:

$$D_0(x_f, x_v, y) = \min_{\emptyset} \{\emptyset > 0 : y/\emptyset \in P(x_f, x_v)\} \text{ where } x_f, x_v \in \mathcal{R}_t^N, y \in \mathcal{R}_t^M \quad (1)$$

The indirect output distance function was given as:

$$ID_0(x_f, p_v/c, y) = \min_{\lambda} \{\lambda > 0 : y/\lambda \in IP(x_f, p_v/c)\} \quad (2)$$

Moutray reported that he used data envelopment analysis from Charnes, Cooper, and Rhodes (1981) and Färe, Grosskopf, and Lovell (1985). As a result "school districts which produce the greatest combination of outputs from a given vector of inputs form an 'envelop' which approximates the production possibilities frontier" (Moutray, 1996, p. 30). Moutray reported that other studies have used this technique "... in assessing the technical efficiency of individual school districts" (Moutray, 1996, p. 31).

This technique produced the foci of innovations he saw from the number of inputs, that "... include the number of students, the number of teachers and the number of administrators ... the percentages of low-income and limited English proficiency students" (Moutray, 1996, p. 8), and outputs, that "... include the graduation rate, retention rate, and various test scores" (Moutray, 1996, p. 8) in his sample population. He used an index of productivity called the Malmquist productivity index that:

> Provides information on the sources of productivity change, which includes changes in efficiency and changes in the frontier (innovation). This is useful, for instance, in determining if a system that recently switched to a voucher or privately-managed system has become more efficient as a result of the change, or

whether these changes actually shifted the frontier. It also could be useful in comparing the changes in efficiency and innovation in both private and public school systems. (Moutray, 1996, p. 7)

After Färe (1989) and Caves, Christensen, and Diewert (1982) the Malmquist productivity index was given as:

$$S_t = \{(x_f, x_v, y): IP_t(x_f, p_v/c), y)\} \text{ where } (x_f, x_v) \in \mathcal{R}_+^N, y \in \mathcal{R}_+^M \quad (3)$$

Moutray used these econometric tools to determine the success of some features associated with charter schools. On the input side of these empirical formulas, he inserted site-based management, that decentralized budget decisions, and local school councils, that decentralized governance. Moutray followed Grosskopf (1996) and Grosskopf, Hayes, Taylor, and Weber (1996) in using the following formula to determine the gain from decentralization:

$$\text{Decentralization Gain} = ID_o(x_f, p_v/c, y)/D_o(x_f, x_v, y) \quad (4)$$

On the output side of the symbolic representations, Moutray inserted the accountability measure of school report cards, that included high school graduation rates, ACT scores, limited English proficiency rates, and the rate of students who qualify for free and reduced lunch assistance. In his applications, Moutray was attempting to measure the value-added effects for schools in Chicago, Illinois and Milwaukee, Wisconsin. He concluded:

> Unfortunately, the results are mixed. While it does tend to confirm the findings of Downes and Horowitz (1995) and others that these schools have not been able to significantly improve since being decentralized, it differs from them in regard to whether or not site-based management is ideal for urban schools.
>
> It is still too early to declare site-based management a success or failure overall, but this research gives us one tool to further explore its performance in the future. (Moutray, 1996, p. 66)

Moutray further concluded:

> Thus, these two studies provide mixed results for Chicago and Milwaukee. While not all schools in Chicago have yet benefited from the switch to site-based management, there are potential gains to be made. Meanwhile, the Milwaukee public school district has operated efficiently in the year's studies. Both studies suggest that individual schools which perform will tend to have a relatively small class size, more extra-curricular activities, and more graduates with post-graduate plans. In addition, per student expenditures tend to be higher in those school district which excel. (Moutray, 1996, p. 86)

Pratt (1996) surveyed the charter school legislation in six states[29] with "strong" charter school legislation and the English grant-maintained schools for their features of freedom and for their measures of accountability. The main accountability activities in the English grant-maintained schools were formative teacher evaluations, fiscal responsibility, student performance standards, and national curriculum goals. Grant-maintained school operators also had to provide at least two reports. One report, of national curriculum implementation, went to the Department of Education. The second report, of summative student achievement tests, went to parents at the benchmark years of 7, 11, 14, and 16. Like most charter school legislation in the U.S., the

English Reform Act of 1988 held the grant-maintained schools accountable for outputs not processes.

In terms of freedom, the English grant-maintained schools were self-governing. Their governing boards had to have a high number of parent representatives. As a measure of autonomy, the schools were not subject to the local education authorities.

Manno, et al. (1997), stated that the viability of charter schools would wax or wane not on their success of exercising freedom, but on their demonstration to be held accountable:

> Charter school accountability is a serious matter. Not only will it make or break the charter "movement" itself, it will also be the primary source of evidence as to whether that movement is making a valuable contribution to the improved education of American children—and the renewal of U.S. public education—or is another half-tried reform fad that sinks into the sand like so many others. Perhaps most important, what we learn from accountability within the relatively small world of charter schools can inform and foster the development of more effective accountability arrangements for U.S. public education as a whole. (Manno, 1997, p. 18)

Rofes' recent study of charter schools in California looked into the assertion that charter schools prompted host district school reform. He looked at charter schools in eight states and discovered that

> ... such schools rarely prompt school reform in the districts where they operate ....
>
> Supporters often claim that charter schools will foster competition by forcing districts to shape up or lose students. But only 24 percent of the districts Mr. Rofes studied had accelerated their reform efforts in response to charters ....
>
> In other districts, officials were relived to see the charters drawing away disgruntled parents or troublesome students. (Viadero, 1998, p. 32)

Summary of the review

The essence of freedom was in the value system of the beholder. Freedom ran the political gamut from freedom for the individual to do what ever he/she chose, to freedom for the group to govern as much as it wanted.

Accountability amounted to answering to those local or state educational agencies that provided the funding for the operation of the charter school. Accountability was virtually non-existent in those states with "strong" charter school laws and was more demanding in those states with "weak" charter school laws.

Chapter Three
Design and Methodology of the Study

Introduction

The purpose of this survey study was to seek information about the variables of freedom and accountability as they affected the success and performance of Alaska's charter schools. Understanding these relationships helped explain the conditions of freedom and accountability that charter schools advocates asserted would lead to an improvement of public school education by compelling schools and school districts to raise the quality of their educational practices.

General Questions

1. How are Alaska's charter schools held accountable and how does that accountability compare with public school accountability in general in the state?
2. What do the founders/operators of Alaska's charter schools perceive to be the importance of freedom and accountability in the implementation of their plans?
3. How do urban and rural charter schools compare in areas such as perceived importance of freedom and accountability?

Research Methodology

Since the project sought answers to questions related to the current status of the perception of freedom and of accountability in charter schools, the researcher used the descriptive method of research. This technique involved the collection of survey responses allowing the researcher quantitatively to assess perspectives, beliefs, demographic data, circumstances, and operations of charter schools with respect to the variables freedom and accountability. The researcher collected the data using questionnaires to measure what currently existed. The researcher adapted for Alaska conditions and for Alaska's unique characteristics the project questionnaires for the superintendents, the principals, and the community members from the "Charter-School District Survey," and the "Charter-School Survey" instruments that Dianda and Corwin (Corwin, 1994, p. 67-78) designed.

The researcher adapted for Alaska conditions and for Alaska's unique characteristics the project questionnaires for the charter schools' principals/lead teachers from the "Phone Survey for the National Charter School Study" downloaded from the study's (U.S. Department of Education,1997) world wide web page: http://carei.coled.umn.edu/Charterschools/NationalCharter/survey.html. With the exception of the charter schools' principal/lead teacher, almost all of the questionnaires were self-completion. The researcher allowed the charter schools' principals/lead teachers to opt for a face-to-face interview, for a telephone interview, or for a self-completion conference.

Research Procedures

The design represented research with the variables of freedom and accountability that were not experimentally manipulated. The researcher deduced information about charter schools in Alaska based on responses from superintendents, principals, charter school principals/lead teachers, and community members. Because of the relatively small size of the population of superintendents, 51, and charter school principals/lead teachers, 15, the researcher chose to use a census survey to canvass these populations.

The population of principals was considerably larger, approximately 490. For the population of principals, the researcher chose to use a random selection technique to derive a sample. The researcher obtained a table of random numbers (Snedcor, 1981, p. 408-409). The researcher identified a sample size of 135 principals. All principals in the population were assigned a number from 000 to 490. The researcher asked his four year old daughter to close her eyes and point to the page of random numbers. Since the population had 490 members, the researcher used the last three digits of the number selected. If the number corresponded to one that was given to one of the principals in the population, then that principal was added to the sample.

The population of community members was 2,000 Alaskans who had applied for 1997 Alaska Permanent Fund Dividend (PFD) checks and who lived in communities that had charter schools. The researcher chose a sample size of 100 community members living in postal zip code areas in which a charter school was located. An interesting anomaly of PFD recipients was that even year-old children might be eligible for the PFD. In order to eliminate the possibility that the sample might include respondents too young to have a considered opinion, the researcher sent surveys in the name of the family, not to an individual.

To understand the logistical difficulties of contacting this population, one must have a clear picture of the geographical immensity of the state of Alaska. Alaska encompassed 586,400 square miles. The average density of the population of the United States was 71.3 persons per square mile. For Alaska it was 1.04 person per square mile with a total population of 611,300. However, as Alaska was 70% urban, 41% of the population lived in Anchorage and the others lived in communities of 2,500 or more gave one a sense of the state's demographics. Since the majority of Alaska's land was designated as national parks, wildlife and wilderness preserves, national forests, national monuments, and easements for wild and scenic rivers, much of the state remained uninhabited. That person not living in urban areas lived in towns, villages or cluster settlements on one of Alaska's many rivers and coastal areas. Some of the school districts covered large geographic areas. The Iditarod Area School District, for example, extended over an area of 44,441 square miles yet served only 420 students.

If one were to overlay a map of Alaska on the map of the contiguous 48 states, it would stretch from Florida in the east to the islands of Hawaii in the West. The northern border would coincide with the northern border of North Dakota and the southern border would lie in the Gulf of Mexico. Alaska, 586,400 sq. mi., was 5.3 times larger than the state of Nevada, 110,540 sq. mi., and 3.6 times larger than the state of California, 158,693 sq. mi. The state of Alaska had approximately 7,000 miles of road. There were vast tracts without roads and most of the state was only accessible by airplane or boat.

Because the size of the potential population was extremely large and geographically dispersed, the researcher chose to select a sample of 100 community members from the population of Permanent Fund Dividend applicants. In order to be eligible for the PFD, recipients must have been residents of Alaska for at least a year. All of the superintendents, all of the principals, and all of the charter school principals/lead teachers were PFD recipients. Therefore, the total sample size drawn from the population of PFD recipients was approximately 215. The reason the researcher chose the population of PFD recipients was because of the residency requirements. These requirements improved the likelihood that individuals in the sample had a longer time to become familiar with the issue of charter schools in Alaska.

The Alaska Division of Elections' regulations state that for a person to be considered an eligible voter, he/she must have been a resident of the state for 30 days. The implication of the Division of Elections' regulations is that 30 days is a reasonable amount of time for a person to become knowledgeable about the issues and candidates to vote in a general or local election. Extending this logic to the requirement that PFD applicants must be residents of the state of Alaska for at least a year, the researcher determined it was reasonable to assume that a year was ample time for residents to become familiar with the statewide public school issue of charter schools. Another reason the researcher chose the sample size was because a large number of the individuals where not readily accessible. The researcher used the same sampling techniques used to select randomly the sample of principals to select the sample of community members.

A cardinal undertaking was to develop questionnaires to acquire data from principals/lead teachers of Alaska's charter schools, superintendents, public school principals, and community members. The researcher began by reviewing national and state charter school survey instruments. Next, a list of the questions and the survey style were developed. A standard style of questions was set up as the text of the question was followed by a list of possible answers. The two choices available were between "literal response" questions, that is, open-ended questions, or multiple response questions with check boxes and Likert scales. The literal response questions allowed for number, number and text, or date responses. The closed questions allowed for either multiple responses or a single response with only one possible answer.

It was rare for a questionnaire to keep its original design. The designing of the questionnaires used in this study was no exception. Many times the sequence of the questions was changed. The researcher chose portrait layout, as opposed to landscape layout, for the presentation of the questionnaires.

The researcher chose two different methods of data collection. The most common method used was the self-completion. The researcher designed the charter school principal/lead teacher questionnaire to collect data by using either the telephone, face-to-face, or self-completion techniques. The self-completion technique was the simplest.

After the questionnaires were designed, the researcher conducted three pilot surveys. The purpose of the pilot survey was to test the questionnaire design, to decide any necessary additions or deletions to the number of responses, and to determine the likely cost of data collection. The potential respondents in Alaska, especially the community members, conceivably came from many different ethnic and linguistic backgrounds. Therefore, since respondents can easily misinterpret the wording of any questionnaire, the researcher decided that this would be the most important reason for conducting the pilots. The researcher conducted a pilot of the superintendents' survey with three superintendents. The researcher conducted an initial pilot of the principals' survey with five principals.

There were five subjects for the initial community member questionnaires. These first five subjects were ethnically Tlingit Indian and were traditional high school graduates. They were primarily English speakers and worked in a modern business office. The wording of the questions emphasized the questions themselves not the range of answers. An experienced interviewer conducted the pilot interviews face-to-face. The interviewer carefully noted whether the respondent provided one answer or more than one answer. The completed questionnaire was reviewed. The questions were redrafted. The interviews were repeated with 10 other respondents. The completed questionnaires were repeated. There was one restraint that limited the pilot work. The respondent population available to the researcher was limited to ethnic Tlingit Indians, some of whom had graduated from high school and others who had not.

The piloting of the charter school principal/lead teacher survey was conducted with a research assistant at the University of Alaska, Fairbanks. In order to determine any problems in conducting a telephone interview, the researcher conducted two telephonic interviews with the research assistant. During the first interview, the researcher polled the research assistant. During the second conference, the research assistant interviewed the researcher. During the practice interviews the researcher explained to the research assistant the goals of the survey and how to conduct the surveys with the charter school principals/lead teachers. In between these two conferences, the researcher conducted a pilot interview with a charter school applicant. After the first five charter school principal/lead teacher questionnaires were returned, the researcher met by teleconference with the research assistant and his supervisor to discuss any problems with the conduct of the interviews and self-completion respondents. Although the pilot testing was not extensive, the responses gave useful information not only about the questions asked but also the presentation of the questionnaires.

Because the questionnaire asked for numerical data that was not readily available to the respondent, many charter school principal/lead teacher respondents opted for self-completion. The researcher placed a time limit on the date that the respondents had to return the questionnaires.

The questionnaires' designs took into account the method of data entry. In order to control for verification of data entry, three separate people where asked to enter data. This technique allowed the other entry clerks to enter selectively completed questionnaires a second or third time. The data entry clerks were permitted to over type the selected questionnaires. If a difference in data entry occurred, the questionnaire software prompted the data entry clerk to check the data.

In order to test the reliability of the questionnaires, the researcher used the test-retest technique. After the piloting of the questionnaires, the researcher conducted the first test. The researcher gave a group made up of two principals, one superintendent, and two community members the questionnaires to fill out. Two weeks later, the researcher asked the group to fill out the questionnaires a second time and the responses were compared to those of the first test. The results of this technique yielded a .98 coefficient of stability.

As with any single method of measuring reliability, there were limitations to the test-retest technique that tests for consistency over time. It was impossible to determine the optimal time in between test episodes. It was impossible determine whether the time lapse would produce too much or too little memory of the first testing episode. Therefore, the researcher performed a specialized split-half reliability test for the internal consistency of 45 of the items on the survey instruments that yielded a Cronbach's alpha measure of reliability coefficient of .7574.

The researcher was aware that it was going to be difficult to get a significant response rate. The response rates for self-completion questionnaires are typically low, around 5-10%. Since most of the questionnaires were distributed by mail, it was likely that many of them would either be undeliverable, primarily due to transience of population, or thrown away. Choosing the appropriate incentive was difficult. A large incentive did not necessarily guarantee a high rate of return. The incentive had to be balanced against the total cost of conducting the survey. The researcher chose to offer respondents to participate in a drawing for a gift certificate at a well-known outdoor outfitter. The respondents were asked to return the questionnaires by a specified date approximately one month after receipt of the questionnaire. The researcher hoped that this technique would motivate respondents to return the questionnaire in a short period of time. The charter school principals/lead teachers were offered the incentive of participating in a study that the University of Alaska and the Alaska Department of Education would use.

Next, the researcher designed a cover letter. This letter explained the purpose of the questionnaire and why the researcher was conducting the survey. The cover letter assured respondents that the researcher arranged for a data tabulation process to guarantee that returned surveys could not be traced back to them and to ensure that the information they provided reflected the reality, the rationale, and the outcome of charter school efforts as they saw them. The cover letter specified a deadline by which the responded should return the survey and become eligible for the drawing for the incentive. The researcher provided each potential respondent with a self-addressed, stamped envelope in which to return the survey.

The introductory envelope contained two copies of an informed consent form. Respondents were asked to sign them, to retain one, and to return one with their completed questionnaire. Although this technique increased administration, it was not overly onerous. It also served to identify the subgroups of rural and urban for later comparisons. The researcher checked postmarks to verify subgroup membership.

The researcher color-coded the questionnaires to facilitate other subgroup comparisons and to determine subgroup rates of response. The superintendents' surveys were printed on white paper. The principals' surveys were printed on ivory paper. The community members' surveys were printed on green paper. The charter schools' principal/lead teacher surveys were printed on goldenrod paper.

The researcher conducted one follow-up activity with the superintendent population. This technique was used to improve the response rate among superintendents. The researcher emphasized the importance of their responses even though their districts did not sponsor a charter school. When the questionnaire return deadline expired, the researcher followed up. The researcher sent a reminder cover letter along with another copy of the survey to the superintendents who had not responded. The cover letter contained a cartoon and a slightly humorous entreaty to send in the new survey. The researcher gave a new deadline and offered another incentive.

To follow up with the charter school principals/lead teachers, the researcher met with the research assistant to discuss a strategy for follow-up. The research assistant was ending his tenure as a research assistant and was due to begin his own doctoral dissertation. The research assistant's supervisor volunteered to take over the task of contacting the charter school principals/lead teachers who had not responded. He called each one and made arrangements with the respondent to complete and return the survey.

The researcher used a different follow-up activity for the community members. The researcher anticipated many, if not all, of the returned community surveys would be anonymous. Therefore, prior to attaching the mailing labels, the researcher made a copy of them. After the deadline for the return of the community questionnaires expired, the researcher sent a postcard reminder to each community member. The postcard informed the potential respondent of the purpose of the study, of the importance of their participation, or of a new deadline. For those who had already returned their questionnaire, the researcher thanked them for their cooperation.

The researcher considered one possible disadvantage of the questionnaire as an instrument: respondent's answer was not included as an option. In order to mitigate this drawback, the researcher provided opportunities for respondents to reply to an "other" category. The researcher also provided space for respondents to supply their own reactions and free-form responses. In order to compile statistics on these open-ended questions, the researcher identified key words within the response and recorded the number of times these key words appeared.

This research was designed to examine the variables of freedom and accountability as they affected the success and performance of Alaska's charter schools. Quantitative methodologies were employed to examine and to compare the variables in Alaska's charter schools.

The Alaska charter school freedom and accountability research examined 15 charter schools. If multiple sites were not studied and if the sites were not intentionally selected for particular characteristics, there would be no justification for generalization. However, the examination of the entire Alaska population of 15 charter schools allowed for some justified generalizations. The researcher acknowledged that since objective population parameters did not exist, the results of this study could not be generalized to the entire population of charter schools in the United States.

Instrumentation

All respondents, with the exception of the principals/lead teachers of the charter schools were given the same instrument. Many of the questions on the charter schools' principals'/lead teachers' were very similar to those on the other questionnaires. The reading level of all survey instruments was the same. The researcher used the built-in readability statistics feature of Microsoft Word for Windows 97© to analyze the survey text. Two readability scores were obtained: "Flesch Reading Ease," and "Flesch-Kincaid Grade Level." The "Flesch Reading Ease" used a readability formula that:

> [wa]s based on the average number of syllables per word and the average number of words per sentence. Scores range from 0 to 100. Standard writing averages 60 to 70. The higher the score, the greater the number of people who can readily understand the document. (User's guide: Microsoft Word version 6.0, 1993, p. 95)

The "Flesch Reading Ease" for the questionnaires was 59.6. The "Flesch-Kincaid Grade Level" was a readability statistic that was

> based on the average number of syllables per word and the average number of words per sentence. The score in this case indicates a grade-school level. A score of 8.0, for example, means that an eighth grader would understand the document. Standard writing averages seventh to eighth grade. (User's guide: Microsoft Word version 6.0, 1993, p. 95)

The "Flesch-Kincaid Grade Level for the questionnaires was 7.8.

Selection of Participating Schools

For this project, the overriding population—charter schools in the State of Alaska—was pre-determined.

Differential Selection of Subjects

The groups of superintendents, principals, and charter school principals/lead teachers were all public school educators. The researcher randomly selected the group of community members from adult residents of school districts with charter schools.

Issues of Generalizability

To the extent that findings within the charter schools were consistent with each other, generalizations were offered about the perceived relationship between freedom and accountability. The identification of purposively selected charter schools and the multi-site examination of freedom and accountability conformed to requirements for internal and external validity and met methodological criteria for generalizability of findings. Factors that effected generalizability are given in Table 6.

Table 6
Factors Affecting Generalizability of Research Findings

Factor	Description
Subjects	Characteristics of subjects such as socioeconomic status, age, gender, racer, and ability. Whether and how subjects are selected from a larger population. Conclusions based on group averages may be inappropriately assumed true for individuals or subgroups within the sample.
Situation	Characteristics of the setting in which the information is collected, e.g., naturally occurring or contrived; time of day; surroundings.
Time	Some explanations change over time, e.g., years or decades.
Treatments	Characteristics of the way in which an experimental treatment if conceptualized and administered.
Measures	Nature and type of measures used to collect information.

Data Sources and Evidence

Data acquisition was conducted on several levels. First, multiple data elements from principals/lead teachers of charter schools, site administrators of public schools, superintendents, and community members was presented on data tables providing information about urban charter schools and rural charter schools. Second, structured interviews were conducted on-site, over the telephone, or self-completed with each principal/lead teacher of charter schools. Dexter (1970) suggested that, "Interviewing is the preferred tactic of data collection when … it will get better data or more data or data at less cost than other tactics" (Dexter, 1970, p. 11).

Interview questions focused on issues of perceived freedom and accountability, exploring each respondent's perceptions of inputs, operations and management, sponsor relations, and relations with other stakeholders in the community.

Data sources for tables include charter school, district-collected data, state-level data, and sources from national groups such as the General Accounting Office, and accreditation associations.

Data Analysis

Fifteen charter schools were included in this study. Each charter school was studied separately, prior to developing urban and rural comparisons.

The design was predicated on a clear definition of freedom and accountability. Indicators of freedom included the charter school's primary control or authority over:

1. Total budget;
2. Purchase of supplies and equipment;
3. School calendar;
4. Daily schedule;
5. Student assessment policies;
6. Student admission policies;

7. Student discipline (suspension and expulsion);
8. Establishment of curriculum; and,
9. Hiring teaching staff.

Sample size/selection.

The study contacted four different populations. First, the principals/lead teachers of the fifteen charter schools in operation in Alaska between March 1, 1996 and May 19, 1998 were interviewed. Second, 51 of the 52 school district superintendents (one superintendent splits a contract with two school districts) received copies of a survey instrument. One superintendent was the researcher and he disqualified himself. Third, nearly 135 principals or site administrators of Alaska's public schools received copies of a survey instrument. Seven principals were withdrawn from the population because they were under the supervision of the researcher, a superintendent. Fourth, Gay (1981) suggested that "30 subjects are generally considered to be minimally acceptable sample size" (Gay, 1981). However, the researcher chose a larger sample size. Out of a total population of over 122,000 recipients of Alaska's Permanent Fund Dividend, 100 families were randomly selected from 53 U.S. Postal Service zip code areas in which the 15 charter schools were located to receive copies of a survey instrument.

Subjects

The subjects of the study included the 15 principals/lead teachers of charter schools in operation in Alaska between March 1, 1996 and May 19, 1999, 51 superintendents of Alaska's school districts, 135 site administrators of Alaska's public schools, and 100 members of communities in which charter schools are located.

Instrumentation

The questionnaire used to collect data from the principals/lead teachers of charter schools may be found in Appendix I. The survey instrument used to gather data from superintendents, site administrators, and community members may be found in Appendix J.

Procedures

After the researcher completed the face-to-face interviews, telephone interviews, or self-completion of the interview questionnaires with the charter school principal/lead teacher, data was clustered according to the categories suggested by the research questions. Data was organized according to the components of freedom and accountability. Multiple data elements were considered to develop this report, examining disparities in freedom and accountability and analyzing possible correlational or explanatory factors.

Research Questions

Research has not developed an explanatory theory of the relationship between freedom from constraints and the amount of accountability in charter schools in Alaska. There was no collection of interdependent ideas, conjectures, and analyses that methodically accounted for and spelled out the consistencies in charter schools. There was no theory, then, that answered the question, did freedom from constraints relate to accountability in Alaska's charter schools? As applied to this project, an emerging theory held that freedom from constraints influenced the accountability a charter school in Alaska would exhibit. This theory was based on two assumptions: (1) "In return for accountability for specific results, the state grants an up-front waiver of virtually all rules and regulations governing public schools" (Nathan, 1996, p. 3); and (2) charter schools "... are freed from most of the rules and regulations that have presumably prevented public schools from innovating" (Corwin, 1994, p. 1).

Data Analysis

When appropriate, the researcher analyzed the raw data using the statistical features of three computer software statistical packages. The snap Professional(r) for Windows(tm) version 4.0 software contained tools to analyze data in a tabular form that allowed the display of frequency tables of absolute values and total percentages. However, if robust analyses of the data were called for, the researcher used either MINITAB® for Windows® 95 Release 1, Lotus 1-2-3® for Windows® 97, or SPSS v. 6.1.

Summary

The methodology for this project conformed to well-established protocols, allowing the development of findings likely to inform discussions about the relationship between perceived freedom and accountability in Alaska's charter schools.

Chapter Four
Presentation and Analysis of Data

Introduction

The purpose of this survey study was to investigate the relationship between freedom from constraints and the amount of accountability for Alaska's charter schools in existence between March 1, 1996 and May 19, 1998. The theory that there was a relationship between freedom and accountability implied that charter schools led to an improvement of public school education by compelling schools and school districts to raise the quality of their educational practices. This study also examined differences between the responses of urban charter schools and of rural charter schools.

Response to Data Collection Strategies

Toward this end, four different data collection efforts were made. The category of respondent by residence classification is given in Table 7. The first data collection effort was conducted with the principals/lead teachers of 15 Alaskan charter schools. Fourteen out the 15 charter school principals/lead teachers responded for a response rate of 93.33%.

The second data collection effort was conducted with the superintendents of Alaska's 52 school districts. Since one superintendent split a contract between two school districts (Aleutian Region School District and the City of Unalaska), surveys were mailed to 51 superintendents of public school districts in Alaska. The response rate for superintendents was 68.6%. In Alaska, 15.69% of the school districts were urban districts, and 84.31% were rural districts. Out of the total number of superintendent respondents, 77.14% were from rural school districts and 22.86% were from urban school districts. In contrast, 75% percent of the urban superintendents had charter schools in their districts, while only 7.4% of the rural school district superintendents had charter schools in their districts.

The third data collection effort was conducted with a random selection of public school principals in Alaska's school districts. Surveys were mailed to 135 public school site administrators of whom 102 returned the surveys. The response rate for the public school site administrators was 75.55%. As was mentioned above, almost 7 out of every 8 school districts were rural. The total number of schools in Alaska was 492, of which 218 or 44.3% were urban schools, and 274 or 55.69% were rural. Out

Table 7
Category of respondent

Residence : Urban	n	%	% with charter schools
Superintendent	8	22.86	75
Principal	44	43	95.45
Community member	71	86.59	100
Principal/Lead Teacher of charter school	12	85.7	150*
Base total	136		

Residence : Rural	n	%	% with charter schools
Superintendent	27	77.14	11.11
Principal	58	56.86	5.17
Community member	11	13.41	100
Principal/Lead Teacher of charter school	2	14.29	9.09
Base total	97		

Total	n	%	% with charter schools
Superintendent	35	100	25.71
Principal	10	100	44.12
Community member	82	100	100
Principal/Lead Teacher of charter school	14	100	100
Base total	233		

Note: *The CSSB 88 legislation permitted the urban school districts of Anchorage, Fairbanks, and Juneau to have more than one charter school.

of the total number of principal respondents, this variance between the urban and rural principals may explain why there were more rural principal respondents (72.9%) than urban principal respondents (28.71%). This, of course, was not the entire story. Another conceivable explanation for the higher rate of response among rural principals was the very high number of small schools with student counts less than 100 in the rural areas. These schools may present lighter work-loads than those of the urban principals of schools with student bodies greater than 500.

The fourth data collection effort was among community members residing in school districts that had operating charter schools. The researcher mailed surveys to a randomly selected population of 100 community members residing in school districts that had charter schools. The response rate of community members was 82%. The variance between the respondent principals and the respondent community members was accounted for by the fact that all of the community members surveyed resided in school districts with charter schools while only 44.12% of principals resided in school districts with charter schools. On the other hand, only three, or 5.17% of the principals lived in rural school districts with charter schools, while all of the community member respondents, 11, or 13.41% resided rural school districts.

Contextual Findings

The researcher found that none of Alaska's charter schools were included in the National Study of Charter Schools' "A Study of Charter Schools: First Year Report–May 1997" (U.S. Department of Education, 1997). This condition existed because the scope of the study encompassed the years 1995-1996 during which no charter schools existed in Alaska.

However, the current project presented information about charter schools according to two dimensions (Table 8). The first dimension was their location, urban or rural. The second dimension was the type, new or pre-existing. Urban charter schools were located in communities with a population of 5,501 or more that were not connected by road or rail to Anchorage or Fairbanks or with a population of 1,501 or more that were connected by road or rail to Anchorage or Fairbanks. Three charter schools were located in rural areas and 11 were located in urban areas.

Table 8
Type of Alaska charter school

	Rural		Urban		Total	
School Type:	n	%	n	%	n	%
Newly created	2	16.67	10	83.33	12	100
Pre-existing	1	50	1	50	2	100
Total	3	21.43	11	78.57	14	100

Source: Alaska Department of Education, June 1997

New charter schools were those that had no previous existence as a private or public school. Pre-existing charter schools were those that had formerly operated as a private or public school and switched over to a charter school. The founders of 16.67% of the newly-created charter schools established their charter schools in rural areas, while the founders of 83.33% of the newly-created charter schools established their charter schools in urban areas. The founders of rural charter schools that sprang out of pre-existing schools accounted for 50% of the pre-existing schools, while the founders of urban charter schools that emerged from pre-existing schools accounted for 50% of the pre-existing schools. Of the total number of charter schools founded, 21.43% were in rural areas and 78.57% were in urban areas.

The charter schools served many different grade span combinations (Table 9). Four schools served students in grades 7-12. Only one school served grades 9-12, and it was located in a rural area. One school served post-secondary students. It was in a partnership with the University of Alaska, Fairbanks, and it was located in a rural area.

With respect to school size (Table 10), 78.5% of the charter schools enrolled less than 100 students and 21.43% had enrollments between 101 and 178. The smallest district from which a charter school reported was Galena City Schools; the largest was Anchorage. Among the responding charter schools, 78.57% (11) were in the urban areas (Table 8). Alaska's student population was concentrated in the urban areas; so were the newly

Table 9
Grade levels in Alaska's charter schools

Grades:	Rural n	%	Urban n	%	Total n	%
K-3	0	0.00	1	9.09	1	7.14
K-4	0	0.00	1	9.09	1	7.14
K-6	0	0.00	1	9.09	1	7.14
K-7	0	0.00	1	9.09	1	7.14
K-8	0	0.00	2	18.18	2	14.28
3-6	0	0.00	1	9.09	1	7.1
4-6	0	0.00	1	9.09	1	7.14
7-12	1	33.33	3	27.27	4	28.57
9-12	1	33.33	0	0.00	1	7.14
9-12,13-14*	1	33.33	0	0.00	1	7.14
Total	3	99.99	11	99.99	14	99.97

Note: *Partnership with the University of Alaska, Fairbanks.
Source: Alaska Departmelnt of Education, June 1997

Table 10
Number of students enrolled in Alaska's charter schools

Number of Students Enrolled:	Rural n	%	Urban n	%	Total n	%
1-20	0	0.00	2	18.18	2	14.29
21-26	0	0.00	1	9.09	1	7.14
27-40	1	33.33	1	9.09	2	14.29
41-50	1	33.33	0	0.00	1	7.14
51-60	0	0.00	1	9.09	1	7.14
61-75	0	0.00	2	18.18	2	14.29
76-84	0	0.00	1	9.09	1	7.14
85-90	0	0.00	0	0.00	0	0.00
91-100	1	33.33	0	0.00	1	7.14
101-120	0	0.00	1	9.09	1	7.14
121-130	0	0.00	1	9.09	1	7.14
131-178	0	0.00	1	9.09	1	7.14
Total	3	99.99	11	99.99	14	99.99

Source: Alaska Department of Education, June 1997

created and the pre-existing charter schools (11). Approximately 85.71% of the charter schools were newly created schools; the rest, 14.29%, were pre-existing schools (Table 8). By comparison, the U.S. Department of Education's study (1997) found that 58.4% of the charter schools studied were newly created.

The newly created schools differed in many ways, including the reasons for forming the charter school and the hazards they faced. When the researcher surveyed them, because school districts and the Alaska Board of Education approved their charters in the spring of 1997, it was expected that many of the newly created charter schools would not be opened in the fall. However, by the fall of 1997 all newly created charter schools were operating. All the pre-existing schools began operations in 1996.

Two cyber-schools, Project Education in Galena, Alaska, and the Delta/Greeley Cyber in Delta Junction, Alaska, were schools that operated as central correspondence schools to which students connected through an Internet link, were among the respondent population of charter schools. These were new schools formed within existing schools. Project Education was located in a remote rural area on the north bank of the mid-Yukon River with no road system. Delta/Greeley Cyber was located in a rural area on the road system between Anchorage and Fairbanks.

In addition, three schools offered parents the choice to have their children exposed to different instructional methods. Two were located in urban communities and one in a rural community. Two charter schools operated their programs for students who had abused drugs or alcohol or who were in danger of dropping out of school. One was in an urban setting. The other was in a rural setting.

The researcher compared charter schools in terms of urban and rural charter schools, and new and converted charter schools. The schools were not uniform in the grade span of students they served. Most charter schools used traditional delivery systems, but two used the Internet or some combination of Internet and distance-delivery methods. Some schools offered parents a choice of instructional methods, and two schools provided programs for troubled students.

Funding to Alaska's Charter Schools

The operational funding for charter schools in Alaska was spelled out in the legislation. Charter schools received funding according to the State of Alaska's educational foundation formula in Alaska Statute: "The 'amount generated by students enrolled in the charter school' is to be determined in the same manner as it would be for a student enrolled in another public school in that school district" (AS 14.03.260 (a)) (Appendix A).

After they became charter schools, all of Alaska's charter schools individually applied for and received a competitive federal grant (Appendix K) under Title X, Part C of the Elementary and Secondary Education Act. The purpose of the federal charter school grant was: "... to increase understanding of the charter schools model by providing financial assistance for the design and initial implementation of charter schools and to evaluate the effects of such schools, including the effects on students, achievement, staff and parents" (Alaska Department of Education, 1997, p. 1). The charter schools used these funds for start-up expenses to cover the expenses of lease-hold improvements, to pay for academic aides, to defray the cost of equipment purchases, to provide money for opening-day celebrations, to settle legal expenses, and to reimburse financial supporters.

Perceived Areas of Freedom

Alaska's charter school legislation did not allow charter schools to be independent of their sponsoring districts, "... because Alaska's charter schools will not be autonomous in any real sense" (A. Gifford, personal communication, March 4, 1996). Although their autonomy was illusory, it was worthwhile to treat charter school freedom as a variable in order to ascertain how much authority Alaska's charter schools perceived they had over key areas. Tables 12, 13, 14, and 15 illustrate the various categories of respondents' replies concerning the nine indicators of perceived freedom of charter schools.

Table 11
Charter schools' reports of key areas they controlled (freedom)

Urban (N = 11) Indicators of freedom	n	% of total	% of response
Total budget	7	9.59	70
Purchase of supplies and equipment	6	8.22	75
School calendar	8	10.96	72.73
Daily schedule	9	12.33	75
Student assessment policies	9	12.33	75
Student admission policies	7	9.59	70
Student discipline (e.g. suspension/expulsion)	9	12.33	75
Establishment of curriculum	9	12.33	75
Hiring teaching staff	9	12.33	75
SUM	73	100	

Rural (N = 3) Indicators of freedom	n	% of total	% of response
Total budget	3	11.54	30
Purchase of supplies and equipment	2	7.69	25
School calendar	3	11.54	27.27
Daily schedule	3	11.54	25
Student assessment policies	3	11.54	25
Student admission policies	3	11.54	30
Student discipline (e.g. suspension/expulsion)	3	11.54	25
Establishment of curriculum	3	11.54	25
Hiring teaching staff	3	11.54	25
SUM	26	100	

Total (N = 14) Indicators of freedom	n	% of total	% of response
Total budget	10	10.1	100
Purchase of supplies and equipment	8	8.08	100
School calendar	11	11.11	100
Daily schedule	12	12.12	100
Student assessment policies	12	12.12	100
Student admission policies	10	10.1	100
Student discipline (e.g. suspension/expulsion)	12	12.12	100
Establishment of curriculum	12	12.12	100
Hiring teaching staff	12	12.12	100
SUM	99	100	

The amount of freedom each charter school had was a function of both the legislation, and the provisions of its contract with its sponsor district. The legislation determined the charter schools' freedoms about the selection of a principal, admissions procedures, budgeting, teacher-student ratio, and the number, the age group, or the grade level(s) of students. The charter school and its sponsoring school district determined the operational freedoms.

Because every charter school in Alaska had to arrange for its operational freedoms with its sponsoring district, this study sought to learn about the freedom the operators of the charter school thought they gained. Charter school directors were invited to indicate the key areas of freedom their schools had. Nearly 74% of the urban charter school operators said they controlled the nine the indicators of freedom (Table 11). By comparison, 96% of the rural charter school heads reported that they controlled the nine indicators of freedom. Of all charter school administrators, 78.57% said they controlled the nine indicators of freedom. The indicators of freedom following "hiring of teaching staff" were responses to the open-ended question of "other." There was no significant pattern among the charter school operators to these additional indicators. Therefore, the researcher did not compile statistics for them.

Nevertheless, it was evident that charter school operators felt they controlled many of the operational areas of their schools. Over 71% of the charter schools chiefs said they had "total budget" freedom. By comparison, less than 1% of all the non-charter school respondents said that charter schools had "total budget" freedom. While charter schools had control of their budgets, it was clear that districts still maintained a high degree of control over the charter school's revenues. Since most charter schools had little or no capability to operate or to pay for their own accounting systems, this was to be expected. The charter schools' source of funding was from their sponsoring districts, which would further account for their perception that they did not have freedom in this area. The absence of waiver requests as a way to obtain more freedom suggested that the charter schools did not want more of it. Failing to expand their freedoms beyond those specified in the legislation, the charter school operators established default boundaries on their capacity for freedom.

The study contrasted the freedoms charter school operators perceived they had with the responses from three other groups. The first group the researcher studied was that of the urban superintendents and rural superintendents (Table 12). Ten percent of the urban superintendents who had charter schools in their districts felt that charter schools had "total budget" freedom. Only 16.7% of the rural superintendents who had charter schools in their districts felt the same way. Almost 20% of the urban superintendents who had charter schools in their districts felt that charter schools had freedom over their daily schedules, but none of the rural superintendents who had charter schools in their districts felt the same way.

Forty percent of the urban superintendents who had charter schools in their districts felt that charter schools had freedom over student discipline, but only 16.7% of the rural superintendents who had charter schools in their districts felt the same way. Ten percent of the urban superintendents with charter schools in their districts felt that the charter schools had freedom to establish their own curriculum. On the other hand, 50% of the rural superintendents with charter schools in their districts felt the same way.

Rural superintendents did not feel that the charter schools' freedoms were adequately described among the operational freedoms listed. A little more than 23%

Table 12
Superintendents' reports of key areas charter schools controlled (freedom)

Urban (N=8)

Indicators of Freedom	With charter school n=8	%	Without n=0	%
Total budget	1	10	0	0
Daily schedule	2	20	0	0
Student discipline (e.g. suspension/expulsion)	4	40	0	0
Establishment of curriculum	1	10	0	0
Hiring teaching staff	2	20	0	0
SUM	10	100	0	0

Rural (N=27)

Indicators of Freedom	With charter school n=3	%	Without n=24	%
Total budget	1	16.7	0	0
Daily schedule	0	0	0	0
Student discipline (e.g. suspension/expulsion)	1	16.7	0	0
Establishment of curriculum	3	50	1	100
Hiring teaching staff	1	16.7	0	0
SUM	6	100	1	100

Total (N=35)

Indicators of Freedom	With charter school n=11	%	Without n=24	%
Total budget	2	12.5	0	0
Daily schedule	2	12.5	0	0
Student discipline (e.g. suspension/expulsion)	5	31.3	0	0
Establishment of curriculum	4	25	1	100
Hiring teaching staff	3	18.8	0	0
SUM	16	100	1	100

of the rural superintendents who had charter schools in their districts felt that the charter schools had freedom in instructional methods. Over 15% of them felt that the charter schools had freedom to attain their goals. Over 23% of them felt that the charter schools had the same freedoms as public schools.

Only 7.7% of the rural superintendents who had charter schools in their districts thought that charters schools had semi-autonomy, and 15.4% felt that charter schools had freedom in management strategies. Only 7.7% of the rural superintendents who had charter schools in their districts felt that charter schools should be free of the collective bargaining agreements. None of the urban superintendents with charter schools in their districts felt the same way.

Table 12 Continued
Superintendents' reports of key areas charter schools controlled (freedom)

Urban (N=8)	With charter school		Without	
Other Indicators of Freedom	n=8	%	n=0	%
Instructional methods	0	0	0	0
Goal attainment	0	0	0	0
Same as public schools	0	0	0	0
Semi-autonomy	0	0	0	0
Management strategies	0	0	0	0
Higher standards	0	0	0	0
Collective bargaining agreement	0	0	0	0
SUM	0	0	0	0

Rural (N=27)	With charter school		Without	
Other Indicators of Freedom	n=3	%	n=24	%
Instructional methods	3	23.1	2	100
Goal attainment	2	15.4	0	0
Same as public schools	3	23.1	0	0
Semi-autonomy	1	7.7	0	0
Management strategies	2	15.4	0	0
Higher standards	1	7.7	0	0
Collective bargaining agreement	1	7.7	0	0
SUM	13	100	2	100

Total (N=35)	With charter school		Without	
Other Indicators of Freedom	n=11	%	n=24	%
Instructional methods	3	23.1	2	100
Goal attainment	2	15.4	0	0
Same as public schools	3	23.1	0	0
Semi-autonomy	1	7.7	0	0
Management strategies	2	15.4	0	0
Higher standards	1	7.7	0	0
Collective bargaining agreement	1	7.7	0	0
SUM	13	100	2	100

No superintendent respondent identified purchase of supplies and equipment, school calendar, student assessment, and student admissions as "Indicators of freedom." No superintendent respondent identified facilities as an "Other indicator of freedom."

The second group the researcher studied was that of the urban principals and the rural principals (Table 13). While over 85% of the charter school chiefs reported that they had the freedom to establish curriculum, 53.8% of urban principals with a charter school in their district thought that charter schools should have the opera-

Table 13
Principals' reports of key areas charter schools controlled (freedom)

Urban (N=44)

Indicators of Freedom	With charter school n=42	%	Without n=2	%
Total budget	0	0	0	0
Purchase of supplies & equipment	0	0	0	0
School calendar	2	15.4	0	0
Daily schedule	1	7.69	0	0
Student assessment	0	0	0	0
Student admissions	1	7.69	0	0
Student discipline	0	0	0	0
Establishment of curriculum	7	53.8	0	0
Hiring teaching staff	2	15.4	0	0
SUM	13	99.9	0	0

Rural (N=58)

Indicators of Freedom	With charter school n=3	%	Without n=55	%
Total budget	3	11.5	0	0
Purchase of supplies & equipment	2	7.7	0	0
School calendar	3	11.5	2	9.52
Daily schedule	3	11.5	2	9.52
Student assessment	3	11.5	2	9.52
Student admissions	3	11.5	1	4.76
Student discipline	3	11.5	2	9.52
Establishment of curriculum	3	11.5	7	33.3
Hiring teaching staff	3	11.5	5	23.8
SUM	26	99.7	21	99.9

Total (N=102)

Indicators of Freedom	With charter school n=45	%	Without n=57	%
Total budget	3	7.69	0	0
Purchase of supplies & equipment	2	5.13	0	0
School calendar	5	12.8	2	9.52
Daily schedule	4	10.23	2	9.52
Student assessment	3	7.7	2	9.52
Student admissions	4	10.3	1	4.76
Student discipline	3	7.69	2	9.52
Establishment of curriculum	10	25.6	7	33.3
Hiring teaching staff	5	12.8	5	23.8
SUM	39	99.9	21	99.9

tional freedom to establish curriculum. None of the urban principals without a charter school in their district category responded to this class of freedom. How-

Table 13 Continued
Principals' reports of key areas charter schools controlled (freedom)

Urban (N=44)

Other Indicators of Freedom	With charter school n=42	%	Without n=2	%
Facility	0	0	1	16.7
Instructional methods	3	20	0	0
Goal attainment	1	6.67	0	0
Same as public schools	4	26.7	0	0
Management Strategies	0	0	1	16.7
Collective bargaining agreement	3	20	1	16.7
Decision making	1	6.67	0	0
District regulations	1	6.67	1	16.7
State regulations	1	6.67	2	33.3
Carnegie units	1	6.67	0	0
SUM	15	100	6	100

Rural (N=58)

Other Indicators of Freedom	With charter school n=3	%	Without n=55	%
Facility	0	0	0	0
Instructional methods	0	0	4	36.4
Goal attainment	0	0	2	18.2
Same as public schools	0	0	1	9.09
Management Strategies	0	0	2	18.2
Collective bargaining agreement	0	0	1	9.09
Decision making	0	0	1	9.09
District regulations	0	0	0	0
State regulations	0	0	0	0
Carnegie units	0	0	0	0
SUM	0	0	11	100

Total (N=102)

Other Indicators of Freedom	With charter school n=45	%	Without n=57	%
Facility	0	0	1	5.88
Instructional methods	3	20	4	23.5
Goal attainment	1	6.67	2	11.8
Same as public schools	4	26.67	1	5.88
Management Strategies	0	0	3	17.65
Collective bargaining agreement	3	20	2	11.76
Decision making	1	6.67	1	5.88
District regulations	1	6.67	1	5.88
State regulations	1	6.67	2	11.76
Carnegie units	1	6.67	0	0
SUM	15	100	17	99.9

ever, 11.5% of the rural principals with a charter school in their district, and 33.3% of the rural principals without a charter school in their district said that they thought that charter schools should have control over establishing their curriculum.

None of the urban principals with a charter school in their district responded to

Table 14
Community Members' reports of key areas charter schools controlled (freedom)

Urban (N=71)	With charter school		Without	
Indicators of Freedom	n=71	%	n=0	%
Purchase of supplies & equipment	2	13.3	0	0
School calendar	1	6.67	0	0
Daily schedule	1	6.67	0	0
Student discipline (e.g. suspension/expulsion)	3	20	0	0
Establishment of curriculum	7	46.7	0	0
Hiring teaching staff	1	6.67	0	0
SUM	15	100	0	0

Rural (N=11)	With charter school		Without	
Indicators of Freedom	n=11	%	n=0	%
Purchase of supplies & equipment	0	0	0	0
School calendar	0	0	0	0
Daily schedule	0	0	0	0
Student discipline (e.g. suspension/expulsion)	0	0	0	0
Establishment of curriculum	0	0	0	0
Hiring teaching staff	0	0	0	0
SUM	0	0	0	0

Total (N=82)	With charter school		Without	
Indicators of Freedom	n=82	%	n=0	%
Purchase of supplies & equipment	2	13.33	0	0
School calendar	1	6.67	0	0
Daily schedule	1	6.67	0	0
Student discipline (e.g. suspension/expulsion)	3	20	0	0
Establishment of curriculum	7	46.67	0	0
Hiring teaching staff	1	6.67	0	0
SUM	15	100	0	0

whether they thought that a charter school should have the freedom to discipline their students. On the other hand, 11.5% of the rural principals with a charter school in their district, and 9.52% of the rural principals without a charter school in their district felt that charter schools have the freedom to discipline students.

Urban principals had more to say about the "other" operational freedoms. Twenty percent of the urban principals with a charter school in their district felt that the charter schools should have freedom over instructional methods, and 6.67% of them felt that charter schools should be free to make decisions.

None of the rural principals with a charter school in their district responded to whether or not they thought that charter schools should have freedom over instructional methods. However, 36.4% of the rural principals in districts without a char-

Table 14 Continued
Community Members' reports of key areas charter schools controlled (freedom)

Urban (N=71)		With charter school		Without	
Other Indicators of Freedom		n=71	%	n=0	%
Instructional methods		5	45.5	0	0
Goal attainment		1	9.09	0	0
Same as public schools		1	9.09	0	0
Higher standards		1	9.09	0	0
Decision making		2	18.2	0	0
District regulations		1	9.09	0	0
	SUM	11	99.9	0	0

Rural (N=11)		With charter school		Without	
Other Indicators of Freedom		n=11	%	n=0	%
Instructional methods		1	100	0	0
Goal attainment		0	0	0	0
Same as public schools		0	0	0	0
Higher standards		0	0	0	0
Decision making		0	0	0	0
District regulations		0	0	0	0
	SUM	1	100	0	0

Total (N=82)		With charter school		Without	
Other Indicators of Freedom		n=82	%	n=0	%
Instructional methods		6	50	0	0
Goal attainment		1	8.33	0	0
Same as public schools		1	8.33	0	0
Higher standards		1	8.33	0	0
Decision making		2	16.67	0	0
District regulations		1	8.33	0	0
	SUM	12	99.99	0	0

ter school responded that they thought charter schools should have freedom over instructional methods.

Over 26% of the urban principals with a charter school in their district thought that the freedom that charter schools had should be the same as that afforded public schools. Twenty percent of the urban principals with a charter school in their district thought that the charter schools should be free of the collective bargaining agreements. One-third of the urban principals without a charter school in their district felt that the charter school should be freed of state regulations. No principal respondent identified semi-autonomy or higher standards as an "Other indicator of freedom."

The third group studied was that of the urban community members and the rural community members (Table 14). All of the community members who responded lived in districts with charter schools. Over 86% of them lived in urban districts, and 13.4% lived in rural districts.

Almost 47% of the urban community members thought that charter schools should exercise freedom over curriculum. A little more than 45% of the urban community members felt that the charter schools should have freedom over their instructional

Table 15
Superintendents: How much freedom do you believe charter schools should have?

Urban (N=8)

Amount of freedom	With charter school n=8	%	Without n=0	%
None - 1	0	0	0	0
Very little - 2	2	25	0	0
Some - 3	2	25	0	0
A lot - 4	4	50	0	0
SUM	8	100	0	0

Rural (N=27)

Amount of freedom	With charter school n=3	%	Without n=24	%
None - 1	1	33.33	0	0
Very little - 2	0	0	2	8.69
Some - 3	1	33.33	13	56.5
A lot - 4	1	33.33	8	34.8
SUM	3	99.99	23	99.9

Total (N=35)

Amount of freedom	With charter school n=11	%	Without n=24	%
None - 1	1	9.1	0	0
Very little - 2	2	18.2	2	8.69
Some - 3	3	27.3	13	56.5
A lot - 4	5	45.5	8	34.8
SUM	11	100	23	99.9

methods. Only one rural community member responded to the indicators of freedom. He/she believed that charter schools should have freedom over instructional methods. No community member respondent identified total budget, student assessment, and student admission as "Indicators of freedom." No community member respondent identified facilities, semi-autonomy, management strategies, or collective bargaining agreement as an "Other indicator of freedom."

To obtain a comparison between the perceived freedoms of the charter schools, superintendents, public school principals, and community members were asked to rate, on a scale from one to five, the relative amount of freedom they believed the charter schools should have. Tables 15, Table 16, and Table 17 respectively display the responses from urban and rural superintendents, urban and rural principals, and urban and rural community members.

Fifty percent of the urban superintendents with a charter school in their district, and 33% of the rural superintendents with a charter school in their district, felt that charter schools should have a lot of freedom. Thirty-three per-

Table 16
Principals: How much freedom do you believe charter schools should have?

Urban (N=44)

Amount of freedom	With charter school n=42	%	Without n=2	%
None -1	0	0	0	0
Very little -2	0	0	0	0
Some -3	13	50	0	0
A lot -4	13	50	0	0
Total freedom -5	0	0	0	0
SUM	26	100	0	0

Rural (N=58)

Amount of freedom	With charter school n=3	%	Without n=55	%
None -1	0	0	2	3.63
Very little -2	0	0	2	3.63
Some -3	1	33.3	23	41.8
A lot -4	1	33.3	26	47.3
Total freedom -5	1	33.3	2	3.63
SUM	3	99.9	55	99.9

Total (N=102)

Amount of freedom	With charter school n=45	%	Without n=57	%
None -1	0	0	2	3.63
Very little -2	0	0	2	3.63
Some -3	14	48.3	23	41.8
A lot -4	14	48.3	26	47.3
Total freedom -5	1	3.45	2	3.63
SUM	29	100	55	99.9

cent of the rural superintendents without a charter school in their district responded that charter schools should have a lot of freedom. Most urban superintendents and rural superintendents, both with and without a charter school in their district, responded that charter schools should have some freedom. Most urban superintendents and rural superintendents who responded that charter schools should have some or a lot of freedom were those superintendents without a charter school in their district. No urban or rural superintendent respondent said that the charter schools should have total freedom.

Table 16 displays the responses of principals with regard to their perception of how much freedom a charter school should have. Urban principals with a charter school in their district were evenly divided between some and a lot of freedom for charter schools. Fifty percent of the urban principals with a charter school in their district and 33% of the rural principals with a charter school in their district felt that charter schools should have some or a lot of freedom. More than 40% of the rural principals without a charter school in their district responded that charter schools should have some freedom, and over 47% felt they should have a lot of freedom. Most urban principals and rural principals, both with and without a charter school in their district, responded that charter schools should have some or a lot of freedom. Most urban principals without a charter school in their district and rural principals without a charter school in their district responded that charter schools should have some or a lot of freedom.

On the other hand, less than 8% of the community member respondents (Table 17) who had a charter school in their district thought that charter schools should have total freedom. Over 58% of urban community members whose districts had a charter school, and over 55% of rural community members whose districts had a charter school felt that charter schools should have a lot of freedom. All of the community members surveyed lived in school districts with a charter school. When results of the two groups were combined, over 57% indicated that charter schools should have a lot of freedom. However, only 7.02% of the two combined groups felt that charter schools should have total freedom. The data suggested that, in the view of the three sample groups (superintendents, principals, and community members), charter schools should have a lot of freedom.

However, as Table 18 indicated, there was little support for charter schools having total freedom. Among those respondents with a charter school in their district, 35.04% indicated that charter schools should have some freedom, 53.61% indicated that charter schools should have a lot of freedom, but only 5.15% indicated that they thought charter schools should have total freedom. Among those respondents without a charter school in their district, 46.15% indicated that charter schools should have some freedom, 43.59% indicated that charter schools should have a lot of freedom, but only 2.56% indicated that they thought charter schools should have total freedom. When the researcher combined the figures, 40% indicated that charter schools should have some freedom, 49.14% indicated that charter schools should have a lot of freedom, but only 4% indicated that they thought charter schools should have total freedom.

Table 19 contains the charter school operators' responses concerning accountability. The researcher broke out the responses of the charter school operators into two categories. Did the charter school operators "use" or "plan to use" the accountability measures? Nearly 29% of the urban charter schools and 47.6% of rural charter schools reported that they used alternative forms of assessment. Of the combined urban and rural charter schools, 32.65% declared that they used alterna-

Table 17
Community members: How much freedom do you believe charter schools should have?

Urban (N=71)

Amount of freedom	With charter school n=71	%	Without n=0	%
None - 1	1	2.08	0	0
Very little - 2	2	4.17	0	0
Some - 3	14	29.2	0	0
A lot - 4	28	58.3	0	0
Total freedom - 5	3	6.25	0	0
SUM	48	100	0	0

Rural (N=11)

Amount of freedom	With charter school n=11	%	Without n=0	%
None - 1	0	0	0	0
Very little - 2	0	0	0	0
Some - 3	3	33.3	0	0
A lot - 4	5	55.6	0	0
Total freedom - 5	1	11.1	0	0
SUM	9	100	0	0

Total (N=82)

Amount of freedom	With charter school n=82	%	Without n=0	%
None - 1	1	1.75	0	0
Very little - 2	2	3.51	0	0
Some - 3	17	29.82	0	0
A lot - 4	33	57.89	0	0
Total freedom - 5	4	7.02	0	0
SUM	57	99.99	0	0

Table 18
All categories of respondents: How much freedom do you believe charter schools should have?

All categories of respondents	With charter school n	%	Without charter school n	%	With & Without charter school n	%
Amount of freedom						
None - 1	2	2.06	2	2.56	4	2.29
Very little - 2	4	4.12	4	5.13	8	4.57
Some - 3	34	35.05	36	46.15	70	40
A lot - 4	52	53.61	34	43.59	86	49.14
Total freedom - 5	5	5.15	2	2.56	7	4
SUM	97	99.99	78	99.99	175	100

tive forms of assessment. By contrast, 24.7% of the urban charter schools, but none of the rural charter schools planned to use alternative forms of measuring student

Table 19, Section 1 of 3
Charter schools' reports of key areas of responsibility (accountability)

Urban (N = 11)	Use		Plan to use	
Indicators of accountability	n	%	n	%
Standardized tests	3	27.3	4	36.4
Iowa Test of Basic Skills	1	9.1	0	0
California Test of Basic Skills	1	9.1	0	0
California Achievement Test	7	63.6	0	0
Scholastic Aptitude Test version 9	0	0	0	0
State assessment program	1	9.1	3	27.3
Alternative forms of assessment				
Performance-based tests developed locally	2	18.2	3	27.3
Performance-based tests developed as part of a national or state effort	1	9.1	1	9.1
Student portfolios	6	54.5	1	9.1
Students' demonstration of work	6	54.5	2	18.2
Parent satisfaction surveys	4	36.4	4	36.4
Student interviews and/or surveys	2	18.2	5	45.5
Behavioral indicators, e.g. attendance, expulsion, and college-going rate, etc.	1	9.1	3	27.3
SUM	35		26	
Rural (N = 3)	Use		Plan to use	
Indicators of accountability	n	%	n	%
Standardized tests	3	100	0	0
Iowa Test of Basic Skills	0	0	0	0
California Test of Basic Skills	1	33.3	0	0
California Achievement Test	3	100	0	0
Scholastic Aptitude Test version 9	1	33.3	0	0
State assessment program	0	0	1	33.3
Alternative forms of assessment				
Performance-based tests developed locally	2	66.7	0	0
Performance-based tests developed as part of a national or state effort	2	66.7	0	0
Student portfolios	2	66.7	0	0
Students' demonstration of work	2	66.7	0	0
Parent satisfaction surveys	0	0	0	0
Student interviews and/or surveys	1	33.3	0	0
Behavioral indicators, e.g. attendance, expulsion, and college-going rate, etc.	1	33.3	0	0
SUM	18		1	

achievement. Of the combined urban and rural charter schools, 19.39% declared that they planned to use alternative forms of assessment.

Even though the state mandated standardized testing using the California Achievement Test version 5, of students in grades 4, 8 and 11, only 27.27% of urban charter

Table 19, Section 2 of 3
Charter schools' reports of key areas of responsibility (accountability)

Total (N = 14)		Use		Plan to use	
Indicators of accountability	n	%	n	%
Standardized tests	6	42.9	4	28.6
Iowa Test of Basic Skills	1	7.1	0	0
California Test of Basic Skills	2	14.3	0	0
California Achievement Test	10	71.4	0	0
Scholastic Aptitude Test version 9	1	7.14	0	0
State assessment program	1	7.14	4	28.6
Alternative forms of assessment				
Performance-based tests				
developed locally	4	28.6	3	21.4
Performance-based tests developed				
as part of a national or state effort	3	27.3	1	7.1
Student portfolios	8	57.1	1	7.1
Students' demonstration of work	8	57.1	2	14.3
Parent satisfaction surveys	4	28.6	4	28.6
Student interviews and/or surveys	3	27.3	5	35.7
Behavioral indicators, e.g.				
attendance, expulsion, and college-				
going rate, etc.	2	14.3	3	21.4
SUM	53		27	

Other Indicators of accountability

Urban (N = 11)		Use		Plan to use	
Other Indicators of accountability	n	%	n	%
Woodcock-Johnson	1	9.1	0	0
District mandated:				
Mathematics	1	9.1	0	0
Language Arts	1	9.1	0	0
Reading	1	9.1	0	0
Analytical writing	1	9.1	0	0
State mandated:				
Direct writing assessment	2	18.2	0	0
National Assessment of Academic				
Progress - Language Arts	1	9.1	0	0
Rubrics	1	9.1	0	0
Social and emotional	1	9.1	0	0
Video	1	9.1	0	0
Projects/Exhibitions	1	9.1	0	0
Calvert tests	0	0	0	0
SUM	7		0	

schools said they used, and 36.36% said they were planning to use standardized tests. By contrast, 100% of the rural charter schools said they used standardized tests. No rural charter schools reported that they planned to use standardized tests, but they did not indicate how they were going to comply with the state requirement for standardized testing. Of the combined urban and rural charter schools, 42.86% declared that they used and 28.57% said that they planned to use standardized

Table 19, Section 3 of 3
Charter schools' reports of key areas of responsibility (accountability)

Rural (N = 3)	Use		Plan to use	
Other Indicators of accountability	n	%	n	%
Woodcock-Johnson	0	0	0	0
District mandated:				
Mathematics	0	0	0	0
Language Arts	0	0	0	0
Reading	0	0	0	0
Analytical writing	1	33.3	0	0
State mandated:				
Direct writing assessment	1	33.3	0	0
National Assessment of Academic Progress - Language Arts	0	0	0	0
Rubrics	0	0	0	0
Social and emotional	0	0	0	0
Video	0	0	0	0
Projects/Exhibitions	1	33.3	0	0
Calvert tests	1	33.3	0	0
SUM	4		0	

Total (N = 14)	Use		Plan to use	
Indicators of accountability	n	%	n	%
Woodcock-Johnson	0	0	0	0
District mandated:				
Mathematics	1	7.1	1	7.1
Language Arts	1	7.1	1	7.1
Reading	1	7.1	1	7.1
Analytical writing	2	14.3	3	21.4
State mandated:				
Direct writing assessment	3	21.4	4	28.6
National Assessment of Academic Progress - Language Arts	1	7.1	1	7.1
Rubrics	1	7.1	1	7.1
Social and emotional	1	7.1	1	7.1
Video	1	7.1	1	7.1
Projects/Exhibitions	2	14.3	3	21.4
Calvert tests	1	7.1	2	14.3
SUM	15		19	

tests. No urban or rural charter school respondent identified the Miller's Analogies Test, the Brigance, the California Test of Basic Skills-Español, the Scholastic Achievement Battery-Español, the Aprenda, or La Prueba as a standardized test he/she would use or plan to use.

Nearly 64% percent of the urban charter schools and 100% of the rural charter schools said they were using the CAT-5. None of the urban charter schools and none of the rural charter schools said they planned to use the CAT-5. These results suggested that the charter schools did not hold standardized testing, in general, and the state mandated CAT-5 tests, in particular, in high esteem. The data implied that the charter school operators felt free to ignore the state mandated assessment program. When this area of freedom was compared, the researcher discovered that there was a significant difference in viewpoints between the responses of the superintendents, principals, and community members (Table 20) and those of the charter school operators.

Table 20, Section 1 of 6
Reports of key areas of responsibility (accountability) of charter schools

Superintendents Indicators of accountability Use and Plan to Use	Urban (n=8) n	 %	Rural (n=27) n	 %	Total (n=35) n	 %
Iowa Test of Basic Skills	3	37.5	4	14.8	7	20
CA Test of Basic Skills	0	0	5	18.5	5	14.3
CA Achievement Test	6	75	16	59.3	22	62.9
Miller's Analogies Test	1	12.5	0	0	1	2.86
Scholastic Aptitude Test version 9	1	12.5	2	7.41	3	8.57
Brigance	0	0	4	14.8	4	11.4
CA Test of Basic Skills - Español	0	0	0	0	0	0
Scholastic Achievement Battery - Español	0	0	0	0	0	0
State assessment	5	62.5	21	77.8	26	74.3
Alternative forms of assessment Local performance-based tests	6	75	17	62.9	23	65.7
National or state performance-based tests	4	50	13	48.2	17	48.6
Student portfolios	7	87.5	23	85.2	30	85.7
Student demonstration	6	75	23	85.2	29	82.9
Parent satisfaction surveys	6	75	21	77.8	27	77.1
Student interviews and/or surveys	4	50	21	77.8	25	71.4
Attendance, expulsion, and college-going rate	7	87.5	22	81.5	29	82.9
SUM	56		192		248	

Table 20 contains the responses of superintendents, principals, and community members concerning charter school accountability. A little more than 40% of the urban superintendents who responded said that they felt that charter schools should use or plan to use some form of standardized testing. Thirty-two percent of the rural superintendents who responded said they thought that the charter schools should use or plan to use some form of standardized testing. A little more than 27% of all superintendents seemed to be comfortable with the use or planned use of some form of standardized

Table 20, Section 2 of 6
Reports of key areas of responsibility (accountability) of charter schools

Principals Indicators of accountability Use and Plan to Use	**Urban** (n=29) n	%	**Rural** (n=72) n	%	**Total** (n=101) n	%
Iowa Test of Basic Skills	4	13.8	15	20.8	19	18.8
CATest of Basic Skills	5	17.2	6	8.33	11	10.9
CA Achievement Test	19	65.5	43	59.7	62	61.4
Miller's Analogies Test	2	6.89	3	4.17	5	4.95
Scholastic Aptitude Test version 9	5	17.2	13	18.1	18	17.8
Brigance	2	6.89	2	2.78	4	3.96
CA Test of Basic Skills - Español	3	10.3	1	1.39	4	3.96
Scholastic Achievement Battery - Español	0	0	1	1.39	1	.99
State assessment	17	58.6	40	55.6	57	56.4
Alternative forms of assessment Local performance-based tests	18	62.1	42	58.3	60	59.4
National or state performance-based tests	13	44.8	34	47.2	47	46.5
Student portfolios	25	86.2	51	70.8	76	75.3
Student demonstration	21	72.4	53	73.6	74	73.3
Parent satisfaction surveys	22	75.9	47	65.3	69	68.3
Student interviews and/or surveys	21	72.4	44	61.1	65	64.4
Attendance, expulsion, and college-going rate	24	82.7	46	63.9	70	69.3
SUM	201		441		642	

testing, including a state assessment program for students of charter schools. Although the state mandates the testing of all public school students with the CAT-5, only 62.85% of all superintendents felt that charter schools should use or plan to use this test.

A little more than 71% of the urban superintendents felt that charter schools should be allowed to use or plan to use alternative forms of assessment. A little more than 74% of the rural superintendents felt that charter schools should be allowed to use or plan to use alternative forms of assessment. Of all superintendents who responded, 73.47% felt that charter schools should be allowed to use or plan to use alternative forms of assessment. CSSB 88 specifically excluded superintendents from the governance structure, including assessment, of the charter school. Consequently, the data collected did not indicate whether or not superintendents knew what accountability measures were in use.

A little more than 24% of the urban principals felt that charter schools should use or plan to use standardized tests for charter school student assessment. Slightly

Table 20, Section 3 of 6
Reports of key areas of responsibility (accountability) of charter schools

Community Members Indicators of accountability	Urban (n=71)		Rural (n=11)		Total (n=82)	
Use and Plan to Use	n	%	n	%	n	%
Iowa Test of Basic Skills	20	28.2	5	45.5	25	30.5
CA Test of Basic Skills	9	12.7	1	9.1	10	12.2
CA Achievement Test	14	19.7	2	18.2	16	19.5
Miller's Analogies Test	8	11.3	2	18.2	10	12.2
Scholastic Aptitude Test version 9	16	22.5	2	18.2	18	21.9
Brigance	5	7.04	0	0	5	6.1
CA Test of Basic Skills - Español	0	0	0	0	0	0
Scholastic Achievement Battery - Español	2	2.81	1	9.09	3	3.66
State assessment	17	23.9	7	63.6	24	29.3
Alternative forms of assessment						
Local performance-based tests	20	28.2	5	45.5	25	30.5
National or state performance-based tests	30	42.3	3	27.3	33	40.2
Student portfolios	29	40.9	4	36.4	33	40.2
Student demonstration	33	46.5	5	45.5	38	46.3
Parent satisfaction surveys	31	43.7	5	45.5	36	43.9
Student interviews and/or surveys	26	36.6	5	45.5	31	37.8
Attendance, expulsion, and college-going rate	31	43.7	5	45.5	36	43.9
SUM	291		52		343	

more than 19% of the rural principals felt that charter schools should use or plan to use standardized tests for charter school student assessment. Almost 20% of all the principals felt that charter schools should use or plan to use standardized tests for charter school student assessment. Of the principals who responded, less than 1% replied that charter schools should use or plan to use Spanish language versions of some standardized tests. Of the urban principals, 70.93% felt that charter schools should use or plan to use alternative assessment instruments. More than 63% of the rural principals felt that charter schools should use or plan to use alternative assessment instruments. A little more than 65% of all the principals felt that charter schools should use or plan to use alternative assessment instruments.

A little more than 60% of the urban community members felt that charter schools should use or plan to use standardized tests (Iowa Test of Basic Skills, California Test of Basic skills, and the California Achievement Test) for charter school student assessment. Although 19.72% of the urban community members indicated that the charter schools should use the California Achievement Test that state law

Table 20, Section 4 of 6
Reports of key areas of responsibility (accountability) of charter schools

Other Indicators of accountability

Superintendents Indicators of accountability Use and Plan to Use	Urban (n=8) n	%	Rural (n=27) n	%	Total (n=35) n	%
National Assessment of Academic Progress - Language Arts	0	0	0	0	0	0
Rubrics	0	0	0	0	0	0
TABE	0	0	0	0	0	0
CAPS	0	0	0	0	0	0
COPES	0	0	0	0	0	0
School-to-work aptitude/Interest	0	0	0	0	0	0
American College Test	0	0	0	0	0	0
Sp. Ed. Incl. Rate	0	0	0	0	0	0
District developed bilingual tests	0	0	0	0	0	0
Level Tests	0	0	0	0	0	0
Curriculum-Based Meas. (CBM)	0	0	0	0	0	0
Student evaluation of teachers	0	0	0	0	0	0
SUM	0		0		0	

required, 23.94% of the urban community members marked that the charter schools should use the state assessment program.

Almost 73% of the rural community members felt that charter schools should use or plan to use standardized tests (Iowa Test of Basic Skills, California Test of Basic skills, and the California Achievement Test) for charter school student assessment. Although 18.18% of the rural community members indicated that the charter schools should use the California Achievement Test that state law required, 63.63% of the rural community members marked that the charter schools should use the state assessment program.

A little more than 62% of all the community members felt that charter schools should use or plan to use standardized tests (Iowa Test of Basic Skills, California

Test of Basic skills, and the California Achievement Test) for charter school student assessment. Although 19.51% of all the community members indicated that the charter schools should use the California Achievement Test that state law required, 29.27% of all the community members indicated that the charter schools should use the state assessment program.

Of the urban community members who responded, 2.82% replied that charter schools should use or plan to use Spanish language versions of Scholastic Achievement Battery. Of the rural community members who responded, 9.09% replied

Table 20, Section 5 of 6
Reports of key areas of responsibility (accountability) of charter schools

Other Indicators of accountability

Principals Indicators of accountability Use and Plan to Use	Urban (n=29) n %	Rural (n=72) n %	Total (n=101) n %
National Assessment of Academic Progress - Language Arts	1 3.45	0 0	1 .99
Rubrics	0 0	0 0	0 0
TABE	1 3.45	0 0	1 .99
CAPS	1 3.45	0 0	1 .99
COPES	1 3.45	0 0	1 .99
School-to-work aptitude/Interest	1 3.45	0 0	1 .99
American College Test	0 0	0 0	0 0
Sp. Ed. Incl. Rate	0 0	1 1.39	1 .99
District developed bilingual tests	0 0	1 1.39	1 .99
Level Tests	0 0	1 1.39	1 .99
Curriculum-Based Meas. (CBM)	0 0	2 2.78	2 1.98
Student evaluation of teachers	0 0	0 0	0 0
SUM	5	5	10

that charter schools should use or plan to use Spanish language versions of Scholastic Achievement Battery. Of all the community members who responded, 3.66% replied that charter schools should use or plan to use Spanish language versions of Scholastic Achievement Battery.

A little more than 81% of all the respondents (superintendents, principals, and community members) felt that charter schools should use or plan to use standardized tests (Iowa Test of Basic Skills, California Test of Basic skills, and the California Achievement Test) for charter school student assessment. This data may have reflected a lack of general knowledge of the Alaska assessment program. Although 45.87% of all the respondents (superintendents, principals, and community members) indicated that the charter schools should use the California Achievement Test that state law required, 49.08% of all the respondents (superintendents, principals, and community members) indicated that the charter schools should use the state assessment program. Only 1.83% of all the respondents (superintendents, principals, and community members) indicated that charter schools should use or plan to use Spanish language versions of the Scholastic Achievement Battery.

Of the urban community members, an average of 28.57, or 40.24% felt that charter schools should use or plan to use alternative assessment instruments. Of the

Table 20, Section 6 of 6
Reports of key areas of responsibility (accountability) of charter schools

Other Indicators of accountability

Community Members Indicators of accountability Use and Plan to Use	Urban (n=71) n	%	Rural (n=11) n	%	Total (n=82) n	%
National Assessment of Academic Progress - Language Arts	0	0	0	0	0	0
Rubrics	1	1.41	0	0	1	1.22
TABE	0	0	0	0	0	0
CAPS	0	0	0	0	0	0
COPES	0	0	0	0	0	0
School-to-work aptitude/Interest	0	0	0	0	0	0
American College Test	0	0	1	9.09	1	1.22
Sp. Ed. Incl. Rate	0	0	0	0	0	0
District developed bilingual tests	0	0	0	0	0	0
Level Tests	0	0	0	0	0	0
Curriculum-Based Meas. (CBM)	0	0	0	0	0	0
Student evaluation of teachers	1	1.41	0	0	1	1.22
SUM	2		1		3	

rural community members, an average of 4.57, or 41.65% felt that charter schools should use or plan to use alternative assessment instruments. A little more than an average of 33.14 of all the community members, or 40.42% felt that charter schools should use or plan to use alternative assessment instruments.

Of all the respondents (superintendents, principals, and community members), an average of 124.71, or 57.21% felt that charter schools should use or plan to use alternative assessment instruments. Of the rural community members, an average of 4.57, or 41.65% felt that charter schools should use or plan to use alternative assessment instruments. A little more than an average of 33.14 of all the community members, or 40.42% felt that charter schools should use or plan to use alternative assessment instruments.

Seven out of the 11 urban charter schools recounted the goals for which their sponsors would hold them accountable. There were no common accountability goals among the respondent charter school administrators. One charter school operator said that his/her sponsoring school district wanted to see performance-based tests with behavioral indicators and a student interview. Another charter school operator reported that his/her sponsoring agency wanted to see attendance reports and parent satisfaction surveys. A third charter school administrator reported that his/her sponsoring school district was looking for a financial audit and the results of a parent questionnaire. Another charter school administrator stated that his/her sponsoring school district expected his/her kindergarten students to be in the top 25% of the district and his/her students had to meet certain goals beyond just a performance test goal. A fifth charter school administrator said he/she did not know the goals for which his/her sponsoring district would hold them accountable. A sixth charter school head said that his/her sponsoring district held them accountable for having CAT-5 test averages that exceeded or were equal to those of the rest

Table 21
Charter school sponsors' action on accountability information

Response:	Urban (N=11) n	%	Rural (N=3) n	%	Total (N=14) n	%
Yes	0	0.00	1	33.33	1	9.1
No	5	62.5	1	33.33	6	54.54
Don't know	3	37.5	1	33.33	4	36.36
SUM	8	100	3	99.99	11	100

of the district for the grades in the charter school. A final charter school head said his/her district wanted a report on his/her charter school's successes and concerns. He/she said the district also wanted to see his/her charter school's CAT-5 and Alaska Direct Writing scores.

Two out of the three rural charter schools recounted the goals for which their sponsors would hold them accountable. There were no common accountability goals among the rural charter school administrators. One charter school chief said that his/her sponsoring district was looking for student achievement at or above the district levels in three years. His/her sponsor also exacted the provision that before a student could advance to the next grade level, he/she would have to attain student mastery at that grade level. The second respondent stated that all his/her sponsoring district wanted was a report on work skills performance.

The researcher was interested to learn from the charter school operators whether or not their sponsors had acted on any of the accountability information they gave to them. Table 21 shows that 11 out of the 14 charter schools that responded to the question, "Has your charter granting agency acted on your accountability information?" eight were urban charter schools and three were rural charter schools.

Five or 62.5% of the urban charter school operators who responded said that their sponsors did not act on the accountability information. One or 33.33% of the rural charter school operators who responded reported that his/her sponsor did act on the accountability information. One other rural charter school operator reported that his/her sponsor did not act on the accountability information. The last rural charter school operator reported that he/she did not know if his/her sponsor acted on the accountability information. The results suggest that, at least from the charter school heads' point of view, the sponsor districts were remiss in their responsibility to monitor for accountability.

To follow-up on the question of whether or not the charter granting agency acted on the accountability information, the researcher asked the charter school heads how their sponsors had acted on that accountability information. Three out of the 11 urban charter

Table 22
Founders' reasons for seeking charter approval

	Type of school		School location		
	New-start (N=12)	Pre-existing (N=2)	Urban (N=11)	Rural (N=3)	Total (N=14)
Control curriculum and instruction	4	1	4	1	5
Implement specific changes	0	1	0	1	1
Form new relationships with parents	6	0	6	0	6
Implement program philosophy	3	0	3	0	3
Parent dissatisfaction with public schools	1	0	1	0	1
Autonomy of home schooling through a charter	1	0	1	0	1
New way to provide funding to start a 2nd Mt. Edgecumbe	1	0	0	1	1
Lack of constancy in district	1	0	1	0	1
Poor district standards	1	0	1	0	1
Lower pupil-teacher ratio	1	0	1	0	1
More parental involvement	1	0	1	0	1
More diversity in curriculum	1	0	1	0	1

school operators responded. One said they did not know. One said that it opened up communication. The third said that he/she had not presented their CAT-5 data yet.

Two of the three rural charter school heads responded. One said that he/she had not formally reported their accountability results. The other reported that the response from his/her sponsoring school district was to assist its local high school to move toward performance-based accountability.

Under the Alaska charter school law, districts were enjoined to hold the charter schools accountable. Before the Alaska Board of Education could approve a charter application, the charter school technical review committee had to affirm two accountability provisions (Table 1). The charter application had to contain provisions for specific levels of achievement for the educational program and it had to specify the accounting for revenues and expenditures. Charter school principals/

lead teachers reported that they used a variety of standardized tests and alternative assessment methods to account for student achievement. However, none reported on the requirement for financial accountability.

Table 23, Section 1 of 3
Charter school operators' most problematic rules and regulations

Charter School	Mission	Problematic rule or regulation
Academy	To create a learning system that encourages and develops students' inherent abilities to be competent, confident, productive and responsible young adults.	None
Aquarian	To create a program philosophy designed for bright, high-achieving children from families with working parents.	Money, facilities, and safety
Aurora Borealis	To provide teachers and parents with the opportunity, responsibility, and accountability for the management and control of the school curriculum and environment; to produce a flexible set of learning outcomes measured with different and authentic forms of assessment; to provide students with an educational opportunity of the highest quality; and to foster students, parent, and community involvement through the uses of community resources and partnerships.	Two or three parents who wanted the school run their way (miscommunication); getting online through the district and learning to operate within the system; lack of funds and need for approval to spend the funds.
Bay View	To provide a school option where all members, students, staff, and parents, function democratically.	Recognition of the Academic Policy Committee as the governing body.
Chinook	To create a dynamic educational environment which fosters educational excellence and cultivates personal, intellectual, and emotional growth and responsibility.	Opposition from school board.
Delta Greely	To prepare students with the knowledge and technological skills to compete and succeed in the 21st century.	None

Table 22 lists the reason respondents gave for wanting to form a charter school. The approved charter schools sought to become charter schools primarily to forge and strengthen ties with family and parents as students' first and continuing educators. The second most popular reason the respondents gave was to be able to use curriculum and instructional methods for students. Only one of the respondents indicated that his/her reason for forming his/her charter schools was for financial reasons.

More than 43% said they started their charter school in order to forge new

Table 23, Section 2 of 3
Charter school operators' most problematic rules and regulations

Charter School	Mission	Problematic rule or regulation
Family Partnership	To be a non-sectarian partnership between students, professional educators, parents, and community members where as many families as desire will customize an education for their children.	School district unwillingness to bend from established practice.
Homer	To provide a compassionate learning environment that gives students, parents, teachers and community members the power to develop self-reliance, cooperation, intellect, creativity, reasoning ability, and personal growth.	District central office rules and regulations, teacher burnout, collective bargaining agreement.
Juneau	To provide a balanced education using developmentally appropriate techniques which tap into the child's need to explore and create in all fields of learning.	Health and safety regulations related to facilities, union.
Ketchikan	To create a learning environment that fosters growth of character, high academic achievement, and the love of learning, resulting in responsible, productive citizens.	Collective bargaining agreements; Inadequate finances; Local bargaining unit opposition.
Midnight Sun	To provide a safe, nurturing, family oriented, multi-age learning environment supporting a highly rigorous academic program for higher education preparation with high standards of responsible citizenship.	Did not respond.

relationships with parents that permitted involvement to foster a family atmosphere in the school. Respondents said that the major gain in obtaining approval of their charter school was the freedom from local policies regarding curriculum and textbooks. Charter schools could also obtain waivers from state

Table 23, Section 3 of 3
Charter school operators' most problematic rules and regulations

Charter School	Mission	Problematic rule or regulation
New Beginnings	To provide quality education services exclusively for junior and senior high school students whose emotional, physical, social and intellectual development has been affected by substance abuse in an academic environment where learning opportunities promote healthy life choices, abstinence, a life of recovery and educational success for them to build their futures upon.	Finances, external partners, and local facilities.
Project Education	To provide a quality education in an environment that encourages innovative modes of teaching and learning in order to empower each individual student to develop academically, socially, and physically as a global citizen of the 21st century.	Collective bargaining agreement; hiring staff; inadequate finances; union or bargaining unit opposition; staff conflict; teacher burnout.
Takotna Training Center	To allow willing participants to take risks as they foster educational excellence and cultivate personal, intellectual and emotional growth, technological skills, responsibility, and citizenship.	Facilities, finances, teacher turnover
Walden Pond	To provide a challenging educational program for students in grades 7 through 12, with emphasis upon serving students presently "falling through the cracks," through small class sizes, multi-level instructional units, varied methods instruction, a well-rounded curriculum, and strong parental involvement.	Collective bargaining agreements, school district board opposition

regulations. Although somewhat more problematic, charter schools, with the permission of their local collective bargaining units, could obtain waivers from the collective bargaining agreement.

A prime rationale advocates for charter schools have given as a reason for forming a charter school was the desire for independence from their sponsoring school district. However, no Alaska charter school principal/lead teacher mentioned that a desire to be independent of his/her sponsoring school district was a motive for the founders of the charter school. The Alaska charter school law explicitly required charter school applications to contain a statement that allowed the founders the freedom to select the school's principal (Table 1). However, no charter school principal/lead teacher reported that the selection of the principal was a reason for forming the charter school.

It was evident that urban charter schools tended to have less functional control over decisions and operations than did the rural charter schools. The greatest differences were between budgetary control (63.64% vs. 100%) and student admissions policies (63.64% vs. 100%). In general, the prevailing pattern of differences suggested more control among the rural charter schools. For example, rural charter schools were more likely to have control over the establishment of curriculum (100% v. 81.82%), student discipline (100% v. 81.82%), and hiring teaching staff (100% vs. 81.82%). The reader may recall that the major reason charter school principals/lead teachers gave for pursuing charter school status was to gain control over curriculum and instruction.

Table 23 contains the charter schools' mission statement and the most problematic rule or regulation the charter school operators reported they had. None of the respondents reported that resistance or regulations of the Alaska Department of Education were problems for them. Twenty percent of the charter school principals/lead teachers reported that collective bargaining agreements and union or bargaining unit opposition were most difficult problems for them.

Twenty percent of charter school principals/lead teachers reported that school district board opposition was a "most difficult problem." Twenty percent of charter school principals/lead teachers reported that the conflict between the charter school and the district was also a "most difficult problem." Two urban charter school operators, or 13.33%, cited regulations and policies as the most difficult problem areas for their charter schools. No charter school principals/lead teachers reported that federal regulations or court rulings interfered with their operations as a charter school.

Summary

The study investigated the relationship between freedom and accountability in Alaska's charter schools. The researcher queried a broad cross-section of Alaska's population including superintendents, principals, community members, and operators of charter schools.

Charter school operators and non-charter school operators were supportive of increased freedom for charter schools. However, the public did not support total freedom for them. On the other hand, except for the state-mandated assessments, increased accountability was not forthcoming.

Chapter Five
Summary, Conclusions and Recommendations

Summary

The purpose of this study was to investigate the relationship freedom from constraints and the amount of accountability for charter schools in Alaska. All charter schools were formed according to the elements of the contract their sponsors approved. The Alaska charter school legislation outlined the required details of a charter school contract. Since the policy requirements for a charter school contract varied from district to district, the charter schools varied in goals and programs from district to district. In districts permitted more than one charter school, each charter, within the policy guidelines, varied significantly. This difference was the result of the specific elements of each contract. Charter school contracts with their sponsoring school districts provided the operational definition of each charter school, including accountability expectations. This project investigated the literature on the topics of freedom and accountability both as they related to public schools in general and also as they connected to charter schools in particular. One of the intents of this project was to make a significant contribution to the charter school literature so that policy makers and educators can have a basis for making decisions about charter schools as an educational reform measure. This project provided a philosophical framework for understanding the complexity of the dynamic educational system of which charters schools were a part.

During the waning days of Governor Walter Hickle's administration, the Alaska legislature's interest in school reform surfaced. After the 1994 general election, the Republican party gained a majority in the legislature. One of their primary election promises was to reduce the spending of state government. It was evident, then, that the legislature did not want to pay very much for educational reform. Charter schools promised inexpensive educational reform. Freedom in exchange for accountability seemed an attractive lure.

This study conformed to the quantitative method of surveying information from four different audiences. The researcher requested copies of all approved charter school applications from the Alaska Department of Education's charter school liaison. All charter school proposals were analyzed. The data obtained from the surveys and the charter school applications were discussed in Chapter IV.

Another source of input on the issue of charter school freedom was the legislative testimony. During the legislative hearings there was very little discussion of the freedom afforded charter schools and almost no discussion of the accountability expected of them. The comments were mostly confined to parent, community, or teacher control issues.

During the legislative public testimony, members of the audience raised several essential points about charter schools. Charter school legislation should allow for creativity. The charter schools should be free of collective bargaining agreements, but provide for teacher tenure. The legislation should provide for start-up funding. In the bill, legislators should include an outline for a charter school approval process and spell out charter school operational guidelines. The legislation should protect students with low academic achievement from discrimination. The establishment of a charter school should have no negative effect on the regular school program. The charter schools should not divert current funds from public schools. The statute should provide for voluntary staff and student assignment to charter schools. The bill should guarantee direct involvement of all effected school employees, parents, and community members in the charter school's design, implementation, and governance. The law should provide adequate contract and employment provisions for all employees. The code should establish appropriate procedures for assessment and evaluation at predetermined periods within the term of the charter. The charter school would have to employ licensed professional staff, and to ensure health and safety standards for all students and employees. The charter schools would have to assure non-discrimination and to provide for equal educational opportunities. The charter schools would have to abide fiscal accountability. The charter schools would have to have equitable procedures regarding student admission and retention and have no limit on the number of students. The charterschool contract would have to provide appropriate safeguards against racial and ethnic segregation. The statute should provide for the right to appeal a decision that denied a charter school application. The public testimony covered mostly operational aspects of charter school administration.

In the Alaska House of Representatives Health, Education, and Social Services committee, Senator Bert Sharp testified (1995) that the push for more freedom came from teachers so that they could escape the stifling conditions of "regimentation." Catherine Portlock said that the charter schools should have the freedom to experiment with instructional models to suit the different learning styles of students. While 35.71% of the non-charter school operators agreed that charter schools should have the freedom to decide their instructional methods, the public was not so ready to grant charter schools total freedom. This condition may have two roots. One was the fact that many school districts provided alternative schooling programs within the current regulatory climate. Examples of alternative schools were the Leonard Seppala Alternative High School in Nome, Alaska, the Howard Luke Academy in Fairbanks, Alaska, and the Craig Alternative & Correspondence Schools. The second was the concern that charter schools may divide a community.

In response to the three research questions that guided this study, the results are presented in the following pages.

Research Questions

1. How are Alaska's charter schools held accountable and how does that accountability compare with public school accountability in general in the state?

Student achievement levels were fixed as a requirement in the charter school legislation as indicated in Table 1. None of the charter schools of this study consistently mentioned the statewide assessments as a measure of accountability. The data suggested that the charter schools' principals/leader teachers paid scant attention to accountability issues. In general, no one seems to hold Alaska's charter schools accountable.

None of the charter school operators reported that giving accountability information was a problem. The legislature left the issue of accountability up to the sponsor districts. With the one time exception of the Delta Cyber Charter School, that had to report to the Alaska Board of Education on March 28, 1998, the Alaska Department of Education did not require charter schools to report accountability information to it.

When the charter school operators were asked how often they have to report accountability data to their sponsors, most of them responded that they were expected to report once a year. When asked if their sponsors took any action on the accountability information they were given, the founders/operators responded ten to one either "no" or "don't know." Only one responded "yes." The researcher concluded that neither the sponsor nor the charter school operators regarded accountability very highly.

All the charter schools that the researcher canvassed confirmed that the more ephemeral the goals and mission of the charter school were, the more subjective assessment was. The evidence indicates a laissez-faire disposition with regards to accountability of charter schools. On the other hand, the state mandated the administration of the CAT-5 tests for students in grades 4, 8, and 11.

However, because of the disruption the administration of the norm-referenced tests already inflicted on the students in regular public schools, most schools, including charter schools, simply administered the test to all members of the student body. Most school districts had enough experience with giving the tests to students in grades 4, 8, and 11, to know that testing days were very disruptive of the school programs. Consequently, most school districts opted to administer the tests to the entire student body rather than just to three grade groups. The standardized tests were also used for evaluation of entitlement programs in the regular public school program. The state also mandated a direct writing assessment of public school students' writing at least once a year.

Although the legislation did not mandate the use of performance-based assessments, most charter schools indicated their preference for this form of assessment. Fifty percent of the charter schools that responded preferred locally developed performance-based tests. Sixty-four percent of the charter schools that responded preferred student portfolios. Seventy-one percent of the charter schools that responded preferred students' demonstration of their work. The evidence indicated that the charter school operators did not give a high degree of perceived importance to accountability, including the state mandated student assessment.

2. What do the founders/operators of Alaska's charter schools perceive to be the importance of freedom and accountability in the implementation of their plans?

The founders/operators of charter schools mentioned as important many expressions of freedom. They wanted the freedom to create a learning system or to have a flexible set of learning outcomes. They preferred to have the freedom to create a program philosophy and to provide teachers and parents with the opportunity for the management and control of the school curriculum and environment. They felt that families should have the freedom to customize an education for their children that included the development of self-reliance, and cooperation. They wanted the freedom to provide quality education for students affected by substance abuse.

The expressions of accountability were pale in the glow of the expressions of freedom. Out of the 14 charter school founders/operators who responded only one mentioned the importance of accountability: accountability for the management and control of the school curriculum and environment. Six of the responding charter schools reported that they used standardized tests for accountability. However, none of the charter schools specified attainment levels as goals. None of the charter schools held their administrators or teachers accountable for the improvement of student achievement, nor did they report that they would report student achievement levels teacher by teacher. The Alaska legislation did not require charter schools to attain the minimal requirements of their host district's curriculum. Accountability was not foremost in importance to the charter school founders/operators.

3. How do urban and rural charter schools compare in the area of perceived importance of freedom and accountability?

Operators of urban and rural charter schools perceived freedom as a way to form new relationships with parents. The perceived freedom elements that appeared most often among the urban charter schools were as follows: daily schedule; student assessment policies; student discipline; establishment of a curriculum; and, hiring teaching staff. The perceived freedom elements that appeared most often among the rural charter schools were as follows: total budget; school calendar; daily schedule; student assessment policies; student admission policies; student discipline; establishment of a curriculum; and, hiring teaching staff. As applied to charter schools, Roberts (1993) reported that: "The most prevalent areas in reform ... were in one or more of the following areas: curriculum ... school-based management, personnel roles ... parental involvement, and parental choice" (Pratt, 1996, p. 170).

The researcher noted Newmann's (1997) criteria for judging accountability of charter schools. None of Alaska's charter schools provided, "Explicit standards for student performance, provisions for information on student performance, and consequences to the school or teachers for student success or failure" (Newmann, 1997, p. 49). None of Alaska's charter schools provided, "Information, standards, and/or consequences that were required by an external agent (district and/or state) or developed by the school itself, or both" (Newmann, 1997, p. 49-50). None of Alaska's charter schools had, "An external agent that required something specific beyond mandatory standardized testing as part of the school's accountability system or that required the school to develop its own accountability system" (Newmann,

1997, p. 49-50). The evidence suggests a confirmation of the findings of the 1995 U.S. General Accounting Office that there was considerable variation in the amount of accountability in charter schools nationwide. Alaska's educational standards were not firmly rooted in the fabric of every school district's curriculum. Alaska did not have any student assessment system aligned with student content and performance standards.

The need for an aligned student assessment system was related to the warnings of Finn, Bierlein, Manno, and Vanourek's (1997) who said that this condition did not auger well for the " ... long term viability of the charter idea" (Finn, 1997, p. 3). Furthermore, Alaska Department of Education Commissioner Holloway's intervention into the area cost differential for correspondence students and into the area of curriculum added some measure of credence to Manno, Finn, Bierlein, and Vanourek's (1997) portent that some states would tighten regulations for charter schools because of shortcomings in accountability. Lastly, the study found that the charter school operators used or planned to use a combination of standardized tests, student portfolios, and locally developed performance-based tests as the predominant means of assessment. This finding was consistent with Cheung's 1998 study of 31 charter schools in eight states. That study found: "Charters use a variety of measures to assess student achievement. The most frequently cited combinations are standardized tests, student portfolios, and teacher evaluations" (Cheung, 1998, p. 12). The researcher mentioned above that districts were required to report only composite standardized test scores as part of each district's report card to the public. Even though legislation required all public schools to conduct standardized testing of students, the scores were not dis-aggregated. Consequently, the researcher did not find the evidence for individual charter school compliance with regulations mandating standardized testing.

Conclusions

The survey findings provided a general perception of Alaska's charter schools and suggested patterns of perceived freedom and perceived accountability worth following. Alaska's charter school law left no question of the charter schools' autonomy; there simply was none.

The survey found a chasm between charter schools in urban areas and those in the rural areas. Urban charter schools encountered a much larger array of obstacles than did the rural charter schools. The obstacles went from union opposition to sponsor district regulations. In spite of these obstacles, urban charter schools had a strong desire to obtain as much freedom from their sponsoring districts as possible.

The following conclusions were based on an analysis of the literature on freedom and accountability as well as the data collected from the surveys of charter school principals/lead teachers, superintendents, principals, and community members:
1. Alaska's charter schools have unique characteristics as a result of the unique programs they offer their students.
2. School choice supporters were concerned with the effects of equity and the solidarity of the community. These concepts also concern those who support the public schools.

3. All of the respondents overwhelmingly supported the concept of freedom.
4. There was a large measure of diversity among the charter schools studied.
5. Parental involvement has long been a cornerstone of public school education in Alaska. The charter school legislation continued the emphasis on lay person representation in school governance.
6. Charter school proponents would benefit from an investigation of charter schools in other states to learn from their experiences.
7. Legislators, the Department of Education, and local school boards should become interested in the tendency for some charter schools to become elitist institutions.
8. Charter schools are public schools and all public schools are mandated to use the CAT-5 standardized test and the Alaska Direct Writing Assessment as their main accountability measures of student achievement. However, the findings of this study indicated a lack of crucial understanding as to the applicability of state mandated testing. Some charter schools used other forms of assessment including authentic assessment for student performance evaluations. Alaska public school operators should investigate the benefits of these alternative forms of assessment as part of the over-all assessment of their schools.
9. At the end of each charter school's contract, legislators, the Department of Education, local school boards, and educators should scrutinize the self-determined goals of the charter school and any research analysis to assess whether or not the programs brought about success of the goals and to see if they have any benefits to give to public schools in general.

Returning to a statement made earlier, the results of this project seem to confirm the finding that autonomy (freedom) " ... creates an accountability policy that is implausible in broader contexts and undercuts efforts to boost the external legitimacy of schools" (Macpherson, 1996, p. 88). This finding mirrors the statement made in the NCREL (1998) material:

> If there is to be freedom, then surely there must be accountability. For nearly a decade, Chicago schools have enjoyed a high degree of local autonomy. Unfortunately, as in many other large urban systems, this freedom did not result in greater student achievement. Indeed, by nearly all measures, student achievement in these systems has fallen to levels beyond the unacceptable. And yet, it has proven extremely difficult to bring these systems to task and to fundamentally change them.
>
> There are many who believe that what these systems lack is accountability, the real consequences that follow from actions. Competition is, of course, a form of accountability, but many who care deeply about the state of inner city education want more direct, controllable, and disciplined means to hold educators responsible. The accountability provided by charter schools is another beach-head in the battle to hold educators responsible for the quality of the education they deliver ....
>
> Greg Richmond, Deputy Assistant to the C.E.O. of the Chicago Public Schools, " ... while accountability is the core of this whole approach, there really wasn't the kind of high quality accountability processes in place to really be able to answer is this school really doing a good job?" (NCREL, 1998)

It was interesting to note that two systems archetypes provided some cautionary insight into the dangers of providing grant money for start-up charter school expenses. The system archetype, "Fixes That Fail" declared that money that was given to solve the problem of start-up expenses of charter schools rapidly led to unplanned after-effects that worsened the problem. The additional funding may, in the short run, take care of the problem of start-up expenses, but eventually the financial problems of the charter schools will come back to where they were before, or even be worse in the long-run (Archetype behavior pairs, 1994, p. 5). It will be interesting to watch if this theory is confirmed.

The system archetype "Growth and Underinvestment" asserts that when the growth of a charter school reaches its maximum potential it can only exceed that potential if investments in capacity are made. In other words, as the demand for the charter school's services increases, the school's operators attempt to take further action to increase the school's ability to meet the demand. This cycle is a reinforcing loop that the balancing loop of performance changes offsets. On the other hand, if a charter school attempts to expand beyond its current capacity, the operators make the compensatory effort of lowering its ideals. Of course charter school operators want to avoid this at all costs. When they lower the school's standards, the supporters of the school no longer see the need to make further investments in the school. Coupled with the lowering performance balancing loop, further investment in the school diminishes over time (Archetype behavior pairs, 1994, p. 5). When charter schools practice living beyond their means, systems thinking theory suggests they are contributing to their own dissolution.

Contemporaneous to systems thinking theory was chaos theory. What chaos theory told us about this phenomenon was that we may not immediately observe the dissolution of charter schools. However, when the forces of dissipation exceeded enthusiasm for founding charter schools, chaos emerged. The responsiveness of the regular public schools to the observable and measurable results of the positive student achievement of charter schools was one example of a force of dissipation. What forestalled the dissolution of the charter schools was the infusion of capacity building resources, such as the federal charter school grants, that were not justified by the system. Further discussion of the implications of chaos theory on the concept of the charter schools appears in Appendix L.

Recommendations

The benefit of studying Alaska's charter schools accrued from the identification of school reform measures, be they programmatic, curricular, pedagogic, or governance, for application to Alaska's public schools wishing to try successful practices. As a result, this researcher recommends that further charter school studies consider:
1. In this study, the researcher did not try to determine how much innovation was evident in Alaska's charter schools, but this issue is cardinal to the charter school concept and it justifies further scrutiny.
2. A study of the effects of charter schooling on student performance using not only standardized, norm-referenced test, but also a number of authentic assessments including performance-based examples of student work is needed.

3. Site-visits should be conducted to corroborate daily performance. At a minimum, a performance review team should be made up of charter school operators, business people, community members, parents, educators, and Department of Education personnel.
4. Research should dis-aggregate and study elementary charter schools, middle school charter schools, secondary charter schools, combined enrollment charter schools, charter schools that serve at-risk students, distance education charter schools, and cyber-charter schools.
5. Studies should be conducted to scrutinize the financial allocations of charter school funds to determine programmatic equity and adequacy as compared to how those funds are spent in the parent school district as a whole.
6. This project should be replicated in other states with charter school legislation.
7. Any study that purports to be a national study, in particular the Department of Education sponsored four-year National Study of Charter Schools, should collect data from a significant number of Alaska's charter schools.

"In *Charter Schools in Action*, authors Finn, Bruno, and Bierlein (1996) say they have not seen a single state with a thoughtful and well-formed plan for evaluating its charter school program" (Saks, 1997, p. 25). This researcher said earlier that Alaska's school accountability system was virtually non-existent and as a consequence had no accountability system for charter schools. Therefore, the researcher recommends looking to Massachusetts for some guidance. "Real accountability can be recognized by looking for three necessary elements: worthy objectives, credible measures of progress toward those objectives, and consequences (both rewards and penalties) based on performance (Hamilton, 1997b). The Massachusetts Department of Education believes that the answers to three cardinal questions can show the way to charter school accountability:

1. Is the academic program a success? An affirmative answer would be based on evidence that the school has made reasonable progress in meeting internally established goals over fours years, and that student performance significantly improved and/or is persistently strong on internal and external academic assessments.

2. Is the school a viable organization? Yes would mean that the school is financially solvent and stable, enrollment is stable and near capacity, school governance is sound, and professional staff are competent and resourceful.

3. Is the school faithful to the terms of its charter? If the school's program and operation are consistent with the terms of its charter, and if the school is within the bounds of essential statutory and regulatory requirements, then the answer will be yes. (Hamilton, 1997b)

Another consideration for further research is to compare achievement in a charter school with achievement in a control school that uses essentially the same processes under the same conditions.

It would also be interesting to see research on Alaska's charter schools' provision of services to children with disabilities. Specifically, what is their record of compliance with section 504 of the Rehabilitation Act of 1973 (29 U.S.C. 794); Individuals with Disabilities Education Act (29 U.S.C. 1401 et seq.); and the Americans with Disabilities Act (42 U.S.C. 12131 et seq.)?

It has been four years since Alaska's charter school law was enacted, but there has been no definitive study of academic progress. Therefore, an area for further study is the conditions that are perceived to lead to enhanced student achievement for those students who attend charter schools. What evidence is needed to indicate whether or not charter schools have been successful? Certainly a review of standardized test data would be called for.

The Alaska Board of Education's recent actions with regard to correspondence study programs' uniform "area cost differential" raised the question about independent study, cyber-schools, and charter schools. This was one area of charter school regulation that has spilled over into the regular correspondence study programs as well. The concerns have come about primarily because school districts, such as the Copper River School District, may have unintentionally discovered this omission as a way to generate greater revenues while minimizing their costs. Another concern comes about because of the lack of clear academic standards for such schools. A final concern came about because of the potential for religious materials to enter the public school arena. Commissioner Holloway's Numbered Memorandum 97-13 addressed this issue.

While not a focus of this study, the funding of cyber charter schools emerges as an issue for further research. It was also clear that there was little control over the performance and the monitoring of the results of these schools. On March 28, 1998, the Alaska Board of Education asked the Delta Cyber School to provide it with a status report. However, the Alaska Board of Education did not ask other cyber school operators to report on their status. It is suggested, then, that the legislature structure the centralized study option so that districts can have flexibility to meet the needs of students without reaping a windfall in funding. A good place to start exploring alternatives and attending to problems would be with a baseline study that would look at the status of centralized correspondence programs in every district and throughout the state.

The Alaska legislature, the Alaska Department of Education, and a research institute have not collected academic performance data on charter schools in Alaska. However, many charter schools stated that they made annual, or quarterly, reports to their local district. It is presumed that local school districts are collecting accountability data. Consequently, researchers may have to wait until the year 2001 when most charter school applications will be up for renewal to learn the individual test scores of the charter schools.

Summary

The debates over the success of charter schools have been around for a decade. They have evoked contrasting visions for education. Many participants in the educational community see evidence of a developing polarization and politicization of the issue of charter schools. Most charter school teachers work diligently in their classrooms which do not look anything like the schools that the zealous advocates on each side of the issue see. It seems that these advocates have set up the boundaries of their positions, in some cases even staking their reputations on them. On the other hand, the charter school teachers look on as the school districts, the parents, and the state escalate the arguments. The teachers see little research to inform them about the successes that can benefit the children in their classrooms.

Effective charter school founders and teachers know that there should be a balance between freedom and accountability. They are also aware that going to so far in one direction or the other may prove to be the undoing of the charter school idea. If the contentions are to serve a constructive purpose, they must provide a foundation for practical conversations and allied striving to take a look at and to use the research that is available. We must do this in ways that indicate that they will assist parents, teachers, and students improve student achievement.

Unfortunately, the prominent impression gained from many recent contributions to the pedestrian and non-refereed literature on charter schools is that their authors have dramatized their importance. Furthermore, they succeed in portraying themselves more as zealots than researchers, advancing conclusions supported mostly by data-free subjective assumptions or by information that has alternative interpretations. Consequently, when researchers gather and evaluate charter school information from the literature, they encounter a daunting task.

Appendix

Appendix A
Alaska's Charter School Law

TITLE 14 EDUCATION, LIBRARIES, AND MUSEUMS
CHAPTER 03 PUBLIC SCHOOLS GENERALLY
ARTICLE 02 CHARTER SCHOOLS
SECTION 14.03.250 Establishment of charter schools.

(a) A charter school may be established as provided under AS 14.03.250 - 14.03.290 upon the approval of the local school board and the Alaska Board of Education of an application for a charter school. The Alaska Board of Education may not approve more than 30 charter schools to operate in the state at any one time and shall approve charter schools in a geographically balanced manner as follows: not more than 10 schools in Anchorage; not more than five schools in Fairbanks; not more than three schools in the Matanuska-Susitna Borough; not more than three schools in the Kenai Peninsula Borough; not more than two schools in the City and Borough of Juneau; not more than seven schools located in other areas of the state, and these seven schools shall be allocated as nearly as possible in a geographically balanced manner throughout the rest of the state.

(b) A local school board shall prescribe an application procedure for the establishment of a charter school in that school district. The application procedure must include provisions for an academic policy committee consisting of parents of students attending the school, teachers, and school employees and a proposed form for a contract between a charter school and the local school board, setting out the contract elements required under AS 14.03.255(c).

(c) A local school board shall forward to the Alaska Board of Education applications for a charter school that have been approved or denied by the local board.

HISTORY
(Sec. 1 ch 77 SLA 1995)
POSTPONED REPEAL EFFECTIVE DATE.
Under Sec. 9, ch. 77, SLA 1995, this section is repealed July 1, 2005.
REVISORS NOTES.
Enacted as Sec. 1, ch. 77, SLA 1995 and codified in 1995, at which time "AS 14.03.250 - 14.03.290" was substituted for "this Act" in subsection (a), and "AS 14.03.255(c)" was substituted for "sec 2(c) of this Act" in subsection (c).

TITLE 14 EDUCATION, LIBRARIES, AND MUSEUMS
CHAPTER 03 PUBLIC SCHOOLS GENERALLY
ARTICLE 02 CHARTER SCHOOLS
SECTION 14.03.255 Organization and operation of a charter school.

(a) A charter school operates as a school in the local school district except that the charter school

    (1) is exempt from the local school district's textbook, program, curriculum, and scheduling requirements;

    (2) is exempt from AS 14.14.130(c); the principal of the charter school shall be selected by the academic policy committee and shall select, appoint, or otherwise supervise employees of the charter school; and

    (3) operates under the charter school's annual program budget as set out in the contract

between the local school board and the charter school under (c) of this section. A local school board may exempt a charter school from other local school district requirements if the exemption is set out in the contract.

(b) A charter school shall

(1) keep financial records of the charter school;

(2) oversee the operation of the charter school to ensure that the terms of the contract required by (c) of this section are being met;

(3) meet regularly with parents and with teachers of the charter school to review, evaluate, and improve operations of the charter school; and

(4) meet with the academic policy committee at least once each year to monitor progress in achieving the committee's policies and goals.

(c) A charter school shall operate under a contract between the charter school and the local school board. A contract must contain the following provisions:

(1) description of the educational program;

(2) specific levels of achievement for the education program;

(3) admission policies and procedures;

(4) administrative policies;

(5) statement of the charter school's funding allocation from the local school board and costs assignable to the charter school program budget;

(6) method by which the charter school will account for receipts and expenditures;

(7) location and description of the facility;

(8) name of the teacher, or teachers, who, by agreement between the charter school and the teacher, will teach in the charter school;

(9) teacher-to-student ratio;

(10) number of students served;

(11) the term of the contract, not to exceed a term of five years;

(12) a termination clause providing that the contract may be terminated by the local school board for the failure of the charter school to meet educational achievement goals or fiscal management standards, or for other good cause;

(13) a statement that the charter school will comply with all state and federal requirements for receipt and use of public money;

(14) other requirements or exemptions agreed upon by the charter school and the local school board.

(d) A charter school may be operated in an existing school district facility or in a facility within the school district that is not currently being used as a public school, if the chief school administrator determines the facility meets requirements for health and safety applicable to other public schools in the district.

HISTORY
(Sec. 2 ch 77 SLA 1995)
POSTPONED REPEAL EFFECTIVE DATE.
Under Sec. 9, ch. 77, SLA 1995, this section is repealed July 1, 2005.
REVISORS NOTES.
Enacted as Sec. 2, ch. 77, SLA 1995. Codified in 1995.
TITLE 14 EDUCATION, LIBRARIES, AND MUSEUMS
CHAPTER 03 PUBLIC SCHOOLS GENERALLY
ARTICLE 02 CHARTER SCHOOLS
SECTION 14.03.260 Funding for charter school.

(a) A local school board shall provide an approved charter school with an annual program budget. The budget shall be not less than the amount generated by the students enrolled in the charter school less administrative costs retained by the local school district, determined by applying the indirect cost rate approved by the Department of Education. The "amount generated by students enrolled in the charter school" is to be determined in the same manner as it would be for a student enrolled in another public school in that school district.

(b) The program budget of a charter school is to be used for operating expenses of the educational program of the charter school, including purchasing textbooks, classroom materials, and instructional aids.

(c) The charter school shall provide the financial and accounting information requested by the local school board or the Department of Education, and shall cooperate with the local school district or the department in complying with the requirements of AS 14.17.190.

HISTORY
(Sec. 3 ch 77 SLA 1995)
POSTPONED REPEAL EFFECTIVE DATE.
Under Sec. 9, ch. 77, SLA 1995, this section is repealed July 1, 2005.
REVISORS NOTES.
Enacted as Sec. 3, ch. 77, SLA 1995. Codified in 1995.
TITLE 14 EDUCATION, LIBRARIES, AND MUSEUMS
CHAPTER 03 PUBLIC SCHOOLS GENERALLY
ARTICLE 02 CHARTER SCHOOLS
SECTION 14.03.265 Admission.

(a) The program of a charter school may be designed to serve
  (1) students within an age group or grade level; or
  (2) students who will benefit from a particular teaching method or curriculum.

(b) A charter school shall enroll all eligible students who submit a timely application, unless the number of those applications exceeds the capacity of the program, class, grade level, or building. In the event of an excess of those applications, the charter school and the local school board shall attempt to accommodate all of those applicants by considering providing additional classroom space and assigning additional teachers from the district to the charter school. If it is not possible to accommodate all eligible students who submit a timely application, students shall be accepted by random drawing. A school board may not require a student to attend a charter school.

(c) In addition to other requirements of law, a charter school shall be nonsectarian.

HISTORY
(Sec. 4 ch 77 SLA 1995)
POSTPONED REPEAL EFFECTIVE DATE.
Under Sec. 9, ch. 77, SLA 1995, this section is repealed July 1, 2005.
REVISORS NOTES.
Enacted as Sec. 4, ch. 77, SLA 1995. Codified in 1995.
TITLE 14 EDUCATION, LIBRARIES, AND MUSEUMS
CHAPTER 03 PUBLIC SCHOOLS GENERALLY
ARTICLE 02 CHARTER SCHOOLS
SECTION 14.03.270 Teacher or employee transfers, evaluations, and negotiated agreements.

(a) A teacher or employee may not be assigned to a charter school unless the teacher or employee consents to the assignment.

(b) All provisions of an existing negotiated agreement or collective bargaining agreement applicable to a teacher or employee of a district apply to that teacher or employee if employed at a charter school in that district, unless the district and the bargaining unit representing the teacher or employee agree to an exemption.

(c) A teacher in a charter school shall be evaluated in an equivalent manner as all other teachers in the district, except that if there is no administrator assigned to the charter school, the local school board, with the agreement of the charter school, shall designate a school district administrator in that district to evaluate a teacher in a charter school.

HISTORY
(Sec. 5 ch 77 SLA 1995)
POSTPONED REPEAL EFFECTIVE DATE.
Under Sec. 9, ch. 77, SLA 1995, this section is repealed July 1, 2005.
REVISORS NOTES.
Enacted as Sec. 5, ch. 77, SLA 1995. Codified in 1995.
TITLE 14 EDUCATION, LIBRARIES, AND MUSEUMS
CHAPTER 03 PUBLIC SCHOOLS GENERALLY
ARTICLE 02 CHARTER SCHOOLS
SECTION 14.03.275 Contracts; duration.
A contract for a charter school may be for a term of no more than five years and may not extend beyond July 1, 2005.

HISTORY
(Sec. 6 ch 77 SLA 1995)
POSTPONED REPEAL EFFECTIVE DATE.
Under Sec. 9, ch. 77, SLA 1995, this section is repealed July 1, 2005.
REVISORS NOTES.
Enacted as Sec. 6, ch. 77, SLA 1995. Codified in 1995.
TITLE 14 EDUCATION, LIBRARIES, AND MUSEUMS
CHAPTER 03 PUBLIC SCHOOLS GENERALLY
ARTICLE 02 CHARTER SCHOOLS
SECTION 14.03.280 Regulations.
The state Board of Education may adopt regulations under AS 44.62
(Administrative Procedure Act) necessary to implement AS 14.03.250 -14.03.290.
HISTORY
(Sec. 7 ch 77 SLA 1995)
POSTPONED REPEAL EFFECTIVE DATE.
Under Sec. 9, ch. 77, SLA 1995, this section is repealed July 1, 2005.
REVISORS NOTES.
Enacted as Sec. 7, ch. 77, SLA 1995. Codified in 1995, at which time
AS 14.03.250 - 14.03.290" was substituted for "this Act."
TITLE 14 EDUCATION, LIBRARIES, AND MUSEUMS
CHAPTER 03 PUBLIC SCHOOLS GENERALLY
ARTICLE 02 CHARTER SCHOOLS
SECTION 14.03.290 Definitions.
In AS 14.03.250 - 14.03.290

(1) "academic policy committee" means the group designated to supervise the academic operation of a charter school and to ensure the fulfillment of the mission of a charter school;

(2) "charter school" means a school established under AS 14.03.250 - 14.03.290 that operates within a public school district;

(3) "local school board" means a borough or city school board or a school board of a regional educational attendance area;

(4) "parent" means a biological, adoptive, or foster parent, or an adult who acts as guardian of a child and makes decisions related to the child's safety, education, and welfare;

(5) "parent advisory group" means a group that is recognized by the school as representative of those parents having children attending that school, that has regular meetings, and in which membership is open to all parents within that school's attendance area;

(6) "teacher" means a person who serves a school district in a teaching, counseling, or administrative capacity and is required to be certificated in order to hold the position.

HISTORY
(Sec. 8 ch 77 SLA 1995)
POSTPONED REPEAL EFFECTIVE DATE.
Under Sec. 9, ch. 77, SLA 1995, this section is repealed July 1, 2005.
REVISORS NOTES.
Enacted as Sec. 8, ch. 77, SLA 1995. Codified in 1995, at which time "AS 14.03.250 - 14.03.290" was substituted for "this Act" in the introductory language and paragraph (2) to reflect the codification, and "school board of a regional educational attendance area" was substituted for "regional school board" in paragraph (3) to correct a manifest error in ch. 77, SLA 1995.

Appendix B
4 AAC 05.080
School Curriculum and Personnel

(a) The curriculum of a local school may be supplemented through the use of correspondence course materials approved by the commissioner.
This use is not grounds for shortening the day in session, as prescribed by AS 14.03.040, for any student.
(b) The governing body of a district shall employ, for each school, certificated teachers for the instruction of the pupils enrolled in it as necessary to provide the educational program described in the plan developed under 4 AAC 05.070(a).
(c) The governing body of a district may make provision for the employment of qualified residents of the community served by the school who hold an appropriate certificate (e.g., emergency or recognized expert) to teach particular skills or courses, and for the employment as teacher aides of qualified residents of the community served who do not hold an appropriate certificate.
(d) The governing body of a district shall adopt, in the manner required by AS 14.14.100(a), a curriculum which describes what will be taught students in grades kindergarten through 12. The curriculum must contain at least
    (1) a statement that the document is to be used as a guide for planning instructional strategies;
    (2) a statement of goals that the curriculum is designed to accomplish;
    (3) content which can reasonably be expected to accomplish the goals; and
    (4) a description of a means of evaluating the effectiveness of the curriculum.
(e) The governing body of a district shall provide for the systematic evaluation of its curriculum on an ongoing basis with each content area undergoing review at least once every six years. This requirement does not relieve a school district of the independent annual planning and evaluation requirement imposed by 4 AAC 05.070.
(f) The governing body of a district shall provide for the annual assessment of academic progress made by students in attendance in the district using a test, administered at appropriate grade levels, that is appropriate for the grade tested, and that is designed to assess student skill level or achievement in at least reading and mathematics. The test required by this subsection must be approved by the commissioner before it is administered for the first time.
(g) The governing body of a district shall ensure that each school provides the educational program described in the plan developed under 4 AAC 05.070(a) and the curriculum required by this section. (Eff. 9/3/76, Register 59; am 11/21/84, Register 92)
Authority:
    AS 14.07.020
    AS 14.07.060

Appendix C
4 AAC 06.075
High School Graduation Requirements

(a) Each chief school administrator shall develop and submit to the district board for approval a plan consisting of district high school graduation requirements. The plan must require that, before graduation, a student must have earned at least 21 units of credit.

(b) Specific subject area units-of-credit requirements must be set out in each district plan and must require that, before graduation, a student must have completed at least the following:

    (1) language arts - 4 units of credit;
    (2) social studies - 3 units of credit;
    (3) mathematics - 2 units of credit;
    (4) science - 2 units of credit;
    (5) health/physical education - 1 unit of credit.

(c) Repealed 2/11/89.

(d) Transfer students who have earned 13 units of credit while in attendance outside the district may, at the discretion of the district, be excused from the district subject area units-of-credit requirements.

(e) Repealed 2/11/89.

(f) As used in this section, "unit of credit" means the credit that a student is awarded for achieving a passing grade in a course of study consisting of at least 8,100 minutes of class time during the school term. (Eff. 3/1/78, Register 65; am 6/16/84, Register 90; am 3/24/85, Register 93; am 2/11/89, Register 109)

Authority:
AS 14.07.020
AS 14.07.060

Appendix D
Sec. 14.14.130
Chief School Administrator

(a) Each school board shall select and employ a qualified person as the chief school administrator for the district. In this subsection, "employ" includes employment by contract.

(b) The chief school administrator of the district shall administer the district in accordance with the policies which the school board prescribes by bylaw.

(c) The chief school administrator shall select, appoint, and otherwise control all school district employees that serve under the chief school administrator subject to the approval of the school board.

(d) This section does not prohibit two or more school districts from sharing the services of a chief school administrator.

HISTORY
(Sec. 1 ch 98 SLA 1966; am Sec. 1 ch 29 SLA 1969; am Sec. 3, 4 ch 136 SLA 1990)
AMENDMENT NOTES
The 1990 amendment added the second sentence in subsection (a) and added subsection (d).
DECISIONS
Applied in Skagway City School Bd. v. Davis, Sup. Ct. Op. No. 1216 (File No. 2265), 543 P.2d 218 (1975).

Quoted in Begich v. Jefferson, Sup. Ct. Op. No. 481 (File No. 894), 441 P.2d 27 (1968).

Appendix E
4 AAC 33.110
Alaska's Charter School Regulations

TITLE 04 EDUCATION
CHAPTER 33 SPECIAL PROGRAMS
ARTICLE 01 SPECIAL SCHOOLS
SECTION 4 AAC 33.110 CHARTER SCHOOLS.

(a) A local school board shall prescribe the application procedure described in AS 14.03.250(b) no later than June 30, 1996. The procedure must be in writing and must be available upon request at the local school board's central office.

(b) A local school board in Anchorage, Fairbanks, the Matanuska-Susitna Borough, the Kenai Peninsula Borough, or the City and Borough of Juneau may not approve an application for a charter school if operation of the charter school as proposed in the application would cause an allocation established in AS 14.03.250(a) to be exceeded.

(c) For purposes of allocating charter schools in the rural areas of the state, the following seven rural school district regions are established:

(1) region one, consisting of Annette Island School District, Craig City School District, Hydaburg City School District, Ketchikan Gateway Borough School District, Klawock City School District, and Southeast Island School District;

(2) region two, consisting of Chatham School District, Haines Borough School District, Hoonah City School District, Kake City School District, Pelican City School District, Petersburg City School District, Sitka Borough School District, Skagway City School District, Wrangell City School District, and Yakutat Borough School District;

(3) region three, consisting of Alaska Gateway School District, Chugach School District, Copper River School District, Cordova City School District, Delta-Greely School District, Denali Borough School District, Valdez City School District, and Yukon Flats School District;

(4) region four, consisting of Galena City School District, Nenana City School District, North Slope Borough School District, Northwest Arctic School District, Tanana City School District, and Yukon Koyukuk School District;

(5) region five, consisting of Bering Strait School District, Iditarod Area School District, Kashunamiut School District, Lower Yukon School District, Nome City School District, and St. Mary's City School District;

(6) region six, consisting of Dillingham City School District, Kuspuk School District, Lower Kuskokwim School District, Southwest Region School District, and Yupiit School District;

(7) region seven, consisting of Adak Regional School District, Aleutian Region School District, Aleutians East Borough School District, Bristol Bay Borough School District, Kodiak Island Borough School District, Lake and Peninsula Borough School District, Pribilof Island School District, and Unalaska City School District.

(d) Before July 1, 1997, the Board of Education will approve no more than one charter school application from each of the seven rural school district regions established in (c) of this section.

(e) On or after July 1, 1997, the Board of Education will approve a charter school application from a school district in the rural areas of the state if, in addition to the requirements in (i) of this section, the Board of Education determines that approval would meet the geographically balanced distribution required in AS 14.03.250(a).

(f) A local school board in the rural areas of the state may not approve an application for a charter school if operation of the charter school as proposed in the application would result in more than one charter school operating in the school district at any one time.

(g) No later than 20 working days after a local school board's decision to approve or deny an application for a charter school, the local school board shall mail the application and the decision to the commissioner.

(h) The Board of Education will review applications for charter schools in the order that they are received under (g) of this section.

(i) The Board of Education will approve an application for a charter school if the

(1) application has been approved by the local school board; and

(2) Board of Education, in its discretion, determines that the application and other information available to the Board of Education demonstrates that the local school board and the charter school have complied with, and will continue to comply with, state and federal laws and regulations, including the requirements of AS 14.03.250 - 14.03.290 and this section.

(j) In this section,

(1) "Board of Education" means the Alaska State Board of Education;

(2) "charter school" has the same meaning given that term in AS 14.03.290;

(3) "commissioner" means the commissioner of the Department of Education;

(4) "local school board" has the same meaning given that term in AS 14.03.290;

(5) "rural areas of the state" means those geographic areas of the state that are not in Anchorage, Fairbanks, the Matanuska-Susitna Borough, the Kenai Peninsula Borough, or the City and Borough of Juneau.

HISTORY

Eff. 4/27/96, Register 138

AUTHORITY.

AS 14.03.250

AS 14.03.290

AS 14.07.020

AS 14.07.060

Appendix F
Senate Bill 182

IN THE LEGISLATURE OF THE STATE OF Alaska
TWENTIETH LEGISLATURE–FIRST SESSION

BY SENATOR WARD
Introduced: 4/21/97
Referred: HESS, Finance

A BILL
FOR AN ACT ENTITLED
"An Act relating to the establishment and operation of charter schools."
BE IT ENACTED BY THE LEGISLATURE OF THE STATE OF Alaska:
Section 1. AS 14.03.250 is repealed and reenacted to read:
Sec. 14.03.250. Establishment of charter schools. A charter school may be established as provided under AS 14.03.250 - 14.03.290 when preliminary approval of application for the charter school has been given by
　(1) a local school board of the school district under AS 14.03.252 and final approval of the application has been given by the state Board of Education;
　(2) a local charter school board authorized by municipal ordinance under AS 29.35.160 (c) or 29.35.260 (c) and final approval of the application has been given by the state Board of Education; or
　(3) the state Board of Charter Schools under AS 14.03.252 and final approval of the application has been given by the state Board of Education; however, an application may not be submitted for preliminary approval under this paragraph unless
　　　(A) preliminary approval was denied when the application was first submitted for preliminary approval under AS 14.03.252 or under an ordinance enacted under the authority of AS 29.35.160 (c) or 29.35.260 (e), as appropriate; or
　　　(B) an ordinance establishing a local charter school board has not been enacted under AS 29.35.160 (c) or 29.35260 (e), as appropriate, in the district in which the charter school is to be located.
Sec. 2. AS 14.03 is amended by adding new sections to read:
Sec. 14.03.252. Preliminary approval by local school board. (a) Preliminary approval of a charter school may be given by a local school board.
　(a) A local school board shall prescribe an application procedure for the establishment of a charter school in that school district. The application procedure must include provisions for an academic policy committee consisting of parents of students attending the school, teachers, and school employees and a proposed form for a contract between a charter school and the local school board, setting out the contract elements required under AS 14.03.255 (c).
　(b) A local school board shall forward to the state Board of Education an application for a charter school that has been
　　(1) given preliminary approval by the local school board; or
　　(2) denied preliminary approval by the local school board if the applicant appeals the denial under AS 14.03.254 (a) (1).

New Text Underlined [DELETED TEXT BRACKETED]

(c) When a charter school application is denied under (c) (2) of this section, the reasons for the denial must be set out in writing and specifically identify the reason for the denial.

Sec. 14.03.252. State Board of Charter Schools; preliminary approval of charter schools by board. (a) There is established in the Department of Education the state Board of Charter Schools. The charter school board consists of seven members. The member of the charter school board shall be appointed by the governor from a list of persons nominated by chief school administrators of all charter schools in operation at the time of the making of the appointment and are subject to confirmation by the legislature under AS 39.05.070 - 39.05.200. The charter school board shall annually elect from its members a chair and vice-chair.

(b) Board members appointed under (a) of this section serve three-year terms.

(c) Board members appointed under (a) of this section are entitled to per diem and travel expenses authorized for boards and commissions under AS 39.20.180.

(d) Board members appointed under (a) of this section shall be appointed with due regard to their demonstrated interest in advocating diversity and improvement in the quality of public education.

(e) The charter school board shall consider applications for preliminary approval of charter schools submitted by applicants whose charter school applications have been denied preliminary approval under AS 14.03.252 or under an ordinance enacted under the authority of AS 29.35.160 (c) or 29.35.260 (e), as appropriate, or that are presented to it when an ordinance establishing a local charter school board has not been enacted in AS 29.35.160 (c) or 29.35.260 (e), as appropriate, in the district in which the charter school is to be located. Preliminary approval of a charter school may be given only by a majority of the members of the charter school board.

(f) The charter school board shall prescribe an application procedure for the establishment of a charter school. The application must include the elements specified in AS 14.03.252 (b) except that the proposed form of the contract shall be between the charter school and the charter school board.

(g) When a charter school application is denied under this section, the reasons for the denial must be set out in writing and specifically identify the reasons for the denial.

(h) The charter school board shall forward to the state Board of Education an application for a charter school that has been

(1) given preliminary approval by the charter school board; or

(2) denied preliminary approval and the applicant appeals the denial under AS 14.03.254 (b).

(i) The charter school board may conduct meetings by telephone, by teleconference, or by video conference.

Sec. 14.03.254. Action on denials. (a) If an application for a charter school is denied under AS 14.03.252 or under an ordinance enacted under authority of AS 29.35.160 (c) or 29.35.260 (e), the applicant may

(1) appeal the denial to the state Board of Education under procedures established by the state Board of Education by regulation; or

(2) amend its application and submit the amended application to the state Board of Charter Schools.

(b) If an application for a charter school is denied under AS 14.03.252, the applicant may appeal the denial to the state Board of Education under procedures established by the state Board of Education by regulation.

*Sec. 3. AS 14.03.255 (a) is amended to read:

(a) A charter school operates as a school in the local district in which it is located. However,

(1) [EXCEPT THAT] the charter school [(1)] is exempt from the local school district's textbook, program, curriculum, and scheduling requirements;

(2) the charter school is exempt from AS 14.14.130 (c); the chief school administrator [PRINCIPAL] of the charter school shall be selected by the academic policy committee and shall select, appoint, or otherwise supervise employees of the charter school; [AND]

(3) the charter school operates under the charter school's annual program budget as set out in the contract [BETWEEN THE LOCAL SCHOOL BOARD AND THE CHARTER SCHOOL] under (c) of this section;

(4) when the charter school operates under a contract with a local school board, the [. A] local school board may exempt the [A] charter school from other local school district requirements if the exemptions is set out in the contract; and

New Text Underlined [DELETED TEXT BRACKETED]

(5) if there is a conflict between a provision of AS 14.03.250-14.03.290 or a charter school contract and a provision of another requirement of this title relating to a public elementary or secondary school, the provision of AS 14.03.250 - 14.03.290 or the charter school contract prevails.

***Sec. 4. AS 14.03.255** (c) is amended to read:

(b) A charter school shall operate under a contract between the charter school and the local school board, the state charter school board, or the municipality, as appropriate. A contract must contain the following provisions:

(1) description of the charter school's mission, philosophy, and educational program; if the charter school's mission, philosophy, or educational program is modeled after one or more existing schools, the description must include reference to the schools and their philosophies;

(2) [SPECIFIC LEVELS OF ACHIEVEMENT] for the education program,

(A) specific goals for the education of students at each grade level, and the expected levels of achievement at each grade level; and

(B) the tests or methods of assessment to be applied to determine students' performance when compared to the goals for the education of the students at each grade level;

(3) admission policies and procedures;

(4) administrative policies;

(5) statement of the charter school's funding allocation from the local school board and costs assignable to the charter school program budget;

(6) method by which the charter school will account for receipts and expenditures;

(7) location and description of the facility;

(8) name of the teacher, or teachers, who, by agreement between the charter school and the teacher, will teach in the charter school;

(9) teacher-to-student ratio;

(10) number of students served;

(11) the term of the contract, not to exceed a term of five years;

(12) a termination clause providing that the contract may be terminated by the local school board, the state charter school board, or the municipality for the failure of the charter school to meet educational achievement goals or fiscal management standards, or for other good cause;

(13) a statement that the charter school will comply with all state and federal requirements for receipt and use of public money

(14) other requirements or exemptions agreed upon by the charter school and the local school board, the state charter school board, or the municipality.

***Sec. 5. AS 14.03.255** is amended by adding new subsections to read:

(e) In a contract entered into under (c) of this section, the local school board, the state charter school board, or the municipality, as appropriate, may not require the chief school administrator of the charter school to hold a valid administrative certificate with sufficient endorsements for the person to qualify as an administrator under a regulation adopted under authority of AS 14.07.060 and AS 14.20.020.

(f) In a contract entered into under (c) of this section, a teacher employed in the school shall hold a valid teaching certificate under AS 14.20.010-14.20.040, but the local school board, the state charter school board, or the municipality, as appropriate, may not otherwise limit the chief school administrator of the charter school in the hire of any person who holds a valid teaching certificate.

***Sec. 6. AS 14.03.265** (b) is amended to read:

(b) A charter school shall enroll all eligible students strictly in accordance with the order of their application. If [WHO SUBMIT A TIMELY APPLICATION, UNLESS] the number of [THOSE] applications exceeds the capacity of the program, class, grade level, or building [. IN THE EVENT OF AN EXCESS OF THOSE APPLICATIONS]. the charter school and the local school board shall attempt to accommodate all [OF THOSE] applicants by considering providing additional classroom space. However, if [AND ASSIGNING ADDITIONAL TEACHERS FROM THE DISTRICT TO THE CHARTER SCHOOL. IF] it is not possible to accommodate all eligible students who submit an [A TIMELY] application by providing additional classroom space, the [,] students shall be accepted strictly in accordance with the order of their application, as the capacity of the charter school permits [BY RANDOM DRAWING]. A school board may not require a student to attend a charter school.

New Text Underlined [DELETED TEXT BRACKETED]

Sec. 7. AS 14.03.270 (b) is amended to read:
(b) All provisions of an existing negotiated agreement or collective bargaining agreement applicable to a teacher or employee of a district apply to that teacher or employee if employed at a charter school in that district, unless exception is otherwise explicitly provided in AS 14.03.250 - 14.03.290 or unless [THE DISTRICT AND] the bargaining unit representing the teacher or employee agrees [AGREE] to an exemption.

Sec. 8. AS 14.03.275 is amended to read:
Sec. 14.03.275 Contracts; duration. A contract for a charter school may be for a term of no more than five years and may not be extended beyond July 1, 2015 [2005].

Sec. 9. AS 14.03.275 is amended to read:
(b) If, at the end of the five-year term, a charter school has met or exceeded specific levels of achievement for its educational program set out in the contract entered into under A 14.03.255, the contract shall be extended for an additional five-year period between the parties to the original contract.

Sec. 10. AS 14.03.280 is amended to read:
Sec. 14.03.280 Regulations. The state Board of Education may adopt regulations under AS 44.62 (Administrative Procedure Act) necessary to implement AS 14.03.250 - 14.03.290. The regulations may not limit the number of charter schools that may operate within the state.

Sec. 11. AS 14.03.290 (6) is amended to read:
(6) "teacher" means a person who is employed in [SERVES] a school district in a [TEACHING, COUNSELING, OR ADMINISTRATIE] capacity for which the person has primary responsibility to plan, instruct, and evaluate learning of elementary or secondary school students in the classroom or an equivalent setting, for which a valid teacher certificate is required by AS 14.20.010 or for which a limited certificate may be issued under AS 14.20.025 [AND IS REQUIRED TO BE CERTIFICATED IN ORDER TO HOLD THE POSITION].

Sec. 12. AS 14.03.290 is amended by adding a new paragraph to read:
(7) "charter school board" means the state Board of Charter Schools established under AS 14.03.253.

Sec. 13. AS 29.35.160 is amended by adding a new subsection to read:
(c) A borough that constitutes a borough school district may, by ordinance, provide for preliminary approval of charter schools through a borough charter school board. The ordinance approved under this subsection must impose on the borough charter school board the same requirements imposed on a local school board under AS 14.03.252 (b) - (d) except that the proposed form of the contract shall be between the charter school and the borough assembly.

Sec. 14. AS 29.35.260 is amended by adding a new subsection to read:
A city that constitutes a city school district may, by ordinance, provide for preliminary approval of charter schools through a city charter school board. The ordinance approved under this subsection must impose on the city charter school board the same requirements imposed on a local school board under AS 14.03.252 (b) - (d) except that the proposed form of the contract shall be between the charter school and the city council.

Sec. 15. Section 9, ch 77, SLA 1995, is repealed.

Sec. 16. AS 14.03.250, 14.03.252, 14.03.253, 14.03.254, 14.03.255, 14.03.260, 14.03.265, 14.03.270, 14.03.275, 14.03.280, 14.03.290, AS 29.35.160 (c), and **29.35.260** (e) are repealed July 1, 2105.

Sec. 17. APPOINTMENT OF INITIAL MEMBERS OF STATE BOARD OF CHARTER SCHOOLS. (a) The governor shall appoint the first members of the state Board of Charter Schools under AS 14.03.253 as follows:
(1) two members shall be appointed for one-year terms;
(2) two members shall be appointed for two-year terms;
(3) three members shall be appointed for three-year terms;

(b) The governor shall make appointments required by AS 14.03.253 and (s) of this section within 30 days of the effective date of this Act.

(c) Notwithstanding AS 14.03.253 (a), in making appointments under this section, the governor is not required to select appointees from a list of persons nominated by the chief school administrators of all charter schools in operation on the effective date of this Act, but the members appointed are subject to legislative confirmation under AS 39.05.070 - 39.05.200.

New Text Underlined [DELETED TEXT BRACKETED]

Appendix G
Sec. 14.30.010
When Attendance Compulsory

TITLE 14 EDUCATION, LIBRARIES, AND MUSEUMS
CHAPTER 30 PUPILS AND EDUCATIONAL PROGRAMS FOR PUPILS
ARTICLE 01 COMPULSORY EDUCATION
SECTION 14.30.010 When attendance compulsory.

(a) Every child between seven and 16 years of age shall attend school at the public school in the district in which the child resides during each school term. Every parent, guardian or other person having the responsibility for or control of a child between seven and 16 years of age shall maintain the child in attendance at a public school in the district in which the child resides during the entire school term, except as provided in (b) of this section.

(b) This section does not apply if a child

(1) is provided an academic education comparable to that offered by the public schools in the area, either by

(A) attendance at a private school in which the teachers are certificated according to AS 14.20.020;

(B) tutoring by personnel certificated according to AS 14.20.020; or

(C) attendance at an educational program operated in compliance with AS 14.45.100 - 14.45.200 by a religious or other private school;

(2) attends a school operated by the federal government;

(3) has a physical or mental condition that a competent medical authority determines will make attendance impractical;

(4) is in the custody of a court or law enforcement authorities;

(5) is temporarily ill or injured;

(6) has been suspended or denied admittance according to AS 14.30.045;

(7) resides more than two miles from either a public school or a route on which transportation is provided by the school authorities, except that this subsection does not apply if the child resides within two miles of a federal or private school that the child is eligible and able to attend;

(8) is excused by action of the school board of the district at a regular meeting or by the district Superintendent subject to approval by the school board of the district at the next regular meeting;

(9) has completed the 12th grade;

(10) is enrolled in

(A) the state boarding school established under AS 14.16; or

(B) a full-time program of correspondence study approved by the department; in those school districts providing an approved correspondence study program, a student may be enrolled either in the district correspondence program or in the centralized correspondence study program;

(11) is equally well-served by an educational experience approved by the school board as serving the child's educational interests despite an absence from school, the request for excuse is made in writing by the child's parents or guardian, and approved by the principal or administrator of the school that the child attends.

HISTORY

(Sec. 37-7-1 ACLA 1949; am Sec. 36 ch 98 SLA 1966; am Sec. 5 ch 71 SLA 1972; am Sec. 5 ch 190 SLA 1975; am Sec. 1 ch 30 SLA 1976; am Sec. 1 ch 10 SLA 1977; am Sec. 4 ch 126 SLA 1978; am Sec. 3 ch 11 SLA 1984; am Sec. 1 ch 78 SLA 1987; am Sec. 4 ch 73 SLA 1988)

NOTES TO DECISIONS

Quoted in L.A.M. v. State, 547 P.2d 827 (Alaska 1976).

Stated in In re S.D., 549 P.2d 1190 (Alaska 1976).

Cited in Matthews v. Quinton, 362 P.2d 932 (Alaska 1961); D.R.C. v. State, 646 P.2d 252 (Alaska Ct. App. 1982).

COLLATERAL REFERENCES.

Religious beliefs of parents as defense to prosecution for failure to comply with compulsory attendance law. 3 ALR2d 1401.

Applicability of compulsory attendance law covering children of a specified age, with respect to a child who has passed the anniversary date of such age. 73 ALR2d 874.

Power of public school authorities to set minimum or maximum age requirements for pupils in absence of specific statutory authority. 78 ALR2d 1021.

Residence for purpose of admission to public school. 83 ALR2d 497; 56 ALR3d 641.

What constitutes a private, parochial, or denominational school within statute making attendance at such school a compliance with compulsory school attendance law. 65 ALR3d 1222.

NOTES TO ARTICLE

Collateral References.- 68 Am. Jur. 2d Schools, Sec. 216 et seq.

78A C.J.S. Schools and School Districts, Sec. 734-739.

Teacher's civil liability for administering corporal punishment. 43 ALR2d 469.

Regulations as to fraternities and similar associations connected with educational institution. 10 ALR3d 389.

Student organization registration statement, filed with public school or state university or college, as open to inspection by public. 37 ALR3d 1311.

What constitutes a private, parochial, or denominational school within statute making attendant at such school a compliance with compulsory school attendance law. 65 ALR3d 1222.

Student's right to compel school officials to issue degree, diploma, or the like. 11 ALR4th 1182.

TITLE 14 EDUCATION, LIBRARIES, AND MUSEUMS
CHAPTER 30 PUPILS AND EDUCATIONAL PROGRAMS FOR PUPILS
ARTICLE 01 COMPULSORY EDUCATION
SECTION 14.30.020 Violations.

A person who knowingly fails to comply with AS 14.30.010 is guilty of a violation. Each five days of unlawful absence under AS 14.30.010 is a separate violation.

HISTORY

(Sec. 37-7-2 ACLA 1949; am Sec. 37 ch 98 SLA 1966; am Sec. 2 ch 78 SLA 1987)

CROSS REFERENCES.

For fines for violations, see AS 12.55.035.

TITLE 14 EDUCATION, LIBRARIES, AND MUSEUMS
CHAPTER 30 PUPILS AND EDUCATIONAL PROGRAMS FOR PUPILS
ARTICLE 01 COMPULSORY EDUCATION
SECTION 14.30.030 Prevention and reduction of truancy.

The governing body of a school district, including a regional educational attendance area, shall establish procedures to prevent and reduce truancy.

HISTORY

(Sec. 37-7-3 ACLA 1949; am Sec. 1 ch 32 SLA 1949; am Sec. 38 ch 98 SLA 1966; am Sec. 55 ch 6 SLA 1984; am Sec. 23 ch 85 SLA 1988; am Sec. 3 ch 59 SLA 1996)

EFFECT OF AMENDMENTS.

The 1996 amendment, effective September 10, 1996, rewrote this section.

Appendix H
Standards for Evaluating State Assessment Systems

Standard 1: Assessment supports important student learning.
   1.1. Assessments are based on and aligned with standards.
   1.2. Multiple-choice and very-short-answer (e.g. "gridded-in") items are a limited part of the assessments; and assessments employ multiple methods, including those that allow students to demonstrate understanding by applying knowledge and constructing responses.
   1.3. Assessments designed to rank order, such as norm-referenced tests (NRT), are not used or are not a significant part of the assessment system.
   1.4. The test burden is not too heavy in any one grade or across the system.
   1.5. High stakes decisions, such as high school graduation for students or probation for schools, are not made on the basis of any single assessment.
   1.6. Sampling is employed to gather program information.
   1.7. The evaluation of work done over time, e.g. portfolios, is a major component of accountability and public reporting data.
   1.8. Students are provided an opportunity to comment on or evaluate the instruction they receive and their own learning.
   1.9. Appropriate contextual information is gathered and reported with assessment data.

Standard 2: Assessments are fair.
   2.1. States have implemented comprehensive bias review procedures.
   2.2. Assessment results should be reported both for all students together and with disaggregated data for sub-populations.
   2.3. Adequate and appropriate accommodations and adaptations are provided for students with Individual Education Plans (OEP).
   2.4. Adequate and appropriate accommodations and adaptations, including translations or developing assessments in languages other than English, are available for students with limited English proficiency (LEP).
   2.5. Multiple methods of assessment are provided to students to meet needs based on different learning styles and cultural backgrounds.
   2.6. Students are provided an adequate opportunity to learn about the assessment.

Standard 3: Professional development
   3.1. States have requirements for beginning teachers and administrators to be knowledgeable about assessment, including appropriate classroom practices.
   3.2. States provide sufficient professional development in assessment, including classroom assessment.
   3.3. States survey educators about their professional development needs in assessment and evaluate their competence in assessment.
   3.4. Teachers and other educators are involved in designing, writing and scoring assessments.

Standard 4: Public education, reporting, and parents' rights.

4.1. Parents and community members are educated about the kinds of assessments used and the meaning and interpretation of assessment results.

4.2. The state surveys parents/public to determine information they want on assessments and whether assessment reports are understandable.

4.3. Reports should be available in languages other than English if a sizable number or significant percentage of the student population come from homes where another language is commonly used.

4.4. Parents and/or students have the right to examine assessments, appeal assessment scores, or challenge flawed items.

Standard 5: System review and improvement.

5.1. The assessment system is regularly reviewed.

5.2. The review includes participation by various stakeholders and evaluation by independent experts.

5.3. The review studies how well the system actually is aligned to standards.

5.4. The review studies the impact of the assessment(s) on curriculum and instruction.

5.5. The review studies whether assessments assess critical thinking or the ability to engage in cognitively complex work within a subject.

5.6. Reviews for assessments in grade 3 or below study whether the assessments are developmentally appropriate.

5.7. Reviews study the impact of assessment programs on student progress and particularly the impact of any high stakes tests, such as high school exit exams, on graduation rates.

5.8. Reviews study the technical quality of assessments.

5.9. The state reviews local assessment practices.

5.10. Reviews help guide improvements in the assessment system that will bring the program more in line with the *Principles and Indicators for Student Assessment Systems*.[30] (Neill, 1997, p. 30-31)

Appendix I
Alaska Charter Schools' Principals/Lead Teachers' Questionnaire

A. Hello, my name is _____ and I am calling on behalf of the Alaska Charter School Study.

B. May I please speak to (NAME/THE PRINCIPAL) or (NAME/LEAD TEACHER) or the person who is most knowledgeable about the school and its history?

When correct person is on the phone, repeat A and then:

C. This telephone survey is one part of a study of charter schools in Alaska. The purpose of the study is to examine how each charter school came about and how these schools differ from other public schools regarding goals, expectations, curricula, teacher qualifications, methods of assessing achievement, and the students these schools serve. Once completed, the Alaska Charter School Study will send you the Executive Summary from this survey's findings, including the information you provide about your charter school during this telephone survey. The survey will take approximately 40 minutes to complete. Would now be a good time to complete this survey?

1. Continue **(GO TO D)**   2. Make appointment for callback

If okay to continue:

D. We appreciate your time. Your answers will be combined with all other respondents so you can't be identified in any way. If there are questions you do not care to answer we can skip over them.

Before we begin, I need to ask a few questions for background purposes.

Q1	Are you the school administrator?	YES _____ NO _____ REFUSED _____
Q2	What is your position at the school? _____	
Q3	For this survey, we are only concerned with charter schools. Has your charter been granted?	Yes, charter granted **(GO TO Q.4)** _____ No, not granted a charter **(ASK Q.5)** _____
Q4	When was your charter granted?	MONTH _____ YEAR _____

189

Alaska's Charter Schools

	DON'T KNOW	____
	REFUSED	____

IF NOT GRANTED, ASK:
Q5 What was the reason your charter was not granted?
_____
_____

THANK RESPONDENT AND EXIT INTERVIEW BY SAYING: For this survey, we are interviewing administrators of charter schools in operation. We will include you in our next survey if you are offering instruction by then. Thank you for your time.

Q6 Is your charter school a newly created school or was it a preeexisting school?
IF NECESSARY, Don't know ____
SAY: "Pre-existing" means the   Refused ____
charter school was originally all
or part of a public or a private
school.

IF RESPONDED "PRE-EXISTING" SCHOOL, ASK:

Q7	Was the previous school a public or a private school?	Public	____
		Private	____
		Don't know	____
Q8	Have you started providing instruction to students under your charter?	Yes	____
		No	____
		Don't know	____
Q9	When did you start providing instruction?	MONTH	____
		YEAR	____

IF DON'T KNOW: You have been very helpful thus far, but we may need to speak to someone else at your school to effectively complete this project, because the survey asks a lot of detailed questions. Is there someone else we could speak with who might know more about the history and details of your charter school? **(IF NOT SPEAKING TO THE SCHOOL ADMINISTRATOR SAY:** The school administration may be the best person – is she/he available to respond to this survey?) **OBTAIN NAME AND PHONE NUMBER OF OTHER PERSON AND TERMINATE INTERVIEW.**

IF NO GO TO Q.10:

Q10	When do you plan to begin instruction as a charter school?	MONTH	____
		YEAR	____
		DON'T KNOW	____

THANK RESPONDENT AND EXIT INTERVIEW BY SAYING: For this survey, we are interviewing administrators of charter schools in operation. We will include you in any future surveys, if you are offering instruction in the future. Thank you for your time,
IF YES:

Q11	How would you describe the community(ies) in which your school instruction takes place? Would you describe it as urban, suburban, rural, or small town?	Urban	____
		Suburban	____
		Rural	____
		Small Town	____
		Don't know	____
Q12	Does your charter school <u>primarily</u>	Yes	____

provide either independent study or home-based learning?	No	____
	Don't know	____

IF DON'T KNOW: You have been very helpful thus far, but we may need to speak to someone else at your school to effectively complete this project, because the survey asks a lot of detailed questions. Is there someone else we could speak with who might know more about the history and details of your charter school? (**IF NOT SPEAKING TO THE SCHOOL ADMINISTRATOR, SAY**: The school administrator may be the best person - is she/he available to respond to this survey?) **OBTAIN NAME AND PHONE NUMBER OF OTHER PERSON AND TERMINATE INTERVIEW.**

IF YES TO Q. 13:
FOR INDEPENDENT STUDY/HOME SCHOOLS ONLY: (ALL OTHERS SKIP TO Q. 17)

Q13	At what location(s) are students instructed?	At student's home	____
		Both at student's home and at school site	____
		Other	____
		Don't know	____

Q14   If students are instructed at some other location, PLEASE SPECIFY:
_____

IF DON'T KNOW: You have been very helpful thus far, but we may need to speak to someone else at your school to effectively complete this project, because the survey asks a lot of detailed questions. Is there someone else we could speak with who might know more about the history and details of your charter school? (**IF NOT SPEAKING TO THE SCHOOL ADMINISTRATOR, SAY:** The school administrator may be the best person - is she/he available to respond to this survey?) **OBTAIN NAME AND PHONE NUMBER OF OTHER PERSON AND TERMINATE THE INTERVIEW.**

Q15	Do you have a common curriculum and assessment system in place for all students or does curriculum and assessment vary from student to student?	Same for all students	____
		Varies student to student	____
		Don't know	____

Q16   Other (Please specify)
_____
_____

Q17   What were the principal reasons for founding your charter school? What other reasons were there? Anything else? (**PROBE FULLY**) (**RECORD EACH REASON INDIVIDUALLY**)

_____
_____
_____
_____
_____
_____
_____

Q18   Of all the ones you've mentioned, which one was the most important reason for founding your charter school?

_____
_____

Alaska's Charter Schools

Q19 Has your charter enabled you to depart from any existing state laws or regulations?

Yes ____
No ____
Don't know ____

IF YES, ASK:

Q20 Which ones have been the MOST important to the operation of your school?

_____
_____

Q21 Before your charter school opened, did you receive any of the following kinds of external support in <u>planning</u> your charter school? "Planning" costs should not include start-up costs. For <u>planning purposes only</u>, did you receive:......(**READ EACH**)

	Yes	No	Don't know
Monetary support such as loans, grants, donations, etc.	____	____	____
Paid technical assistance	____	____	____
In-kind expertise or technical assistance	____	____	____
Other in-kind support (such as release time, loan or donation of equipment)	____	____	____
Staff training	____	____	____
Did you receive any other type of support for planning?	____	____	____

Q22 Please specify the other type of support you received

_____

IF YES TO PAID TECHNICAL ASSISTANCE OR IN-KIND EXPERTISE, ASK:

Q23 Was the technical assistance you received....

	Yes	No	Don't know
Advice relating to legal matters?	____	____	____
Advice relating to business operations?	____	____	____
Advice relating to organizational matters?	____	____	____
Advice relating to curricula and instructional issues?	____	____	____

IF ANY YES IN Q.23, ASK:

Q24 Who provided these types of support? Did you receive <u>planning</u> support of some kind from: (**READ EACH AND RECORD AS MANY AS APPLY**)

	Yes	No	Don't know
University or college	____	____	____
School district	____	____	____
Foundation	____	____	____
Business or private company	____	____	____
Community agency	____	____	____
Government agency	____	____	____
Parents or community members	____	____	____
Did you receive planning support of some kind from anyone else?	____	____	____

Q25 Please specify the source of the planning support

_____

Q26 Since your charter school has opened, have you received any of the following kinds of external support? Did you receive (**ITEM**) after your school opened? (**READ EACH**)

	Yes	No	Don't know
Monetary support such as loans, grants, donations, etc.	____	____	____
Paid technical assistance	____	____	____
In-kind expertise or technical assistance	____	____	____
Other in-kind support (such as release time, loan or donation of equipment)	____	____	____
Staff training	____	____	____
Did you receive any other type of support?	____	____	____

Q27 If your school received any other type of support, PLEASE SPECIFY:
_____

IF YES TO PAID TECHNICAL ASSISTANCE OR IN-KIND EXPERTISE (in Q.26), ASK:

Q28 Was the technical assistance you received after your school opened...

	Yes	No	Don't know
Advice relating to legal matters?	____	____	____
Advice relating to business operations?	____	____	____
Advice relating to organizational matters?	____	____	____
Advice relating to curricula and instructional issues?	____	____	____

I'd now like to ask about your paid staff. For each of the following job categories, please estimate the number of full-time equivalent (FTE) staff in these positions. We need an unduplicated count of the staff at your school. If staff members are part-time or split their time between two categories, please give the proportion of time, to the nearest tenth, devoted to each category. I will begin by reading the whole list of the categories, divided by the instructional and non-instructional staff, and then we can go back to record your responses. The categories are: (LIST)

Q29 INSTRUCTIONAL STAFF   FULL-TIME EQUIVALENT
Certified classroom teachers   _____
Non-certified classroom teachers   _____
Resource teachers   _____
Classroom aides   _____
Certified special education teachers _____
Special education aides   _____
Other instructional staff?   _____

Q30 Please specify the types of other instructional staff
_____
_____

Q31 NON-INSTRUCTIONAL STAFF   FULL-TIME EQUIVALENT
Administrative staff   _____
Parent liaisons, attendance coordinators, or home-school coordinators   _____
Social workers, counselors, or psychologists   _____
Librarian(s)   _____
Curriculum coordinator   _____
Other non-instructional staff?   _____

Q32 Please specify the types of other non-instructional staff
_____
_____

ADD UP TOTAL AND VERIFY BY ASKING:
That totals _____ full-time equivalent staff in your school, _____ instructional staff and _____ non-instructional staff.

Q33 Is that correct?   Yes ____
                                                   No   ____

If "NO" repeat Q.29 & Q.31. IF DOES NOT ADD SECOND TIME, GO TO Q.34.

Q34 Since the information does not seem to add, we can obtain this later, rather than spending time on the phone now to correct this. If you need to consult records or someone else at your school to complete this question, I can arrange to have a paper version of the question mailed (or faxed) to you after the interview. You can return it either by mail or by fax.

                                                   Mail/fax   ____
                                                   Not mail/fax ____

Q35 What grades or grade equivalents does your charter school serve?

Pre-school	____	Grade 7	____
Kindergarten	____	Grade 8	____
Grade 1	____	Grade 9	____
Grade 2	____	Grade 10	____
Grade 3	____	Grade 11	____
Grade 4	____	Grade 12	____
Grade 5	____	Ungraded	____
Grade 6	____	Other	____

Q36 IF OTHER/UNGRADED, PLEASE SPECIFY:
_____

Q37 IF OTHER/UNGRADED, what ages does your charter school serve?
_____

Q38 What is your current total student enrollment? **IF NECESSARY, SAY:** "Current" or "currently" always means the most recent date of data collection.
_____

Q39 What is the ethnic/racial composition of your student body, using the following census categories? How many are...IF NECESSARY, SAY: "Hispanic" includes Mexican, Puerto Rican, Cuban, Central or South American, or other Hispanic culture or origin. "Alaska Native" includes Aleut, Alaska Indian (Athabascan), Yupik Eskimo, and Inupiat Eskimo. "Asian or Pacific Islander" includes Japanese, Chinese, Filipino, Korean, Asian Indian, Vietnamese, Hawaiian, Guamanian, Samoan, and other Asian

White, but not of Hispanic origin	_____
Black, but not of Hispanic origin	_____
Hispanic	_____
Asian or Pacific Islander	_____
American Indian or Alaska Native	_____
DO NOT READ: Other	_____

IF OTHER:
Q40 Please specify and give the number
_____

IF DON'T KNOW, ASK:
Q41 If you need to consult records or someone else at your school to complete this question, I can arrange to have a paper version of the question mailed (or faxed) to you after the interview. You can return it either by mail or by fax.

Mail/fax	_____
Not mail/fax	_____

Q42 How many students are...

Male	_____
Female	_____

Q43 Does your school participate in the National School Lunch Program?

Yes	_____
No	_____
Don't know	_____

Q44 Regardless of the school's participation in the National School Lunch program, are there any students in the school eligible for free or reduced-price lunch?

Yes	_____
No	_____
Don't know	_____

IF NO OR DON'T KNOW IN Q.44, SKIP TO Q.46

IF YES:
Q45 How many students currently enrolled at your charter school are eligible for free or reduced price lunch?

_____

Q46 How many students currently enrolled at your charter school received special education services prior to enrolling at your charter school? **IF NECESSARY, SAY**: "Special Education" services are those provided to students who have an Individualized Education Program (IEP) because of a disability. An individualized education program is a written statement for a child with a disability that is developed in accordance with federal regulations. "Disability" is defined as a learning disability, mental retardation, speech or language impairments, serious emotional disturbance, visual impairments, including blindness, hearing impairment including deafness; deaf blindness; orthopedic impairments, autism, traumatic brain injury, multiple disabilities; or other health impairments.

Number of students	_____
Don't know	_____
Declined to respond	_____

Q47 How many of the students currently enrolled at your charter school are now eligible under the federal Individuals with Disabilities Education Act (IDEA) for special education as specified on an individual education program (IEP)?

Number of students	_____
Don't know	_____
Declined to respond	_____

Q48 How many of your current students have been identified as Limited English Proficient?

Number of students	_____
Don't know	_____
Declined to respond	_____

Q49 Next, a few questions about possible problems at your school. To what extent is each of the following matters currently a problem at your school? For each, please tell me whether it is a SERIOUS problem, a MODERATE problem, a MINOR problem, or NOT A PROBLEM at your school. (READ EACH)

Alaska's Charter Schools

	Serious Problem	Moderate Problem	Minor Problem	Not a Problem
Student tardiness	___	___	___	___
Student absenteeism	___	___	___	___
Teacher absenteeism	___	___	___	___
Student violence	___	___	___	___
Vandalism	___	___	___	___
Student drug or alcohol abuse	___	___	___	___
Any other problems?	___	___	___	___

Q50 Any other problems? Yes (SPECIFY)
_____

Q51   No   ___

IF YES TO Q.50, ASK:
Q52 How much of a problem is that?   Serious   ___
                                         Moderate ___
                                         Minor   ___

Q53 Next, I want to learn about the features of your school that are powerful in attracting parents and students. For each of the following items, please indicate how powerful you feel this feature is in attracting parents and students to your school by using a scale from 1 to 5, where a score of 1 means "not powerful," a score of 2 means "slightly powerful," a score of 3 means "somewhat or moderately powerful," a score of 4 means, "quite powerful," and a score of 5 means "very powerful." If your school does not have that feature, please let me know.

	Do Not Have 0	Not Powerful 1	Slightly Powerful 2	Somewhat Powerful 3	Quite Powerful 4	Very Powerful 5
Don't Know ___						
Small classes	___	___	___	___	___	___
Services for students with disabilities ___	___	___	___	___		
Strict dress and/or behavior codes	___	___	___	___	___	___
Extensive use of technology	___	___	___	___	___	___
Flexible school schedule	___	___	___	___	___	___
Specialized curriculum focus (SPECIFY IN Q54)	___	___	___	___	___	___
Structured environment	___	___	___	___	___	___
Central role for parents	___	___	___	___	___	___
Clear goals for each student	___	___	___	___	___	___
Extensive community service projects	___	___	___	___	___	___
Focus on needs of a special cultural, ethnic, or language group (Native American, African-Am., Bilingual Student)	___	___	___	___	___	___
Longer school year	___	___	___	___	___	___
Quality of academic program	___	___	___	___	___	___
Nurturing environment	___	___	___	___	___	___
Value system	___	___	___	___	___	___

	Do Not Have 0	Not Powerful 1	Slightly Powerful 2	Somewhat Powerful 3	Quite Powerful 4	Very Powerful 5
Safe environment	___	___	___	___	___	___
High standards for student achievement	___	___	___	___	___	___
Support for home schooling	___	___	___	___	___	___
Adaptive environment	___	___	___	___	___	___

Q54 What specialized curriculum focus attracts parents, PLEASE SPECIFY:
_____

Q55 Are there any other features of your school that are important to parents and students? (SPECIFY):
_____

ASK EVERYONE:

Q56 Does your school have Internet access?
- Yes ___
- No ___
- Don't know ___

IF YES:

Q57 What percentage of your students have access to the Internet through school?
- None ___
- 1-25% ___
- 26-50% ___
- 51-75% ___
- 76-100% ___
- Don't know ___

Q58 Does your school provide distance learning opportunities?
- Yes ___
- No ___
- Don't know ___

IF YES:

Q59 What percentage of your school's students are involved in distance learning?
- None ___
- 1-25% ___
- 26-50% ___
- 51-75% ___
- 76-100% ___
- Don't know ___

Q60 How many computers in your school are used for instruction? _____

IF NONE, SKIP TO Q. 63

Q61 What proportion of these computers are capable of running multimedia or advanced applications?
- None ___
- 1-25% ___
- 26-50% ___
- 51-75% ___
- 76-100% ___
- Don't know ___

Q62 What percentage of your classrooms have computers that are used for
- None ___
- 1-25% ___

Alaska's Charter Schools

	instruction?	26-50%	_____
		51-75%	_____
		76-100%	_____
		Don't know	_____

Q63 Does your school have e-mail? Yes _____
　　　　　　　　　　　　　　　　　　　　No _____
　　　　　　　　　　　　　　　　　　Don't know _____

Q64 Do you currently administer any standardized tests to students in your school?　　Yes _____
　　　　　　　　　　　　　　　　　　　　No _____

IF YES, ASK:
Q65 Do you administer.....?

	YES	NO	DON'T KNOW
ITBS	___	___	___
CTBS	___	___	___
CAT	___	___	___
MAT	___	___	___
SAT-9	___	___	___
Brigance	___	___	___
CTBS - Espanol	___	___	___
SABE	___	___	___
Any others?	___	___	___
Aprenda	___	___	___
La Prueba	___	___	___
No others	___	___	___
Other	___	___	___

Q66 Other (PLEASE SPECIFY)
　　　_____

Q67 In what month is the test usually administered?

	Jan	Feb	Mar	Apr	May	Jun	Jul	Aug	Sep	Oct	Nov	Dec
ITBS												
CTBS												
CAT												
MAT												
SAT-9												
CTBS - Espanol												
SABE												
Other (listed in Q.66)												
Aprenda												
La Prueba												
No others												

Q68 Which of the following means of assessing your school's performance are you using this year or planning to use in subsequent years? Do you use or plan to use....(**READ EACH**)?

	USE	PLAN TO USE	NO/ NEITHER	DON'T KNOW
Standardized tests	___	___	___	___
State assessment program	___	___	___	___
Performance-based tests developed locally	___	___	___	___
Performance-based tests developed as part of national or state effort	___	___	___	___
Student portfolios*	___	___	___	___
Students' demonstration of their work**	___	___	___	___
Parent satisfaction surveys	___	___	___	___
Student interviews and/or surveys	___	___	___	___
Behavioral indicators such as attendance, expulsion,				

	USE	PLAN TO USE	NO/ NEITHER	DON'T KNOW
and college-going rate, etc.	___	___	___	___
Other assessments you currently use?	___	___	___	___
Any others you plan to use?	___	___	___	___

Q69 If you plan to use others, PLEASE SPECIFY:
_____

Q70 For which goals will your school be held accountable by your charter granting agency as part of your charter? Any other goals? (**PROBE FULLY**)
_____
_____
_____
_____
_____
_____

Q71 How often do you report accountability data to your charter granting agency?
Once a school year ___
Twice a school year ___
More often ___

Q72 IF "more often", PLEASE SPECIFY
_____

Q73 Does/has your charter granting agency act(ed) on your accountability information?
Yes ___
No ___
Don't know ___

IF "YES" IN Q73
Q74 In what way(s) has/have your charter granting agency acted on your accountability information?
_____
_____
_____

Alaska's Charter Schools

Q75 How does the school procure each of the following services? Does the school provide the service, does the district provide the service, or does your school contract independently with an outside provider? IF NECESSARY, SAY: "Outside provider" includes a person or organization hired or under contract to the school to provide a service or goods. "School" may include students, staff and/or community volunteers.

	SCHOOL	DISTRICT	OUTSIDE PROVIDER	NOT PROVIDED	DON'T KNOW
Payroll/personnel	____	____	____	____	____
Budget and accounting	____	____	____	____	____
Insurance	____	____	____	____	____
Purchasing	____	____	____	____	____
Health services/school nurse	____	____	____	____	____
Social services	____	____	____	____	____
Nutrition and food programs	____	____	____	____	____
Legal services	____	____	____	____	____
Custodial	____	____	____	____	____
Transportation	____	____	____	____	____
Before and/or after school programs	____	____	____	____	____
Building maintenance services	____	____	____	____	____

FOR PRE-EXISTING SCHOOLS (From Q.6):

Q76 Earlier (SEE Q.6), you mentioned that this was a pre-existing school. Did you switch providers for any of these services we just mentioned when you became a charter school?

Yes ____
No   ____

IF YES:

Q77 For which services?

Payroll/personnel ____
Budget and accounting ____
Insurance ____
Purchasing ____
Health services/school nurse ____
Nutrition and food programs ____
Legal services ____
Custodial ____
Transportation ____
Before and/or after school programs ____
Building maintenance services ____

Q78 Is your charter facility....(**READ CATEGORIES**)

	Yes	No	Don't know
Leased from a commercial source	____	____	____
Provided by the district free or at a nominal cost	____	____	____
Leased at (or near) market price from the district	____	____	____

Q79 If your charter school facility is provided through another arrangement? (PLEASE SPECIFY)

_____

Q80 Who has primary control or authority over your charter school's....(**READ ITEM**)? Is it your school or the district?

	Your School	District	Other	Don't Know
Total budget?	___	___	___	___
Purchase of supplies and equipment?	___	___	___	___
School calendar?	___	___	___	___
Daily schedule?	___	___	___	___
Student assessment policies?	___	___	___	___
Student admission policies?	___	___	___	___
Student discipline? (e.g. suspension/expulsion)	___	___	___	___
Establishment of curriculum?	___	___	___	___
Hiring teaching staff?	___	___	___	___

Q81   If respondent answered "Other" to any of the above, **PLEASE SPECIFY** the other authority who has primary control over that item.

_____

Q82   Does your school have any special requirements for admission other than proof of immunization, age, and/or residence?

Yes ___
No ___
Don't Know ___

IF YES, ASK:
Q83   Which of these requirements does the school use for admission? Does your school use...

	YES	NO	DON'T KNOW
Admission tests	___	___	___
Academic records	___	___	___
Special student needs (SEE Q84)	___	___	___
Special student aptitudes (SEE Q85)	___	___	___
Personal interviews	___	___	___
Racial/ethnic background to attain diversity	___	___	___
Are there any other requirements? (SEE Q86)	___	___	___

Q84   If your school uses special student needs as a requirement for admission, PLEASE SPECIFY

_____

Q85   If your school uses special student aptitudes as a requirement for admission, PLEASE SPECIFY

_____

Q86   If your school uses any other requirements for admission, PLEASE SPECIFY

_____

Q87   Does your school have more applicants for admission than it has the capacity to serve?

Yes ___
No ___
Don't know ___

IF YES, ASK:
Q88   How does the school select among applicants?

A lottery or other random selection process ___
A "first-come-first-served"

Alaska's Charter Schools

		selection process	___
		Other (SEE Q89)	___

Q89 If "other" in Q.88, PLEASE SPECIFY
_____

Q90 Does your school have plans to increase its enrollment?
- Yes ___
- No ___

Q91 Are parents or family members required to participate or volunteer at your school?
- Yes (SEE Q92) ___
- No ___
- Don't know ___

Q92 IF YES, ASK: How many hours are required per child each year? _____

Q93 Is there a maximum time commitment per family?
- Yes ___
- No ___
- Don't know ___

Q94 Which of the following means of home-school collaboration are in place at your school? For this question, "parents" include parents and other family members. Do you have...

	YES	NO	DON'T KNOW
Parent education workshops or courses	___	___	___
Staff member assigned to work on parent involvement	___	___	___
Written contract between school and parent	___	___	___
Parent-child learning activities	___	___	___
Parents or staff maintain a log of parent participation	___	___	___
Parents involved in instructional issues	___	___	___
A reliable system of communication established (e.g. newsletters, phone trees, etc.)	___	___	___
Parents involved in governance	___	___	___
Support services so parents can attend meetings (e.g. child care, transportation)	___	___	___
Drop-in center or parent lounge	___	___	___
Parents involved in budget decisions	___	___	___
At-home learning activities to support school objectives	___	___	___
Any other home collaboration efforts	___	___	___

Q95 If your school has other home collaboration efforts, PLEASE SPECIFY
_____

Q96 Which of the following ways do school staff communicate with parents? Do you have:

	YES	NO	DON'T KNOW
Parent phone conferences	___	___	___
In-person parent conferences	___	___	___
Newsletters/mailings	___	___	___
Home visits	___	___	___

	YES	NO	DON'T KNOW
Progress reports	___	___	___
Personal letters	___	___	___
e-mail to parents	___	___	___
Open houses	___	___	___
Calendars of events	___	___	___
Work folders sent home	___	___	___
School-wide meetings	___	___	___
Information line/voice mail	___	___	___
Informal communication	___	___	___
Community events	___	___	___
Any other ways in which your school communicates with parents? (SEE Q97)	___	___	___

Q97 If there are other ways in which your school communicates with parents, PLEASE SPECIFY:
_____

FOR PRE-EXISTING SCHOOLS ONLY (From Q.6):

Q98 You mentioned that this was a pre-existing school (before becoming a charter school). Which of these methods of communicating with parents began only after your school became a charter school?

Calendars of events		___ In-person parent conferences	___
Work folders sent home		___ Newsletters/mailing	___
School-wide meetings		___ Home visits	___
Information line/voice mail		___ Progress reports	___
Informal communication		___ Personal letters	___
Community events		___ e-mail to parents	___
Open houses		___ Other (SEE Q99)	___

Q99 If there are other ways your school communicates with parents after your school became a charter schools, PLEASE SPECIFY:
_____

Q100 Approximately what percentage of the teachers in your school have participated in the following professional development activities since June 1996?

	0-25%	26-50%	51-75%	76-100%	Don't Know
Workshops sponsored by your school					
Professional conferences or workshops					
Peer observation and critique					
Release time to work collaboratively with other instructional staff at your school					
Release time for independent professional development activities other than workshops and conference					
Any other professional development activities?					

Q101 If the teachers in your school participate in other professional development activities, PLEASE SPECIFY:
_____

IF DON'T KNOW TO ANY, ASK:

Q102 If you need to consult records or someone else at your school to complete this question, I

Alaska's Charter Schools

can arrange to have a paper version of the question mailed (or faxed) to you after the interview. You can return it either by mail or by fax.   Mail/fax   _____
Not mail/fax   _____

Q103   Which of the following have you found to be barriers to implementing your charter school during the 1997-1998 school year? Please note the level of difficulty in overcoming each potential barrier by using a scale from 1 to 5, with a score of 1 meaning "not at all difficult," a score of 2 meaning "slightly difficult," a score of 3 meaning "somewhat or moderately difficult," a score of 4 meaning "quite difficult," and a score of 5 meaning "most difficult."

	Not at all Difficult 1	Slightly Difficult 2	Somewhat Difficult 3	Quite Difficult 4	Most Difficult 5
Local facilities	___	___	___	___	___
Collective bargaining agreements	___	___	___	___	___
School district board opposition	___	___	___	___	___
Hiring staff	___	___	___	___	___
Conflict between school and district	___	___	___	___	___
State Department of Education resistance or regulations	___	___	___	___	___
Internal processes within school	___	___	___	___	___
Conflict with external partners	___	___	___	___	___
Conflict over school governance	___	___	___	___	___
Communication within school	___	___	___	___	___
Administration and management	___	___	___	___	___
Administrator turnover	___	___	___	___	___
Disagreement among parents of enrolled students	___	___	___	___	___
Communication with community members	___	___	___	___	___
Community opposition	___	___	___	___	___
Inadequate finances	___	___	___	___	___
Accountability requirements	___	___	___	___	___
Health and safety regulations	___	___	___	___	___
Federal regulations	___	___	___	___	___
Union or bargaining unit opposition	___	___	___	___	___
Teacher certification requirements	___	___	___	___	___
District central office resistance/regulations	___	___	___	___	___
Staff conflict	___	___	___	___	___
Teacher burnout	___	___	___	___	___
Teacher turnover	___	___	___	___	___
Difficulty in recruiting students	___	___	___	___	___
Lack of parental support	___	___	___	___	___
Communication with parents	___	___	___	___	___
Issues between charter board and school administration	___	___	___	___	___
Any other barriers? (SEE Q104)	___	___	___	___	___

Q104   If there were any other barriers, PLEASE SPECIFY:
_____

IF MORE THAN ONE ITEM IN Q103 WAS RATED AS 3, 4, or 5, ASK:
Q105   Which was the most problematic?
_____

Q106 Which was the next most problematic?
_____

Q107 Which was the third most problematic?
_____

IF RESPONDENT RATED "FEDERAL REGULATIONS" 3, 4, or 5, ASK:
Q108 Can you specify the Federal regulations that are problematic?
_____

Q109 Title I is a federally funded program that provides aid to schools andschool districts to service childrenwho live in areas with high concentrations of low-income families. Is your school eligible to receive federal Title I funding?

    Yes (SEE Q110) _____
    No _____
    Don't Know _____

IF YES:
Q110 Is your school actually receiving Title I funding for the 1997-1998 school year?

    Yes _____
    No _____
    Don't Know _____

Q111 Do you plan to extend the grades or grade equivalents covered by your charter school?

    Yes (SEE Q112) _____
    No _____
    Don't know _____

IF YES:
Q112 What month and year do you plan to expand?

    MONTH _____
    YEAR _____

Q113 Has your school received a grant from the federal charter school program?

    Yes _____
    No _____
    Don't Know _____

IF NEED TO SEND WORK SHEET (Q.34, Q.41, Q.102), SAY:
Q114 You indicated that you need to consult school records or someone else at your school to answer some of these questions. I will arrange to send you a work sheet to record your responses to these questions. Can you tell me how you'd prefer us to send the work sheet, by mail or by fax?

    Mail _____
    Fax _____

Let me make sure I have the correct mailing address for the school, or can I have the fax number at the school?

Q115 VERIFY NAME AND ADDRESS
_____
_____
_____

Q116 RECORD FAX NUMBER
_____

THANK RESPONDENT AND EXIT INTERVIEW

Appendix J
Alaska Charter Schools Administrator's Survey

Q1 Please check the response that best describes how familiar you are with:

	Know Very Little 1	2	3	4	Very Well Informed 5
Alaska's charter school legislation	___	___	___	___	___
The charter school(s) in your district	___	___	___	___	___
Other charter schools in Alaska	___	___	___	___	___
Prospects and problems associated with charter schools	___	___	___	___	___

Q2 If one or more charter schools are operating or being planned in your region. What is its (their) relationship with:

	Adversarial 1	2	Mixed 3	Neutral 4	5	Cooperative 6
Your district's administration?	___	___	___	___	___	___
The local teacher's union?	___	___	___	___	___	___
The local school board?	___	___	___	___	___	___

Q3 To what extent do you agree or disagree with the statements below? (Check one box for each statement)

	Strongly Disagree 1	2	3	4	Strongly Agree 5
Our district encourages people to start charter schools	___	___	___	___	___
In deciding whether to grant a charter, our district weighs probable outcomes against administrative burdens on district staff	___	___	___	___	___
Our district has added (or will add) more conditions before it approves a charter school petition	___	___	___	___	___
Someone in the district helps the charter school(s) cut through the red tape	___	___	___	___	___
In deciding to grant a charter, our district weighs probable outcomes against legal risks	___	___	___	___	___
There is a real risk that charter schools will abuse their freedom	___	___	___	___	___
Partially in response to the charter school legislation, our district has

	Strongly Disagree				Strongly Agree
	1	2	3	4	5
liberalized policies pertaining to school restructuring	___	___	___	___	___
Our district provides visibility and recognition for its charter school(s)	___	___	___	___	___
Our school board has lost authority, but it is still responsible for what happens at charter schools	___	___	___	___	___
Charter schools impose enormous administrative burdens on districts	___	___	___	___	___
Our district risks losing Average Daily Membership (ADM) if a charter school is approved	___	___	___	___	___
The leadership in our district is committed to facilitating what each charter school(s) propose(s) to do (or is doing)	___	___	___	___	___
Our district maintains good communication with its charter school(s)	___	___	___	___	___
Our district encourages other schools to adopt practices used in charter schools	___	___	___	___	___
What our district permits a charter school to do depends largely on the opinions of auditors and/or lawyers	___	___	___	___	___
Charter schools drain ADM needed for critical programs	___	___	___	___	___
Partially in response to the charter school legislation, schools in our district have begun to experiment with new programs and practices	___	___	___	___	___
Districts are liable for the actions of its charter schools without benefit of the usual safeguards	___	___	___	___	___
Charter schools should be held accountable to the district	___	___	___	___	___
Charter schools should be held accountable to the public	___	___	___	___	___
The public is holding charter schools accountable	___	___	___	___	___
Our district has not received clear guidance from the state about what charter schools can and cannot do	___	___	___	___	___
Charter schools put districts at risk of being out of compliance with court rulings	___	___	___	___	___

Q4   Which statement below most closely characterizes your opinion of charter schools? (Check only one). Charter schools ...

Could significantly improve the education of children	___
Might achieve useful but limited reforms	___
Are not necessary to implement the reforms and changes that are really needed	___
Could make it easier to implement change/reform already underway	___
Are more trouble than they are worth	___

Open the door to serious problems
that could ultimately hurt public education ____
Could have public relations advantages,
but not much more ____
Are likely to do things our district does not approve ____
Act as a "safety valve" by offering
parents another educational option ____

Q5 Public Education is regulated with rules generated by the state, school district, and teacher and other unions. What is your assessment of the necessity of such rules? (Check one box for each item.)

	Most are Necessary 1	Some Are Necessary 2	Many Are not Necessary 3	Most Should be Rescinded 4
State rules	____	____	____	____
School district policies	____	____	____	____
Union contract provisions	____	____	____	____
Federal regulations	____	____	____	____
Court rulings	____	____	____	____

Q6 Which statement most accurately describes your opinion of the waiver process? (Check only one.)

It is useful and effective ____
It works, but it is time consuming
and cumbersome ____
It is inefficient and not effective ____
It can actually make matters worse ____

Q7 Which of the following measures of charter school accountability do you believe districts should use?

	USE	PLAN TO USE	NO/ NEITHER	DON'T KNOW
ITBS	____	____	____	____
CTBS	____	____	____	____
CAT	____	____	____	____
MAT	____	____	____	____
SAT-9	____	____	____	____
Brigance	____	____	____	____
CTBS-Español	____	____	____	____
SABE	____	____	____	____
Aprenda	____	____	____	____
La Prueba	____	____	____	____
Other	____	____	____	____
State assessment program	____	____	____	____
Performance-based tests developed locally	____	____	____	____
Performance-based tests developed as part of a national or state effort	____	____	____	____
Student portfolios	____	____	____	____
Students' demonstration of their work	____	____	____	____
Parent satisfaction surveys	____	____	____	____
Student interviews and/or surveys	____	____	____	____
Behavioral indicators such as attendance, expulsion, and college-going rate, etc.	____	____	____	____

Q 8 Do you think they should use others? PLEASE SPECIFY:
_____

Q 9 For which goals do you think districts should hold the charter school accountable as part of its charter?
_____

Q 10 How often do you think districts should require the charter school(s) to report accountability data?

Once a school year	___
Twice a school year	___
More often	___

Q 11 If "more often," PLEASE SPECIFY: _____

Q 12 How do you think districts should act upon charter school accountability information?
_____
_____
_____

Q. 13 How much freedom do you believe charter schools should have?

None - 1	___
Very Little - 2	___
Some - 3	___
A Lot - 4	___
Total - 5	___

Q. 14 What do you believe that freedom should look like?
_____
_____
_____

Q. 15 Which of the following do you believe charter school(s) find to be barriers to implementation? Please note the level of difficulty in overcoming each potential barrier by using a scale from 1 to 5, with a score of 1 meaning "not at all difficult," a score of 2 meaning "slightly difficult," a score of 3 meaning "somewhat or moderately difficult," a score of 4 meaning "quite difficult," and a score of 5 meaning "most difficult.

	Not at all Difficult 1	Slightly Difficult 2	Somewhat Difficult 3	Quite Difficult 4	Most Difficult 5
Local facilities	___	___	___	___	___
Collective bargaining agreements	___	___	___	___	___
School district board opposition	___	___	___	___	___
Hiring staff	___	___	___	___	___
Conflict between school and district	___	___	___	___	___
State Department of Education resistance or regulations	___	___	___	___	___
Internal processes within school	___	___	___	___	___
Conflict with external partners	___	___	___	___	___
Conflict over school governance	___	___	___	___	___
Communication within school	___	___	___	___	___
Administration and management	___	___	___	___	___
Administrator turnover	___	___	___	___	___
Disagreement among parents of enrolled students	___	___	___	___	___
Communication with community members	___	___	___	___	___
Community opposition	___	___	___	___	___
Inadequate finances	___	___	___	___	___

	Not at all Difficult 1	Slightly Difficult 2	Somewhat Difficult 3	Quite Difficult 4	Most Difficult 5
Accountability requirements	___	___	___	___	___
Health and safety regulations	___	___	___	___	___
Federal regulations	___	___	___	___	___
Union or bargaining unit opposition	___	___	___	___	___
Teacher certification requirements	___	___	___	___	___
District central office resistance/regulations	___	___	___	___	___
Staff conflict	___	___	___	___	___
Teacher burnout	___	___	___	___	___
Teacher turnover	___	___	___	___	___
Difficulty in recruiting students	___	___	___	___	___
Lack of parental support	___	___	___	___	___
Communication with parents	___	___	___	___	___
Issues between charter board and school administration	___	___	___	___	___
Any other barriers? (Please list below)	___	___	___	___	___

_____
_____

Q. 16 Listed below are issues charter schools have raised. To what extent do you agree or disagree with each statement? (Check one box for each statement.)

	Strongly Disagree 1	2	3	4	Strongly Agree 5
The school attracts (or will attract) the best students from other schools	___	___	___	___	___
New rules and authority structures are as constraining as old ones	___	___	___	___	___
Managing nonacademic services diverts energy from academics	___	___	___	___	___
The school must meet higher accountability standards than other schools	___	___	___	___	___
Some in the community feel the program could be done without a charter	___	___	___	___	___
A charter means more work for teachers	___	___	___	___	___
Teachers' authority in charter schools is being eroded by parents' increased influence	___	___	___	___	___
The school receives (or will receive) less ADM funds than hoped	___	___	___	___	___
Restrictive state rules are a great obstacle for charter schools	___	___	___	___	___
The local teachers' union encourages teachers to work in charter schools	___	___	___	___	___
One of the great obstacles to charter schools is district policies	___	___	___	___	___
Charter schools have opened (or reopened) complex issues related to accountability, liability, compliance, and/or equity	___	___	___	___	___
A restrictive local union contract is a great obstacle to charter schools	___	___	___	___	___
The state may not give charter					

	Strongly Disagree				Strongly Agree
	1	2	3	4	5
schools the freedom needed for their programs to work	___	___	___	___	___
The relationship between the bodies that govern charter schools and school boards is unclear	___	___	___	___	___
Charter schools are not really going to avoid rules and regulations	___	___	___	___	___
If a charter school raises private funds to support educational programs, it risks being sued for providing special treatment to some students that is not available to others	___	___	___	___	___
Securing funding to start or run a charter school is a major obstacle	___	___	___	___	___

Q. 17 If you have any other comments to make, please feel free to add them here. (If necessary, please use additional sheets)

_____
_____
_____

Appendix K
Alaska Charter School Grantees

CHARTER SCHOOL	DISTRICT	Urban	Rural	FY97 Total	FY98 Total
Bay View Charter School	Kenai Peninsula School District	X		$118,850	
Juneau Community Charter School	Juneau Borough School District	X		$125,000	
Chinook Charter School	Fairbanks North Star School District	X		$106,567	
Walden Pond Charter School	Anchorage School District	X		$104,658	
Aurora Borealis Charter School	Kenai Peninsula School District	X		$100,850	
Takotna Training Center Charter School	Iditarod Area School District		X	$59,000	
Homer Charter School	Kenai Peninsula School District	X			$144,995
Academy Charter School	Matanuska-Susitna Borough School District	X			$145,000
Village Charter School	Anchorage School District	X			$144,524
New Beginnings Charter School	Fairbanks North Star School District	X			$143,127
Delta Cyber Charter School	Delta-Greely School District		X		$143,500
Family Partnership Charter School	Anchorage School District	X			$49,615
Midnight Sun Charter School	Matanuska-Susitna Borough School District	X			$140,800
S.P.Y.D.E.R. Charter School	Anchorage School District	X			$142,000
Project Education Charter School	Galena City School District		X		$131,684
Aquarian Charter School	Anchorage School District	X			$135,931
Ketchikan Charter School	Ketchikan Borough School District	X			$119,500
	TOTALS	14	3	$614,925	$1,440,676

<u>Sources</u>: (Charter school grant awards, 1997) and (Department of Education to award eleven charter schools $1.4 million, 1997)

Appendix L
Chaos Theory and the Charter School

Some researchers have studied schools as dynamic systems. Their work provided some ideas for analyzing charter schools within the context of dynamic systems and chaos theory. However, there were some caveats about the use of chaos theory in educational research. Griffiths at al. (1991), for example, warned,

> Scholars should take care to avoid a tautology by looking for turbulence, strange attractors, and other social phenomenon named after chaotic systems' concepts and finding them as a result of imprecision of the instrumentation and measures available and the generality of the concepts when applied to social experiences. Interest groups frequently coalesce around strange attractors, pressure points sparking demands for action .... [T]he appeal of chaos [is that] knowledge of an initial position will not help predict where the system will be at a future point, and if the general parameters of the system cannot be mapped because of the limitations of data, then chaos theory may not help us "predict" outcomes any more than more "traditional" or currently employed theories and frameworks from social science and the humanities .... [T]he overall patterning that is the hallmark of chaos, providing long-range, macroscale analysis of human and physical events, remain obscure .... This partly may be the result of the post hoc nature of the analysis, but it also results from a lack of the type of data that can be plotted over time, plotting chaotic patterns in seemingly random events. (Griffiths, 1991, p. 448)

Another researcher pointed out some other limitations of the application of chaos theory to the dynamic system of public education. Sterman (1988) concluded that:

> Aggregate data sufficient for strong empirical tests simply do not exist for many of the most important social systems. Social systems are not easily isolated from the environment. The huge temporal and spatial scales of these systems, the vast number of individual actors, considerations of cost, and ethical concerns make controlled experiments on the systems themselves difficult at best. Finally, the laws of human behavior are not as stable as the law of physics. (Sterman, 1988, p. 172)

When educational researchers wanted to use chaos models in their studies of public school issues, Sterman illustrated some other problems they needed to meet:

> First ... problems in the analysis of social systems models frequently show patterns replicating chaos that fall outside the parameters of plausible spatial analysis (a critical aspect of the application of chaos theory). Second, social scientists lack empirical tests of the decision rules dominating complex social systems ... so many models developed are subject to doubt .... [T]he explanatory value of chaos in larger systems requires elegant

heuristics that can be quantified and rendered through mathematical formulas .... [M]any other complex social interactions within education as a field do not lend themselves to this form of modeling. (Griffiths, 1991, p. 450)

Sterman found that many questions regarding the significance of chaos modeling remained to be solved:
Real social systems are bombarded by broad-band noise, and it is well known that such random shocks severely degrade the point of predictability of most systems .... Similarly, chaos is a steady-state phenomenon that manifests [itself] over very long time frames, but many policy-oriented models are concerned with transient dynamics, and nearly all with time horizons much shorter than those used in the analysis of chaotic dynamics. (Sterman, 1988, p. 172)

On the other hand, Griffiths, et al. expressed both hope and skepticism:
We are hopeful because many of the concepts on which chaos is built hold intuitive and explanatory value for fundamental and important research issues .... Many of the aspects of chaos theory appear to help scholars and practitioners understand the outcomes.

We are skeptical, however, because ... researchers ... should continue to view chaotic models as ad hoc methods for examining critical questions in theory and research unless they can develop quantitative measures possessing the necessary precision to examine chaotic systems. Enthusiasm for the concepts of chaos theory does not easily translate into meaningful research applying chaotic models to social system analysis. (Griffiths, 1991, p. 450)

In their rejoinder to Cziko (1989), Lerher, et al (1990) added notes of caution:
Much of Cziko's commentary about methodology can be understood as an appeal for more circumspection when building models of behavior. Models have virtues of precision, simplicity, and generativity. Precision arises from the symbolic representations used. Simplicity arises from exemplification by models of the statements in a theory without being isomorphic with them. Generativity results from recombining the constituents of models to simulate new conditions and results for a domain.

However, models also contain several dangers than perhaps impede understanding. First, models can lead to an overemphasis on form .... In this regard, Powers (1973) observed that noting regularities and other descriptive aspects of a phenomenon must precede model construction (Powers, 1973).

Second, models may oversimplify. For example, the linear model is a gross simplification of the actual relations between some forms of behavior ....

Third, models may overemphasize rigor, perhaps at the expense of essential details ....

The difficulty with Cziko's recommendations is that they are presented as an endpoint instead of a beginning. He recommends that descriptive research should "lead to the implementation and dissemination of innovative educational practices" (Cziko, 1989, p. 23). It is hard to see how the framework suggested by Cziko could lead to such confidence in the generalization of results. If behavioral indeterminancy is so rampant, how could one hope that one individual could be enough like another to justify implementing innovative practices? ... "This view of educational research is one that takes as its primary goal and responsibility the dissemination of descriptive educational findings to other researchers, teachers, administrators, and policy makers in a form that is meaningful and useful" (Cziko, 1989, p. 24). Yet much of the mainstream practice eschewed by Cziko is intended to bring this about! (Griffiths, 1991, p. 19)

References

Abraham, F., Abraham, R., & Shaw, C. (1990). <u>A visual introduction to dynamical systems theory for psychology</u>. Santa Cruz, CA: Aerial Press.

Accountability for charter schools. (1998, June). <u>The American School Board Journal</u>, 185(6), 9.

AERA. (1996). Home page: American Educational Research Association.

AERA, APA, & NCME. (1985). <u>Standards for educational and psychological testing</u>. Washington, D.C.: American Psychological Association.

Alaska Department of Education. (1997). Alaska public charter schools grant program. Juneau, AK: Author.

Alaska State Board of Education. (1998, March 27). <u>Tentative agenda</u>. Paper presented at the State Board of Education Worksession, Juneau, AK.

Alexander, K., & Alexander, M. D. (1991). <u>American public school law</u>. (3rd ed.). St. Paul, MN: West.

Anrig, G. (1992, September). Testing and accountability. <u>The American School Board Journal</u>, 34-36.

Antonucci, R. V. (1997). <u>Test results from Massachusetts charter schools: A preliminary study</u>. Boston, MA: The Massachusetts Department of Education.

Archetype behavior pairs. (1994). <u>The Systems Thinker</u>, 5(9), 2.

ASCD. (1990). <u>Public schools of choice</u>. Alexandria, VA: Association for Supervision and Curriculum Development.

Association of Alaska School Boards. (1998). <u>Legislative Bulletin</u> (Week 12). Juneau, AK: Association of Alaska School Boards.

Ariz. school loses charter. (1998, April 15). <u>Education Week</u>, 17, 4.

Ariz. wants four-campus charter school closed. (1997, December 10). <u>Education Week</u>, 17, 4.

ASCD. (1990). <u>Public schools of choice</u>. Alexandria, VA: Association for Supervision and Curriculum Development.

Baratz-Snowden, J. (1990). <u>RFP-National Board for Professional Teaching Standards</u>. Washington, D.C.: National Board for Professional Teaching Standards.

Becker, H. (1989). Tricks of the trade. <u>Studies in Symbolic Interaction</u>, 10, 481-490.

Berkley, G. E. (1978). <u>The craft of public administration</u>. Boston, MA: Allyn and Bacon.

Bierlein, L. A., & Mulholland, L. (1994a). Comparing charter school laws: The question of autonomy. Tempe, AZ: Morrison Institute for Public Policy, Arizona State University.

Bierlein, L. A., & Mulholland, L.A. (1994b, September). The promise of charter schools. Educational Leadership, 52, 34-40.

Bierlein, L. A. (1995/1996, December/January). Catching on but the jury's still out. Education Leadership, 53, 90-91.

Bierlein, L. A., & Fulton, M.F. (1996). Emerging issues in charter school financing (Policy Brief). Denver, CO: Education Commission of the States.

Blair, B. G. (1993). What does chaos theory have to offer educational administration? Journal of School Leadership, 3(September), 579-596.

Bogdan, R., & Biklen, S. (1992). Qualitative research for education: An introduction to theory and methods. Boston, MA: Allyn and Bacon.

Boyd, W. L., & Cibulka, J.G. (Ed.). (1989). Private schools and public policy: International perspectives. London: Falmer.

Brandt, R. (1996, October). Choice is here to stay. Educational Leadership, 54, 5.

Brombacher, G. E. (1996). Charter schools: An analysis of the obstacles and opportunities for Georgia public school reform. Unpublished Dissertation, The University of Alabama.

Bronowski, J. (1973). The ascent of man. Boston, MA: Little, Brown and Co,.

Brookover, W. B., & Lezotte, L.W. (1979). Changes in school characteristics coincident with changes in school achievement. East Lansing, MI: Institute for Research on Teaching, Michigan State University.

Brown, P. R. (1990). Accountability in public education. San Francisco, CA: Far West Laboratory.

Bryant-Booker, D. (1995). Shared governance conditions in some League of Professional Schools which lead to improved student outcomes. Unpublished Dissertation, Georgia State University.

Bryk, A. S., & Hermanson, K.L. (1992). Educational indicator systems: Observations on their structure, interpretations, and use. Review of Research in Education, 19, 451-484.

Buechler, M. (1996). Charter schools: Legislation and results after four years (Policy Report PR-B13). Bloomington, IN: Indiana University, Indiana Education Policy Center.

Buechler, M. (1997). Charter school legislation across the states. Washington, D.C.: The Center for Education Reform.

Carnegie Forum on Education and the Economy. (1986). A nation prepared: Teachers for the 21st century. New York, NY: Carnegie Forum on Education and the Economy, Report of the Task Force on Teaching as a Profession.

Caves, D. W., Christensen, L.R., & Diewert, W.E. (1982). The economic theory of index numbers and the measurement of input, output, and productivity. Econometrica, 50, 1393-1414.

Charnes, A., Cooper, W. W., & Rhodes, E. (1981, June). Evaluating program and managerial efficiency: An application of data envelopment analysis to program follow through. Management Science, 27, 668-696.

Charter principal sentenced. (1997, October 22). Education Week, 17, 5.

Charter schools. (1997, December 9). School Board News, 17, 8.

Charter schools (1998, July 8). Education Week, 17, 42.

Charter revoked in D.C. (1998, May 27). Education Week, 17, 4.

Charter school principal fired. (1998, January 28). Education Week, 17, 4.

Charter school grant awards. (1997). Information Exchange, 23 (30).

Charter teachers scrutinized. (1998, April 15). Education Week, 17, 28.

Chenery, G. (1991, December). Chaotic calculations: Seeking the order in apparent randomness. The Science Teacher, 28-33.

Cherkes-Julkowski, M. (1996). The child as a self-organizing system: The case against instruction as we know it. Learning Disabilities: A Multidisciplinary Journal, 7(1), 19-27.

Cheung, S., Murphy, M., & Nathan, J. (1998). Making a difference? Charter schools, evaluation, and student performance. Minneapolis, MN: University of Minnesota, Hubert H. Humphrey Institute of Public Affairs, Center for School Change. Available: www.hhh.umn.edu/centers/school-change/differen.htm

Childs, K., & Reagle, J. (1997, December 15). Charter schools must heed civil rights laws. Leadership News, 11, 1.

Chubb, J. E., & Moe, T. M. (1990). Politics, markets, and American schools. Washington, D.C.: Brookings Institution. (ERIC Document Reproduction Service No. ED 336-851).

Chmelynski, C. (1998, March 24). Arizona school districts find long-distance charters troublesome. School Board News, 18.

Christianson, S. S. (1998, April). Are Alaska's schools in peril? Alaska Business Monthly, 14-20.

Cibulka, J. G. (1991). Educational accountability reforms: Performance information and political power. In S. Fuhrman, & Malen, B. (Ed.), The politics of curriculum and testing (pp. 181-201). London: Falmer Press.

Clayton Foundation. (1997). The Colorado charter schools evaluation. Denver, CO: The Clayton Foundation.

Coleman, J. S. (1966). Equality of Educational Opportunity. Washington, D.C.: Office of Education, U.S., Department of Health, Education and Welfare, National Center for Education Statistics.

Coons, J. E., & Sugarman, S.D. (1978). Autonomy as the goal: A personal view, Education by choice: The case for family control (pp. 71-87). Berkeley, CA: University of California Press.

Corwin, R., & Flaherty, J. (1995). Freedom and innovation in California's charter schools. Los Alamitos, LA: Southwest Regional Laboratory.

Corwin, R. G., & Dianda, M. R. (1993). An early look at charter schools in California. Los Alamitos, CA: Southwest Regional Laboratory. (ERIC Document Reproduction Service No. ED 357-484).

Corwin, R. G., & Dianda, M. R. (1994). Vision and reality: A first-year look at California's charter schools. Los Alamitos, CA: Southwest Regional Laboratory.

Cromer, A. (1998, May). The math and science wars. Northeastern University Magazine, 49-52.

Crutchfield, J. P., Farmer, J. D., Packard, N. H., & Shaw, R. S. (1986). Chaos. Scientific American, 255, 46-57.

Cziko, G. A. (1989, April). Unpredictability and indeterminism in human behavior: Arguments and implications for educational research. Educational Researcher, 18, 19.

Cziko, G. A. (1992, December). Purposeful behavior as the control of perception: Implications for educational research. Educational Researcher, 10-18.

D.C. school retains charter. (1997, November 12). Education Week, 17, 4.

Darling-Hammond, L., & Ascher, C. (1991). Creating accountability in big city schools. New York, NY: National Center for Restructuring Education, Schools and Teaching, Teachers College, Columbia University.

Darling-Hammond, L., & Snyder, J. (1992). Reframing accountability: Creating learner-centered schools. In A. Lieberman (Ed.), The changing contexts of teaching: Ninety-first yearbook of the National Society for the Study of Education (pp. 11-36). Chicago, IL: National Society for the Study of Education.

David, J. L. (1988). Aid or threat to improvement. Phi Delta Kappan, 69(7), 499-502.

David, J. L. (1995,). The who, what, and why of site-based management. Educational Leadership, 53, 4-9.

Davis, A. (1991). Upping the stakes: Using gain scores to judge local program effectiveness in Chapter 1. Educational Evaluation and Policy Analysis (Winter).

Davis, B., & Sumara, D. J. (1997, Spring). Cognition, complexity, and teacher education. Harvard Educational Review, 67, 105-125.

Demitchell, T. A. (1997, November). The legal confines of school reform. The School Administrator, 28-31.

DeMoulin, D. F. (1990). It's not what you see that counts, it's what you don't see. Dubuque, IA: Kendall/Hunt Publishing Company.

DeMoulin, D. F., & Kendall, R. (1993, November). The administrative role in an accountability network: A developmental conceptualization. Journal of School Leadership, 3, 688-698.

Denzin, N. (1978). A theoretical introduction to sociological methods. (2nd ed.). New York, NY: McGraw Hill.

Denzin, N., & Lincoln Y. (Ed.). (1994). Introduction: Entering the field of qualitative research. Thousand Oaks, CA: Sage Publications.

Department of Education sets new policy for out-of-district enrollment. (1998). Information Exchange, 25 (1).

Department of Education to award eleven charter schools $1.4 million. (1997). Information Exchange, 24(13).

Dexter, L. (1970). Elite and specialized interviewing. Evanston, IL: Northwestern University Press.

Diamond, L. (1994, September). A progress report on California's charter schools. Educational Leadership, 52, 41-45.

Dianda, M. R., & Corwin, R.G. (1994, September). Start-up experiences: A survey. Educational Leadership.

Dianda, M. R., & Corwin, R. G. (1994). Vision and reality: A first-year look at California's charter schools. Los Alamitos, CA: Southwest Regional Laboratory.

Edmonds, R. (1979). Some schools work and more can. Social Policy, 9(2), 28-32.

Education choice: A background paper. (1991). Washington, D.C.: Quality Education for Minorities Network.

Education Commission of the States & The Center for School Change at the University of Minnesota. (1995). Preliminary results from a survey of approved charter schools. Denver, CO: Education Commission of the States.

Effect of a public school choice program. (1997, September). ERS Bulletin, 25, 9.

Elmore, R. F. (1990). Choice in public education. In W. L. Boyd, & Kirchner, C.T. (Ed.), The politics of excellence and choice in education. London: The Falmer Press.

Elmore, R. (1990). Choice as an instrument of public policy. In W. Clune, & Witte, J. (Ed.), Choice and control in American public education. New York, NY: Falmer Press.

Ennis, C. D. (1986, Fall). Conceptual frameworks as a foundation for the study of operational curriculum. Journal of Curriculum and Supervision, 2, 38.

Ennis, C. D. (1992, Winter). Reconceptualizing learning as a dynamical system. Journal of Curriculum and Supervision, 7, 115-130.

ERS. (1998, March). Charter schools. ERS Bulletin, 25.

Färe, R., Grosskopf, S., & Lovell, C.A.K. (1985). The measurement of efficiency of production. Boston, MA: Kluwer-Nijhoff.

Färe, R., Grosskopf, S., Lindgren, Bjorn, & Roos, P. (1989). Productivity development in Swedish hospitals: A Malmquist output index approach (Discussion Paper 89-3). Carbondale, IL: Southern Illinois University at Carbondale, Economics Department.

Finn, C. E., Manno, B. V., & Bierlein, L. (1996a). Charter schools in action: What have we learned? Indianapolis, IN: Hudson Institute.

Finn, C. E., Manno, B. V., Bierlein, L., & Vanourek, G. (1997). Charter schools in action project, final report, part III: The policy perils of charter schools [On-line]. Washington, D.C.: Hudson Institute. Available: http://www.edexcellence.net/chart/chart1.htm

Finn, C. E., & Ravitch, D. (1996b). Education reform 1995-1996. Indianapolis, IN: Hudson Institute.

Firestone, W. (1993). Alternative arguments for generalizing from data as applied to qualitative research. Educational Researcher, 4, 16-23.

Fullan, M. (1993). Change forces. (4th ed.). Bristol, PA: Falmer Press.

Garmston, R., & Wellman, B. (1995, April). Adaptive schools in a quantum universe. Educational Leadership, 53, 6-12.

Gay, L. R. (1981). Educational Research: Competencies for analysis & application. (2nd ed.). Columbus, OH: Charles E. Merrill Publishing Co.

Gerzon, M. (1996). A house divided: Six belief systems struggling for America's soul. New York, New York: G.P. Putnam's sons.

Giroux, H. (1986, Spring). Radical pedagogy and the politics of student voice. Interchange, 17, 48-69.

Glaser, B., Strauss, L. (1967). The discovery of grounded theory: Strategies for qualitative research. Chicago, IL: Aldine.

Gleick, J. (1987). Chaos: Making a new science. New York, NY: Penguin Books.

Goetz, J., & LeCompte, M. (1984). Ethnography and qualitative design in educational research. New York, NY: Academic Press.

Griffith, J. E. (1990). Indicators and accountability in the USA. In T. J. Wyatt, & Ruby, A. (Ed.), Education indicators for quality, accountability and better practice: Papers from the [second] national conference on indicators and quality in education. Sydney: Australian Conference of Directors-General of Education.

Griffiths, D. E., Harts, A.W., & Blair, B.G. (1991, August). Still another approach to administration: Chaos theory. Educational Administration Quarterly, 27, 430-451.

Grosskopf, S., Hayes, K., Taylor, L., & Weber, W. (1995). On competition and school efficiency: Authors.

Grosskopf, S., Hayes, K., Taylor, L., & Weber, W. (1996). On the political economy of school deregulation (Working Paper).

Guba, E., & Lincoln, Y. (1981). Effective evaluation. San Francisco, CA: Jossey-Bass.

Guess, D., & Sailor, W. (1993). Chaos theory and the study of human behavior: Implications for special education and developmental studies. The Journal of Special Education, 27(1), 16-34.

Guthrie, J. (1997, September 21). Clintons tout charter schools in San Carlos. San Francisco Examiner, pp. A-12.

Hamilton, S. (1997a). Charter schools technical advisory 97-1 (pp. 27). Malden, MA: The Commonwealth of Massachusetts Department of Education.

Hamilton, S. (1997b). The Massachusetts charter school initiative: Evaluation & accountability policy. Boston, MA: Massachusetts Department of Education.

Hanushek, E. A. (1986). The economics of schooling: Production and efficiency in public schools. Journal of Economic Literature (September), 1141-77.

Hawking, S. W. (1988). A brief history of time: from the big bang to black holes. (1990 ed.). New York, NY: Bantam Books.

Hayles, N. K. (1990). Chaos-bound: Orderly disorder in contemporary literature and science. Ithaca, NY: Cornell University Press.

Heid, C. (1991). The dilemma of Chapter 1 program improvement. Educational Evaluation and Policy Analysis (Winter).

Henry, G. T. (1996, September). Community accountability: A theory of information, accountability, and school improvement. Phi Delta Kappan, 85-90.

Herrington, C. D., Johnson, B., & O'Farrell, M. (1992). A legislative history of accountability in Florida: 1971-1991. Unpublished manuscript.

Hill, P. T., Bonan, J. J., & Warner, K. (1992). Uplifting education. American School Board Journal, 179(3), 21-25.

Hill, P. T. (1994,). Reinventing urban public education. Kappan, 75, 396-401.

Hoke, J. (1997, June 27). Reprisals possible for schools that fail to meet standards. Reno Gazette-Journal.

Holayter, M. C., & Sheldon, D. P. (1994, October). Order out of chaos. The Executive Educator, 23-25.

Holloway, S. (1995). Charter Schools. Juneau, AK: Alaska Department of Education.

Holloway, S. (1997a). Out-of-district correspondence programs (Numbered memorandum 97-12). Juneau, AK: Alaska Department of Education.

Holloway, S. (1997b). Religious curricula (Numbered memorandum 97-13). Juneau, AK: Department of Education.

Hospers, J. (1971). Libertarianism. Los Angeles, CA: Nash.

House Finance Committee. (1995). SB 88 pilot program for charter schools. Juneau, AK: Alaska State Legislature.

House HESS. (1995). SB 88 pilot program for charter schools. Juneau, AK: Alaska State Legislature, House Health, Education, & Social Services Committee.

Howe, D. W. (1979). The political culture of the American Whigs. Chicago, IL: University of Chicago Press.

Hower, W. (1997, April 12). A question of money. Fairbanks Daily News-Miner, pp. A-1, A-8.

Hurst, D. S. (1994, September). We cannot ignore the alternatives. Educational Leadership, 52, 78-79.

Jaeger, R. M., Gorney, B.E., & Johnson, R.L. (1994, October). The other kind of report card: When schools are graded. Educational Leadership, 42-45.

Johnston, R. C. (1997, August 8). 1993 Mich. charter school statute is legal, high court declares. Education Week, 16, 24.

Jones, R. (1994, October). Chaos theory. Executive Educator, 20-23.

Kaagen, S. S., & Coley, R. (1989). State education indicators: Measured strides and missing steps. New Brunswick, NJ: Center for Policy Research in Education, Rutgers University.

Kaestle, C. F., & Vinovskis, M. (1980). Education and social change in nineteenth-century Massachusetts. New York, NY: Cambridge University Press.

Kaku, M. (1994). Hyperspace: A scientific odyssey through parallel universes, time warps, and the tenth dimension. New York, NY: Oxford University Press.

Kaplan, R. (1997). Charter schools are a breath of fresh air: Don't let one bad apple spoil the bunch (97-11). Phoenix, AZ: Goldwater Institute.

Karweit, N. (1993). Driving school improvement with assessments: Some implications from Chapter 1. NASSP Bulletin (October), 1-10.

Kolderie, T. (1990). Beyond choice to new public schools: Withdrawing the exclusive franchise in public education. Washington, D.C.: The Democratic Leadership Council.

Krathwohl, D. (Ed.). (1993). Methods of education and social science research: An integrated approach. White Plans, NY: Longman Publishing Corp.

LaMorte, M. W. (1990). School law cases and concepts. Englewood Cliffs, NJ: Prentice-Hall.

Lane, J. J., & Walberg, H. J. (1989, November 28-31). Site-managed schools: The Chicago plan. Education Digest.

Latham, A.S. (1998, May). Home schooling. Educational Leadership.

Levy, D. C. (1991, June). Review essay: Accountability and private-public comparisons. Educational Policy, 5, 193-199.

Lincoln, Y., & Guba, E. (1985). Naturalistic inquiry. Beverly Hills, CA: Sage Publications.

Lofland, J. (1971). Analyzing social settings: A guide to qualitative observation and analysis. Belmont, CA: Wadsworth.

Louis, K. (1982). Multisite/Multimethod Studies. American Behavioral Scientist, 26, 6-22.

MacCoun, R., & Reuter, P. (1997, October 3). Interpreting Dutch cannabis policy: Reasoning by analogy in the legalization debate. Science, 278, 47-52.

Machan, T. (1989). Individuals and their rights. La Salle, IL: Open Court.

Macpherson, R. J. S. (1996). Educative accountability policy research: Methodology and epistemology. Educational Administration Quarterly, 32 (1), 80-106.

Manno, B. V., Finn, C.E., Bierlein, L.A., & Vanourek, G. (1997). Charter schools in action, final report, part IV: Charter school accountability: Problems and prospects. Washington, D.C.: Hudson Institute.

Mao, T. (1961). Problems of war and strategy, Selected Works of Mao Tse-Tung (Vol. 2). Beijing, PRC: Foreign Languages Press.

Marion, R. (1992). Chaos, Topology, and Social Organization. Journal of School Leadership (April), 144-177.

Massell, D. F., S., Kirst, M., Odden, A., Wohlstetter, R., & Yee, G. (1994). Ten years of state education reform, 1983-1993: Overview with four case studies. Washington, D.C.: Center for Policy Research in Education, Office of Educational Research and Improvement.

Matwick, M. R. (1996). Charter school directors' perceptions of the process of establishing a charter school in Arizona. Unpublished Dissertation, Northern Arizona University.

McCotter, S. (1996). Charter schools (ECS Clearinghouse Issue Brief) . Denver, CO: Education Commission of the States.

McCune, C. (1994). The modification of structural constraints in California charter schools. Unpublished Ed.D. dissertation, University of LaVerne, LaVerna, CA.

McKinney, J. R. (1996, October). Charter schools: A new barrier for children with disabilities. Educational Leadership, 54, pp. 22-25.

McLaughlin, M. W. (1991, November). Test-based accountability as a reform strategy. Phi Delta Kappan, 248-251.

McMillan, J. (1996). Educational research: Fundamentals for the consumer. New York, NY: Harper Collins.

Medler, A., & Nathan, J. (1995). Charter schools... what are they up to? A 1995 survey. Denver, CO: Education Commission of the States.

Mehrens, W. A. (1992). Using performance assessment for accountability purposes. Educational Measurement: Issues and Practice (Spring), 3-9, 20.

Merriam, S. (1988). Case study research in education: A qualitative approach. San Francisco, CA: Jossey-Bass.

Merrow, J. (1997). Education's big gamble: Charter schools (videotape). Columbia, SC: Learning Matters, Inc.

Mich. audit finds charter school problems. (1997, October 22). Education Week, 17, 12.

Miles, M., & Huberman, A. (1984). Qualitative analysis: A sourcebook of new methods. Newbury Park, CA: Sage Publications.

Mill, J. (1993). In D. Krathwohl (Ed.), Methods of education and social science research: An integrated approach. White Plans, NY: Longman Publishing Corp.

Milliron, T. (1995). Charter schools workshop: author.

Morra, L. G. (1995). Charter schools: A growing and diverse national reform movement (GAO/T-HEHS-95-52). Washington, D.C.: General Accounting Office, Health, Education, and Human Services Division.

Moutray, C. M. (1996). Assessing the performance of market-based education reforms. Unpublished Dissertation, Southern Illinois University at Carbondale, Carbondale, IL.

Mulholland, L. (1996). Charter schools: The reform and the research. Phoenix, AZ: Morrison Institute for Public Policy.

Mulholland, L. A., & Bierlein, L.A. (1995). Understanding charter schools (Fastback 383). Bloomington, Indiana: Phi Delta Kappa Educational Foundation.

Naphin, D. (1997). A matter of principal. In M. Safer (Ed.), CBS News 60 Minutes (pp. 8). Livingston, NJ: Burrelle's Information Services.

Nathan, B. R., & Cascio, W.F. (1986). Introduction: Technical & legal standards. In R. A. Berk (Ed.), Performance assessment: Methods and applications (pp. 1-50). Baltimore, MD: The Johns Hopkins University Press.

Nathan, J. (1996). Charter schools: Creating hope and opportunity for American education. San Francisco, CA: Jossey-Bass.

National Center for Education Statistics. (1991). Education counts: An indicator system to monitor the nation's educational health. Washington, D.C.: National Center for Educational Statistics, Special Study Panel on Education Indicators.

National Commission on Excellence in Education. (1983). A nation at risk. Washington, D.C.: U.S. Government Printing Office.

NCREL. (1998). Charters in our midst: The impact of charter schools on school districts [audio-cassettes]. Oak Brook, IL: North Central Regional Educational Laboratory.

Neill, M. (1997). Testing our children: A report card on state assessment systems. Cambridge, MA: National Center for Fair & Open Testing (FairTest).

Newmann, F. M., King, M.B., & Rigdon, M. (1997). Accountability and school performance: Implications from restructuring schools. Harvard Educational Review, 67(Spring), 41-74.

Nolan, J. R., & Nolan-Haley, J.M. (1990). Black's law dictionary. St. Paul, MN: West Publishing Co.

Norris, J. M. (1996). Running from the education code: Measuring how far California's charter schools have come. Unpublished Dissertation, University of La Verne, La Verne, CA.

North Carolina State Board of Education. (1995). Performance-based accountability program: 1993-1994 school year report. Raleigh, NC: North Carolina State Board of Education. (ERIC Document Reproduction Service No. ED 390 882)

Nozik, R. (1974). Anarchy, state, and utopia. New York, NY: Basic Books, Inc.

Nozik, R. (1981). Philosophical explanations. Cambridge, MA: Harvard University Press.

Oakes, J. (1986). Educational indicators: A guide for policymakers. New Brunswick, NJ: Rutgers University, Center for Policy Research in Education.

Ogden, E. L. (1995). A study to explore perceptions of public school superintendents in Michigan regarding charter schools. Unpublished Dissertation, Wayne State University.

O'Neil, J. (1994, August). Charter schools: Newest wrinkle in school choice. Educational Leadership, 3.

Palenske, N. (1995). Questions about charter schools. Palmer, AK: author.

Patton, A. (1993). How to use qualitative methods in evaluation. Newbury Park, CA: Sage Publications.

Peikoff, L. (1991). Objectivism: The philosophy of Ayn Rand. (1 ed.). New York, NY: Dutton.

Perkins-Gough, D. (1997). Charter schools: Whom do they serve, and how well? ERS Spectrum (Summer), 3-9.

Peshkin, A. (1993,). The goodness of qualitative research. Educational Researcher, 22, 23-29.

Purvis, C. S. (1997). Analysis of Nevada school accountability system: School year 1994-1995. Carson City, NV: Nevada Department of Education.

Pogrow, S. (1997, November 12). The tyranny and folly of ideological progressivism. Education Week, 17, 2.

Pollitt, C. (1995). Justification by works or faith? Evaluating the new public management. Evaluation, 1(2), 133-154.

Pool, C. (1996, December). Letters on line. Educational Leadership, 54.

Pool, R. (1989). Is it chaos, or is it just noise? Science, 243, 25-28.

Powers, W. T. (1973). Behavior: The control of perception. Chicago, IL: Aldine.

Pratt, J. (1996). An analysis of selected contracts governing charter schools in six states. Unpublished Dissertation, University of Central Florida.

Pulliam, J. D. (1968). History of education in America. Columbus, OH: Charles E. Merrill.

Ramirez, A., & McClanahan, R. (1992). Reporting to the public. The American School Board Journal (April), 33-35.

Rand, A. (1990). Introduction to Objectivist epistemology. (2nd ed.). New York, NY: Meridian.

Rawls, J. (1971). A theory of justice. Cambridge, MA: Harvard University Press.

Roberts, R. R. (1993). An analysis of state school reform legislation and related litigation. Unpublished Dissertation, University of Central Florida.

Romzek, B. S., & Dubnick, M.J. (1987, May/June). Accountability in the public sector: Lessons from the Challenger tragedy. Public Administration Review.

Rosenblum, B. A. (1997). Guidelines for preparing a charter school accountability plan. Philadelphia, PA: The Massachusetts Department of Education.

Rothbard, M. N. (1978). For a new liberty: The Libertarian manifesto. (Revised ed.). New York, NY: Macmillan Publishing Co.

Rothman, R. (1995). Measuring up: Standards, assessment and school reform. San Francisco, CA: Jossey-Bass.

Ruelle, D. (1989). Chaotic evolution and strange attractors. Cambridge: Cambridge University Press.

Sack, J. L. (1997, November 19). Clinton administration shifts gears on reading bill. Education Week, 17, 1.

Saks, J. B. (1998, January). A close look. The American School Board Journal, 185, 14-19.

Sandham, J. L. (1998, January 8). Isolated no more. Education Week, 17, 96-99.

Sautter, R. C. (1993). Charter schools: A new breed of public schools (Policy Brief). Oak Brook, IL: North Central Regional Educational Laboratory (ERIC Document Reproduction Service No. ED 361-905).

Sawada, D., & Caley, M. T. (1985, March). Dissipative structures: New metaphors for becoming in education. Educational Researcher, 14, 16.

Schnaiberg, L. (1997a, February 19). Charter school laws are all over the map on disabled students. Education Week, 16, 25.

Schnaiberg, L. (1997b, April 9). Off to market. Education Week, 16, 34, 36-39.

Schnaiberg, L. (1997c, April 16). EAI seeks to team with developers to build charter schools in Arizona. Education Week, 16, 1, 27.

Schnaiberg, L. (1998a, February 18). Voucher study finds support for accountability. Education Week, 17, 5.

Schnaiberg, L. (1998b, August 5). Predominantly black charters focus of debate in N.C. Education Week, 17, 43.

School in community gets reprieve. (1998, February 1). The Chapel Hill News, pp. A-1.

Senate HESS. (1995). SB 88 pilot program for charter schools. Juneau, AK: Alaska State Legislature, Senate Health, Education, & Social Services Committee.

Senge, P. (1990). The fifth discipline. New York, NY: Doubleday/Currency.

Sergiovanni, T. J., Burlingame, M., Coombs, F.S., & Thurston, P. W. (1992). Educational governance and administration. (3rd ed.). Boston, MA: Allyn and Bacon.

Shaw, L. (1997, November 19). Test scores: The last word? Think again. Seattle Times, pp. 1.

Shinohara, R. (1995, July 5). State opens door to charter schools: Approach permits more independence. Anchorage Daily News, pp. B-1-2.

Shinohara, R. (1998, September 29). Village charter school folds. Anchorage Daily News, pp. A-1, A-8.

Simmons, T. (1998, January 8). 21 charter school bids get approval. The News & Observer.

Snedcor, G. W., & Cochran, W.G. (1981). Statistical methods. In L. R. Gay (Ed.), Educational research: Competencies for analysis & application (pp. 408-411). Columbus, OH: Charles E. Merrill Publishing Company.

Spring, J. (1997). The American school: 1642-1996. (4th ed.). New York, NY: McGraw-Hill Companies, Inc.

SREB. (1992). School accountability reports: Lessons learned in SREB States. Atlanta GA: Southern Regional Education Board.

State Board June Meeting Actions.)1994). Information Exchange, 26(15)

Statewide assessment systems study. (1998, February). ERS Bulletin, 25, 1-8.

Stake, R. (1995). The art of case study research. Thousand Oaks, CA: Sage Publications.

Sterman, J. D. (1988). Deterministic chaos in models of human behavior: Methodological issues and experimental results. System Dynamics Review, 4, 148-178.

Streshly, W. A., & Newcomer, L. (1994, March). Managing change with accountability: A challenge for educators. NASSP Bulletin, 62-68.

Sungaila, H. (1990). Organizations alive: Have we at last found the key to a science of educational administration? Studies in Educational Administration, 52, 3-26.

Supovitz, J. A. (1997, November 5). From multiple choice to multiple choices. Education Week, 17, 2.

Swanson, A. D., & King, R.A. (1991). School finance its economics and politics. New York, NY: Longman.

Teichroeb, R. (1997, December 22). Flight to private schools grows: Stanford strives to improve city's public education. Seattle Post-Intelligencer.

Texas Education Agency. (1994). Accountability manual. Austin, TX: Texas Education Agency.

Texas Education Agency. (1996). The development of accountability systems nationwide and in Texas: Statewide Texas educational progress study (Report 1). Austin, TX: Texas Education Agency.

Texas school loses charter. (1998, January 28). Education Week, 17, 4.

The compact edition of the Oxford English dictionary. (1971). (Vol. I). Oxford, England: Oxford University Press.

The Massachusetts charter school initiative. (1996). Boston, MA: The Massachusetts Department of Education.

Tian, J. (1998). Important role of developing countries in promoting human rights. Foreign Affairs Journal, 48, 12-18.

Tovey, R. (1995). Despite the promises, school choice can worsen racial and social class inequities. The Harvard Education Letter, XI (3), 1-3.

U.S. Department of Education. (1997). A study of charter schools: first year report (SAI 97-3007) [On-line]. Washington, D.C.: U.S. Department of Education, Office of Educational Research and Improvement, RPP International, and the University of Minnesota. Available: http://www.ed.gov/pubs/charter/

U.S. Department of Labor. (1991). What work requires of schools: A SCANS report for America 2000. Washington, D.C.: U.S. Department of Labor, The Secretary's Commission on Achieving Necessary Skills.

U.S. Department of Labor. (1992). Learning a Living: A SCANS report for America 2000. Washington, D.C.: U.S. Department of Labor, The Secretary's Commission on Achieving Necessary Skills.

U.S. General Accounting Office. (1995). Charter schools: New model for public schools provides opportunities and challenges (Report to Senators Arlen Spector and Edward Kennedy GAO/HEHS-95-42). Washington, D.C.: U.S. General Accounting Office.

Viadero, D. (1998, May 13). Education Week, 17, 35.

Villaneuva v. Carere, 873. F. Supp. 434 (D. Colo. 1994).

Walsh, B., Billick, B., & Peterson, J. (1998). Bill Walsh: Finding the winning edge. Champaign, IL: Sports Publishing Inc.

Webster's third new international dictionary of the English language unabridged. (1981). Boston, MA: Merriam-Webster.

Wells, A. S. (1993). The sociology of school choice: Why some win and others lose in the educational marketplace. In E. Rasell, & Rothstein, R. (Ed.), School choice: Examining the evidence (pp. 29-48). Washington, D.C.: Economic Policy Institute.

Wheatley, M. J. (1992). Leadership and the new science: Learning about organizations from an orderly universe. San Francisco, CA: Berrett-Koehler Publishers.

Willie, C. V. (1997, October 1). Can equity and excellence coexist? Education Week, 17, 56,36.

Willis, S. (1995, November). Charter schools take hold. ASCD Education Update, 37, 1,3, 5, 8.

Wisconsin Dept. of Public Instruction. (1995). 1993-94 Wisconsin statewide school performance report (Statistical Data, Reports, Evaluative/Feasibility Bulletin No. 96138). Madison, WI: Wisconsin State Dept. of Public Instruction. (ERIC Document Reproduction Service No. ED 391 247)

Witcover, J. (1997). 1968: The year the dream died. New York, NY: Warner Books, Inc.

Wohlstetter, P., & Griffin, N. C. (1997). First lessons: Charter schools as learning communities (RB-22). Philadelphia, PA: University of Pennsylvania, Graduate School of Education, Consortium for Policy Research in Education.

Endnotes

1   Arizona's legislature mandated a "statewide student assessment program (Arizona Revised Statutes Annotated, 1992 §15-741, required goals for excellence be established on a statewide and local level; §15-741.01 required the State Board of Education to produce an annual report card which includes results of student assessment, dropout rates, graduation rates and postsecondary employment and education (§15-743))" (Roberts, 1993, p. 63).

2   Dr. Lawndia White Venerable, founder of Phoenix, Arizona's Citizen 2000 charter school, opened in August 1995, was indicted on charges of fraud. Five of the teachers in Citizen 2000 were Kristen Shears, Kelly Gudreau, Don Locke, Eric Helming, and Mary Smith.

3   Anchorage - 3; Delta/Greely - 1; Fairbanks - 2; Galena - 1; Iditarod - 1; Juneau - 1; Kenai - 2; Ketchikan - 1; Matanuska-Susitna - 3.

4   Massachusetts had three charter schools operated by Chris Whittle's Edison Project. (O'Neil, 1994, p. 3).

5   A political subdivision of the state of Alaska that is equivalent to a county in most other states.

6   Rep. Al Vezey introduced HB 229 Charter School Establishment & Operation, in House Health Education and Social Services. In the Senate, Sen. Bert Sharp introduced SB 182.

7   During Governor Hickel's administration, Senators of the 1st session §§ 12 to 19 (1993) of Alaska's Eighteenth Legislature introduced SB 60 and SB 61. Representatives in the House introduced HR 84, 18th Legislature, 1st Session §§ 12 to 19 (1993).

8   A private Montessori school, Bluffview Montessori, converted to a charter school in March 1993.

9   Alaska Administrative Code

10 Alaska Statute

11 Superintendent members of the CSSTF were: Dan Beck, Delta Greeley; Carl Knudsen, Galena; Patrick Doyle, Copper River; Virgie Fryrear, Alyeska Central School; Terry Bentley, Nenana; and Tim McDonald, Klawock. Local School Board Members of the CSSTF were: John Billings, Galena; Doris Fales, Delta Greeley; Endil Moore, Nenana; and Linda Marchini, Copper River. Teacher members of the CSSTF were: Pat Hein, Nenana; Margaret MacKinnon, Alyska Correspondence School; Mary Townsend, Galena; and Laural Jackson, Delta Greeley. Parent members of the CSSTF were: Donna Emerson, Alyeska Correspondence School; Lisa Sites, Galena; Trisha Eaton, Copper River; and Liz Chase, Copper River. Dela Mathis from the Alaska State Library rounded out the CSSTF membership.

12 Elaine Griffin and her husband, Ned, taught at Akiohk School in the Kodiak Island Borough School District. Akiohk is a two-teacher public school. Elaine and Ned job shared with other couples.

Their first job-share partners were Karen and Chuck Tenneson. Their second job share partners were Josh and Vicky Lewis. Their third job share partners were Bridget Platter and Judy Phillips.

13 SB 88 at this point did not support this assertion. The final charter school law, AS 14.03.250-275, also did not support this assertion. For example, Chinook Charter School in Fairbanks did not have a principal; the Midnight Sun Charter School in Wasilla also did not have a principal.

14 At this point in the legislative debate, it was not clear how charter school students would be counted. This point would not be made clear for several more months. Charter school student accounting is imbedded in the foundation formula for an individual funding community.

15 While technically there could be four students in a given elementary or high school, those students are counted as part of a combined K-12 population for a funding unit.

16 Mr. Gottstien is the CEO of a corporation in Alaska.

17 The provisions of SB 88 did not support this assertion. In fact, AS 14.08.115, and AS 14.12.035 adopted in 1976 already required school boards to form advisory school boards for each school in the district, thus providing for mandated parental involvement in governance of each school.

18 A floor action vote in Alaska's Legislative History is designated by Y-Yes, N-No, E-Excused, A-Absent.

19 "… well-ordered, rational, and serene; distinguished from Dionysian" (Webster's third new international dictionary of the English language unabridged, 1981, p. 65).

20 "… of the orgiastic nature of the Dionysia; wild, frenzied; and sensuous: distinguished from Apollonian" (Webster's third new international dictionary of the English language unabridged, 1981, p. 387).

21 An "educational indicator" is defined as "a statistic about the educational system that reveals something about its performance or health" (Oakes, 1986, p. 1).

22 An "indicator system" should further the informed and on-going debate about the process and product of education by expanding awareness of problems and by bringing together new issues" (Bryk, 1992).

23 The educational literature has co-opted this concept from the political context in which it originally occurred. Consequently, as educational authors have done so, the exact definition of this term in the education literature has never been made clear. Therefore, the concept is treated as a "floating abstraction" until more concrete and educational differentia are given for it.

24 Mehrens advises to "[s]ee Watson v. Fort Worth Bank and Trust, 1988, for a discussion of this issue in employment testing" (Mehrens, 1992, p. 9).

25 The Technical Advisory 97-1 was a revision of technical advisories 96-1 and 96-3.

26 "District of Columbia Superior Court Judge Truman A. Morrison III ordered Ms. Angibo to perform 240 hours of unspecified community service. She could have served up to 21 months in jail" (Charter principal sentenced, 1997, p. 5).

27 "There is a particular systems archetype, first identified by ecologist Garrett Hardin and called 'The Tragedy of the Commons'" (Senge, 1990, p. 294).

28 The Uniform System of Financial Records (USFR) and the Arizona Revised Statutes (ARS) § 15-271.

29 Arizona, California, Colorado, Massachusetts, Michigan, and Minnesota.

30 (National Forum on Assessment, 1995).